Blind White Fish in Persia

Anthony Smith, broadcaster and writer, was born in 1926. He graduated in zoology at Balliol College, Oxford, in 1951. As a journalist he worked on the *Manchester Guardian*, first in 1953 and then again in 1956, and also on *Drum* in Africa. He joined the *Daily Telegraph* as science correspondent in 1957 and left in 1963 to write *The Body* (1968, Penguin 1970), which has been translated into thirteen languages. A Scientific Fellow of the Zoological Society, he is also the author of *Sea Never Dry* (1958), *High Street Africa* (1961), *Throw Out Two Hands* (1963), *The Seasons* (1970, Penguin 1973), *The Dangerous Sort* (1970), *Mato Grosso* (1971), *Beside the Seaside* (1972), *Good Beach Guide* (with Jill Southam) (1973, Penguin 1973), *The Human Pedigree* (1975), *Animals on View* (1977), *Wilderness* (1978), *A Persian Quarter Century* (1979), *A Sideways Look* (1983), *The Mind* (1984, Penguin 1985), *Smith and Son* (1984), *The Great Rift* (1988) and *Explorers of the Amazon* (Penguin 1990). *Blind White Fish in Persia* was first published in 1953. Anthony Smith, who has married twice and has five children, enjoys lighter-than-air flying in his spare time.

Blind White Fish
in
PERSIA

ANTHONY SMITH

PENGUIN BOOKS

PENGUIN BOOKS

Published by the Penguin Group
27 Wrights Lane, London w8 5tz, England
Viking Penguin Inc., 40 West 23rd Street, New York, New York, 10010, USA
Penguin Books Australia Ltd, Ringwood, Victoria, Australia
Penguin Books Canada Ltd, 2801 John Street, Markham, Ontario, Canada L3R 1B4
Penguin Books (NZ) Ltd, 182–190 Wairau Road, Auckland 10, New Zealand

Penguin Books Ltd, Registered Offices: Harmondsworth, Middlesex, England

First published by George Allen & Unwin 1953
Published with a new Postscript in Penguin Books 1990
1 3 5 7 9 10 8 6 4 2

Made and printed in Great Britain by
Richard Clay Ltd, Bungay, Suffolk

One knows these modern travellers, these overgrown prefects and pseudo-scientific bores despatched by congregations of extinguished officials to see if sand dunes sing and snow is cold. Unlimited money, every kind of official influence support them; they penetrate the furthest recesses of the globe; and beyond ascertaining that sand dunes do sing and snow is cold, what do they observe to enlarge the human mind?

Nothing.

page 239 THE ROAD TO OXIANA by Robert Byron
John Lehmann Ltd 1950

CONTENTS

ACKNOWLEDGEMENTS

This journey to Persia could not have taken place without the approval of the University of Oxford, which allowed the Expedition to use the name of the University and made it a grant of money.

It is a pleasant duty to acknowledge this help gratefully, and also that provided by the scientific and geographical organizations whose assistance is more explicitly acknowledged in the published scientific work of the expedition. For their part in this book I am indebted to Philip Beckett and Eric Gordon who took all the photographs, to James Leask who made the maps and drawings, and to John Lehmann Ltd and the Peters, Fraser and Dunlop Group Ltd for permission to quote from *The Road to Oxiana*.

A Foreword

A T first it was only one soldier who shouted at me. I didn't understand what he said but it wasn't a greeting. He repeated it several times as if for my benefit, but even with this help I could not understand what he was calling me; so I nodded simply and walked on. This annoyed him apparently, for he began to chant his refrain with increasing fervour; he yelled it so loudly that the children stopped playing in the drain which ran down the centre of the street. Then they too shouted with the same words while everybody else turned to see who was causing the noise.

All they had to look at was their own familiar street and a lanky individual walking along it. His face and legs were burnt by the sun and his clothes were rather old; there was a shapeless beard on his chin which absorbed the sweat from his forehead. They had seen beards and old clothes many times before, but this time the children were shouting at the one who wore them. He was striding along, for there was nothing he could do; a long time has to be spent in a country before a discussion can be carried on with a lot of small boys and he had only been there for three months. They began to call him American, to call him decadent and to say that he was a capitalist. These words he had heard before and understood: there was still nothing that he could say in reply.

He passed another group of soldiers and they began to call him a 'Lus mahi'. The boys were quick to copy this phrase and chanted unceasingly as they followed along beside the striding figure. Now he knew that 'Mahi' meant fish, but 'Lus' conveyed no meaning to him; he did not know why he should be called a fish of any sort. However, the people in the street thought that it was a very suitable name, for they shouted it with a strange seriousness. The few policemen who were there said nothing; the women and old men also were quiet: it was the boys and the soldiers who were making the noise. Soon he came to the end of the road and, after stepping over a dead donkey, disappeared down a smaller street. The soldiers didn't want to leave the shade of the shop awnings; the boys became bored with the game and returned to play in the drain. The street returned to its normal state, the shouting died down and only the braying of donkeys remained.

It was the last day of our stay in southern Persia. Four of us, who were students at Oxford University, had decided to spend our summer vacation learning about the way of life of the village people and the natural history of the area around Kirman. We had arrived in that town in our truck nine weeks previously and during that time had been living and working in some of the villages on the edge of the Kirman plain. The day before we had arrived back in the town in order to prepare for the return journey to England. That morning we had been in the bazaar, buying a few necessities and two small tribal carpets. The others had gone back earlier, but I had been delayed by a useless determination to try and find a pair of shoes that fitted me. Thus it came about that I returned by myself, through the main street to the old English Consulate, our temporary home.

Shaikh-al-Islami was our host and the representative of the Anglo-Iranian Oil Company. Initially he denied that I should have been called a lus mahi; for it is something which children call each other and cannot be properly translated. The others laughed and said they had always been searching for such an expression. Shaikh-al-Islami insisted that the accusation had been meaningless and instructed me to forget it. Whether this was true or not there was nothing that could be done about it, for we had to pack. But the accusation had given us a feeling of guilt and of deep dissatisfaction, and it was not known in which direction the guilt lay.

When we first arrived in Kirman, it was unanimously agreed by the local people that we were Russian spies. Our skin was not so dusky as theirs, nor our hair so dark; therefore we came from the north and from Russia. Our first few days were spent driving around the area and it became obvious to them that we were spying. To our minds four more conspicuous spies had never been seen before: our faces, pink from the sun, stood out like beacons; our lorry, with a large white canopy, was painted light grey and we were all about a foot taller than anybody else. This blatancy of activity did not convince the Persians of our true position in the world; instead they accepted us kindly; for it did not seem unreasonable to them that the Russians should send spies to the town of Kirman. They were intrigued, I think, as to which activities of theirs we had been instructed to examine.

The second phase came when we were living in the villages. The pro-communist faction in the town decided to write an article in their paper against us. They decried our behaviour and our way of life; they cited us as examples resulting from the evils of a capitalistic community. At this we were greatly displeased. The article had influenced quite a few people against us, but these people all lived in the town, where the papers were sold: out in the villages it did not matter; for not only are most unable to read but these politics do not enter into their lives.

Those in the towns despise those outside them; they say that the villages contain only illiterate, uneducated and worthless people. We preferred the villagers, for they had humility. When a villager asked if the hills near London were as high as the Kirman peaks of 13,000 ft. none the less was thought of him. When a town-dweller said English imperialism makes slaves of the English and then asked if the desert around Oxford was the same as at Kirman his education was shown to be unbalanced: a man who says that dates and camels flourish in England can know little of her economy. The villager was respectful and we respected him. The town dweller was arrogant and we wondered why he should be such a very different individual and why his values should be so contrary.

The soldier had instigated the third accusation against us. He spoke neither of Russia nor of America; he referred only to the lus mahi; with that word he, and those who shouted with him, considered that they had aptly described the one who walked down the street. They chanted it proudly and were confident, apparently, that repetition would increase its worth; they continued with it as if there was nothing more to add. But the reiterative wailings of the soldiers were as those of all teasing children when they denounce a solitary child, though children tease mainly for the love of teasing and not for any deep conviction of the truth of their accusation. Yet, in spite of the puerile and guileless manner in which their opinion was being given, it was an opinion and was being given at the end of our two months' stay, when we had done what we had done and lived as we had lived.

Whether the soldier was right or not I did not know; for I did not even know the meaning of his words, but their meaning was clearly derogatory. Therefore it seemed as if we had failed in our attempts to live with the people, for a similar vituperation had not occurred when we first went to Kirman; the remark was for our benefit and resulted from the way we had lived there: it was a condemnation.

But the shouting incident occurred in a town and we had not been living in a town. We never felt that there had been any understanding between us and the people of Kirman; partly because a town is by its size more impersonal, and partly because our associations with it had always been fleeting and transitory. With the villagers we did not believe our failure was so complete; for they are a people who live by the land and such people are less variable and more dependable in their beliefs. They have their sense of values and it is well engrained within them; it has been there for years and will be for many more to come; they do not change so rapidly and any fluctuations will be well drawn out. With them our lives had been, through them we had seen the country of Persia and by them we had appreciated it. In the town all is different; for there is the preliminary mixing of the East and the West: through them we did not view the land and had no inclination to do so; they did not, we felt, represent the country we had come to see, and anyway our work was not with the towns but out in the parts where the villagers lived. It was good that this was so.

The cry of the town people is that they are standing up for their rights. Power in any form is respected. Assertion of personal rights means little respect for the rights of others; motor car smashes frequently occur head-on in the middle of the road, neither driver being prepared to give way. Weakness and stupidity are believed to be as one: as one they are ridiculed. Weakness is replaced by stubbornness; ignorance by aggressive assertion of what is thought to be true. Travellers say the kindness of the Persian prompts him to misdirect you; a Persian, they say, is never so uncharitable as to tell anybody that his present route is wrong. Perhaps this is so. Nowadays its form is distorted; the answer is given because an answer is necessary and something to meet the case is readily produced. Snakes, we were told, ate air. Unfertilized eggs could be made fertile by being placed with fertilized eggs. A driver insisted that he could read English; as proof he pointed out the name Studebaker on the front of his lorry, but moved his finger from right to left. Our denial of these statements met only with more vigorous assertion and the more fallacious their remark the more rapidly was our interruption brushed aside. We never discovered the Persian for 'I don't know'.

However, on that seventh day of September there was not much time for considering the matter of the rights and wrongs of our stay in Kirman, as we had to pack up our kit and load the lorry. On the journey home we thought little about it; travelling in a lorry is not conducive to deep thought and anyway we were all supporting a number of internal parasites which sapped our strength unfairly; the business of getting home was quite sufficient for all of us at that time. And even back at Oxford there were exams to be taken and they loomed up too threateningly for worries on other subjects to be considered.

That did not mean, however, that the question had ceased to exist. What is the result of four students blundering into the village life of Persia? Is it doomed to failure from the outset because of the incompatibility between East and West? This intractable difference is so often declared to exist by those who have been to the East; 'their ways are dissimilar from ours', they say, 'and there can never be an understanding'. We became sceptical of their belief and felt, in spite of another religion and another and harder means of existence and all the minor differences of their country, that it would be possible for us to go there without the total lack of comprehension of which we had been forewarned. Why, in short, should there be any big dichotomy between East and West?

As the Philosopher's stone is never found, it was necessary not to go there with the fixed intention of discovering that which had puzzled so many others, but to go with the idea of treating everything as if it were of importance. How were we, who knew nothing of their ways, to hit upon the focal point, upon the significant and conclusive factors of their existence? Naturally we were not; but, when living in their surroundings, we should force ourselves to be aware of them, to appreciate all factors, to realise all that had occurred to us in that place: the painter can do it with a brush, but it can also be done by writing down the things as they happened; the environment, whether beautiful or ugly or gay or frightening, will assist in the attainment of sincerity for that which has been put on paper.

Fortunately, the work which we had planned to do there would enable us to lead varied lives and bring us into contact with much that was there, with many types of people and with their activities, with the different parts of the countryside and with the customs. Thus, if our daily occurrences were written down, they might form a patchwork of the type of life that is led by the people of southern Persia and of the land on which they live.

But an intense and furious description of all that we saw would lead to a most lengthy and exasperating recitation, full of descriptive connotations and accurate measurements, overflowing with knowledge and tedium. It was only to be hoped that lethargy would erase the lengthy description and a defective memory would retain only the major details of the day: by a conjunction of these two an incidental type of portrayal might occur and be most satisfactory; for he who can describe the blueness of the sea has told of all its mysteries.

Thus, whether they be thoughts or scenes or fears or faces, so long as they have been remembered for a little while, they should be written down. Perhaps, in that way, the inevitable incidentals to the description would show something of the life in Persia and even of those immutable qualities which are said to exist in the East.

But, if any purpose at all is to be served, it must all be told as a tale, of our reasons for going there and of all the happenings which occurred both before and after the day with the soldier: in fact, whether that man had been right.

CHAPTER I

Preparations at Oxford

I⊤ had been in the previous October that four of us had
decided to go to Persia. The decision was made quite simply;
for Oxford is a breeding ground of similar ideas, and rather
more for the sake of the ideas than for achieving any end.
But this one happened to stick. Philip Beckett had wanted to go
into the centre of Turkey and I was thinking of floating a raft
down the Nile: agreement was reached only on Persia and then
the idea remained. We got out maps and looked at the country:
its size, the remoteness of it and the distance from England did
not detract from the idea. As with all notions that have not even
entered the preparatory stages, difficulties are considered good
omens and strengthen the original and tentative scheme.

Within the University there is an Exploration Club; its function
is to assist its members to go on expeditions. As the funds to which
expeditions have access are limited and the Club possesses only a
certain amount of equipment, the expeditions which leave with
its blessings are usually not more than two in the year. They take
place in the long summer vacation. Therefore, in order to judge
between the merits of the plans, an Expedition Council is formed
of some senior members of the University and of the Club. In
January they decide which of the various proposals shall be
allowed to achieve fruition, with principal regard being paid to
their possible utility and general feasibility.

Thus it was necessary for us to find out about Persia in those
three months, to calculate the cost of living there, to discover the
cheapest method and route for the journey and to plan a programme of scientific work. So we read the travel books and
found that most were uninteresting and lengthy; we inquired
at Travel Agencies to find that few were helpful when there

existed no visible signs of ticket buying; we wrote letters to all acquaintances, however casual, who might be able to provide information on the country.

Slowly we collected facts of value. In general, those who tried to be most helpful were those who could do least to help us: a short visit in 1917 is of little use in calculating the cost of living today, but the prices of that time were proffered eagerly.

Some facts came from those incredibly hardy women which England seems to produce in such numbers and who tramp over vast countries with constitutions requiring only a handful of dates at sunset; but they gave us living costs to work on and we adapted them to meet our less humble demands. Most information collected was not required. 'Do you know that the congealed juice of the Persian plant, Gum Tragacanth, will, if mixed with carpet clippings, make an excellent surface for tennis courts?'.

There are a lot of ways by which it is possible to travel to Persia but only a few by which it can be done cheaply and quickly. Philip, at one time, seriously considered four motor bicycles. Helpful letters poured in from the *Motor Cycling* readers; he was told quite politely that he had a European's idea of roads that was misleading him. Hired aeroplanes, the Istanbul Orient express, pleasure cruises and oil tankers were investigated, but no idea seemed so good as that of buying a truck. Beseeching letters were sent to firms informing them that, merely by loaning a vehicle, they could have it tested most stringently: they replied and that was all. Jeeps, 3 tonners, and adapted cars were thought about, but we finally decided upon a Bedford 15 cwt. truck.

Once the idea of going to Persia had been embedded, it was not expected that anything should be able to gouge it out again: the difference between stubbornness and determination is slender but the intention was clear. Yet many people who were not in the Club apparently believed it to be their duty to dishearten us; for fresh facts which could hinder our schemes were constantly laid before us; they were not intended to be helpful, but only to act as discouraging guidance. It is true that these suggestions of theirs were subjective, that the remarks bore a relation to the things they could and would do, but they caused much spleen to rise within us and increased our determination; I did not know before that they formed quite such a large part of the community. They told us that it was impossible to live in a town for less than three pounds a day, that it was quite hopeless to attempt to get there on the truck and that the bribes required at all stages of the journey would force us to return prematurely and penniless. We were informed of bandits and of fierce heat, a heat which would stop us from working in the five hottest hours of the day. Quite apart from the fact that all these remarks were found to be untrue, I can see no virtue in the saying of them. It was obvious that it was our intention to go, that the poor didn't pay three pounds a day to live or rest for five hours in the middle of the day. Other people had been there before. Why shouldn't we? At that time the discouragers merely annoyed us: now, by reflection with the facts, their remarks appear in a still darker light. These advisers were still chirruping on the day that we left.

Shortly after the collection of facts had begun, we learnt of the qanats. It was written that there were 100,000 miles of them in Persia, that they were artificial underground water channels and that the deepest was over 1,000 ft. Naturally we became intrigued and read that their purpose was to bring a constant stream of water onto the surface. This water was not lifted to the surface but flowed down the channel away from the point of seepage, as if a normal well had been pushed over on its side until the water flowed out of its mouth. The books said the channels were often 25 miles long and 1 yard high, that they were unsupported, that the danger in them from asphyxiation was great and that roof collapses were not infrequent. Our curiosity fluctuated.

But then another book said: 'Blind, white fish live in the qanats and make for excellent eating.' Now the loss of pigment and of eyes suggested that the form had long since lived in subterranean regions. Possibly some qanats had penetrated an underground system and other interesting forms might be living in the channels. We decided to study the fauna of the qanats.

There were four of us who were going to make the trip. Philip Beckett was a chemist; he had been to Iceland twice, but knew, like the rest of us, nothing about Asia. Eric Gordon was a geographer, was married and had spent one summer in the Gambia on the west coast of Africa. Louis Armstrong was studying Botany and professed a slight mechanical knowledge that increased inversely with the welfare of an antique car in his possession. I studied Zoology and knew nothing of mechanics, marriage or any other continent.

In January we four produced the programme. It contained our proposed work, proposed route and estimated cost. The council considered that we would justify the probable expense of £850 and approved the plans. Our route was to be from Dunkirk to Genoa and then by boat to Beirut; from there, via Damascus, Baghdad and Tehran to our destination, Kirman. This town was chosen for various reasons. Firstly, we would have to go through most of Persia to get there; this would then give us some under-standing of the rest of the country. Secondly, the town and its villages relied almost entirely upon qanats for their water supply; the qanats would therefore be abundant and in good order. Thirdly, a small Church Missionary Society hospital was there, a comforting factor; for we had been told that living in the East and acquiring diseases were synonymous phrases. The programme of work was extensive and very ready to be modified on our arrival there if conditions were found to be different from those which were expected. Briefly: Eric wished to make maps of some villages with their areas of cultivation and qanat systems; Philip to study the soil and the effect of cultivation upon it; Louis to investigate the botanical aspect of the countryside; and I to see what lived in the qanats. Information was also to be collected on every subject that seemed to be of interest.

Such, in short, was our intention. We had some note paper printed with 'The Oxford University Expedition to Persia, 1950' in large black letters on the top and felt a lot better. With the aid of this paper we pestered people with much more vigour and slightly more authority. Nothing further was discovered about the fish save that one man had considered selling otters to the qanat owners; for, so he thought, the otters would, in their efforts to catch the fish, keep the channels free from the deposition of silt. Some people had heard of the fish, but they were not thought to be white or blind. Anyway we were lent, through the National Coal Board, two miners' helmets with lamps and we promised to send them photographs.

Eric spent time in the building of the Royal Geographical Society borrowing equipment, Louis in the Herbarium at Kew, I in the Zoo and the British Museum. It was Philip who went to buy the lorry. He had an introduction to a man who would take him round a large ex-W.D. dump. All the vehicles were lined up on the perimeter track of a disused aerodrome and he wandered past them with this man who talked continually of John Bunyan, Dorothy Sayers and his daughter in Australia: somehow they were all linked in his mind and brought to the surface by the sight of Philip sitting in lorry after lorry, pulling the self starters, listening to the engines and looking at the tyres. He was a kind man; he took a lot of trouble and made certain that the one which was eventually picked upon was a good machine. Then an arrangement was made with a London garage to collect it from the dump and overhaul it for us. At last it seemed as if something had been achieved.

Negotiations through the Foreign Office with the Persian Government had still not acquired positive results. Letters gave way to telegrams, but formal approval came through only three weeks before we were due to leave. Friendly instructions had warned us not to try and hurry the East, but Persia gave us plenty of encouragement to try and do so. However, three weeks were sufficient time to collect all the other visas and no ill came of the long delay.

We had planned to leave Oxford on the last day of term. The cross channel passage and the deck class accommodation from Genoa to Beirut had been booked, and we sent a letter to our hosts in Tehran saying that our arrival there would be on July 1st; the date was guessed at by us just in order to have a date of arrival, but we did not possess much confidence in its possible accuracy.

It was one week before the end of term that Philip and I went to London to fetch the truck. It had been painted grey; for most other colours seemed excessive and the sand would have turned them grey in time. Outside the garage of Mansell and Fisher the truck looked very fine indeed: grey was the only colour it could have been. I was taken off for a practice drive, while Philip went inside to settle the account. I took over in a back street; the mechanic sat expectantly at my side. In time the gears responded even to my touch and the garage man settled more easily into his seat. Never before had I felt so proud of a thing; the solidity of it, the humming of its tyres and its powerful subservience, made me wish to shout out its praises. How could it be that those pedestrians were paying no attention to this wonderful machine?

Back at Mansell and Fisher we collected the spare parts and took grinning group photographs of those who had worked on it. As a lot of equipment had to be collected, we bowled around in the London traffic going to the various places. Most of it kept well distant from us; for the canopy was off and it was all too plain that both occupants were talking unconcernedly and laughing excitedly. It was at the British Museum that the radiator began to leak. It can't be every day that a lorry in their yard develops such a fault, but one or two men of the mammal department spent a lot of their time in making an extremely effective repair. I took the opportunity to learn how to stuff an animal; I learnt only the difficulties, the principal one being that the stuffed form finishes up being two animals long and half an animal wide.

Philip, by this time, was elsewhere and had told me to meet him on Westminster Bridge. It was on the Embankment and in the centre lane that the engine stopped. At once the frustrated drivers behind all blew their horns to let me know of their angry existence. I managed to persuade the first to come to my aid and then we both persuaded quite an array of the drivers to push the truck into a side street. I hurried off to a garage; they stumped back to their cars.

That particular garage apparently thrived on cars which broke down on its section of the Embankment; certainly one of its hands treated my agitation with much calm and prepared the breakdown lorry with the bored familiarity of a man pulling on his socks in the morning. He said nothing. I was pulled into the garage and went off to find Philip.

Later, the bored one broke his silence to say: "Petrol pump bust, 10/-" and we were off for Oxford. London traffic is difficult; it is always so but especially at five o'clock in the evening. But what did it matter, what did anything matter? Only that it was a beautiful summer evening and we had our truck. Nothing else did; nothing else entered our heads, with the result that we ran out of petrol about half a mile before Tetsworth.

The last week of a summer term at Oxford has a distinctive quality. If there was any order in the daily routine during the preceding seven weeks, then it is lost by the eighth; if there has been no order, then that eighth week is as it should be and the last thing to be forgotten about Oxford. Perhaps there is no time and place as suitable for the preparation of an expedition to Persia as Oxford at that time. Life in my digs in Walton Street was, as the old landlady said, "very eventful". She carried on looking after me in the same way as she had always attended me and those of the years before me. I found her one morning dusting the four spare lorry wheels which I had tried to hide behind the sofa; she worried only because the spare back spring was resting on the bottom of the curtain and she would not have been able to move it and draw the curtain when evening came. I removed the spring and leant it as tidily as I could against the bookshelf. She said she had tried to tidy, but had found it difficult; I implored her to leave it all, for worse was to come, and to add strength to my words, in came Philip carrying a fifty yard roll of wire netting. She agreed to leave it all, but in going out hung up our two miners' helmets on the hooks on the back of the door.

Everything began to accumulate in that room; we all dumped things in it before going hurriedly away to fetch something else. Delivery boys called. Messenger boys. Postmen with vast parcels. "Sir, a gentleman left these petrol cans for you." "Sir, someone put sixty tins of milk in the passage saying he hadn't time to go upstairs". During that week, the four individuals who were going on the expedition saw very little of each other; we met as a body only when we gathered at the Doctor's for another set of inoculations; but there was always evidence of things accomplished. One day twelve boxes, each three feet high, were left in my room with a little note: "How much toilet paper and soap do four people use in three months?" I pencilled some suitable reply and the paper was later replaced by the real thing.

As this was my room it was the natural rendezvous for all those people from whom we were still gleaning information. Perhaps it would be a Persian we had discovered, perhaps it would be someone recently returned from the Middle East or a man who knew something about lorries. So a tea party would go on in the midst of it all. A sense of urgency dominated the conversation: Philip might be testing a primus or a blow-lamp in one corner, Eric might be telephoning very loudly out in the passage, or possibly someone had just backed into a pile of test tubes. The visitor would soon leave, impressed that an awful lot was going on in that room but not being certain what it was. The accumulations continued; range finders, water bottles, sleeping bags, saucepans, butterfly nets, microscopes were brought in and there became less and less space. There was no time to make out lists of what should be done; when you remembered something you did it. "The jerricans haven't come from the War Office, nor has the channel ticket from the A.A." and a minute later you were ringing them up. If you sat down, you found yourself writing notes and letters; if you stood, you found yourself going out to buy or fetch something else.

However, it was term time and I still had an essay to write. It took me a long time to write it; an enormous list of things to be done when it was finished grew steadily by my side. "Sir, there's a policeman outside who wants you to move your vehicle from the bus stop". "Sir, here's a telegram and the boy wants to know if there's an answer". The essay progressed slowly. Further interruptions came from undergraduates who had heard of the trip and wanted to know if there was room for one more; we tried to turn this into a profit-making scheme and sent a circular round to all the colleges: 'To Baghdad for thirty pounds' was its general motif. Quite a few people became interested, but their interest waned when they saw the size of the truck and the quantity to be loaded onto it. I asked my landlady to show them into another room in order that I should try to come to an arrangement before discouragement set in. "But sir, I've shown a man about insurance into the kitchen". Finally, three art students agreed to be taken to Genoa for five pounds each. I sent the completed essay by post, for I was fearful of an encounter.

As our journey entailed passing through twelve Customs houses, it was considered vital to have our boxes sealed in England; it would have been too distressing to have to unload a ton of equipment twelve times. Louis had had trouble of this sort before when going on a small botanical trip to Italy; he had with him, among other things, a Wheatstone's bridge—a gadget of complex appearance for measuring the electrical resistance of the soil. He was told that wirelesses were not allowed to be imported into Italy; he said it was not a wireless but a 'Ponta di Wheatstone' and asked if there was a ruling on them. There was not, but the whole affair took a long time. We thought of our clinometers, soil borers and killing bottles and sent for a Customs man to seal the boxes. The lists of contents were then to be translated into French, Italian, Arabic and Persian. Quite how alidade, plankton net or taxidermine was going to be translated into Arabic was interesting but was not our difficulty; as it was not the Customs man's difficulty either, the job was finished in a day.

Our departure was fixed for Friday, 16th June. It was thus right, proper and inevitable that a big party should be held on Thursday, 15th June. The party began in the evening; the fact that no members of the expedition were there did not cause worry among its participants: an Oxford party needs but little reason for its initiation and none for its continuance. Our healths were drunk with reckless abandon; the success of the trip was toasted with similar enthusiasm, Customs men of the world were united, Anglo-Persian relations were strengthened, Vive les Arabes, Vive les Pèrses—the noise billowed out from the room to be dispersed in the evening air. It did not billow as far as Philip, who was preparing for a viva that had been arranged to take place on the Friday morning. Nor did it reach Eric, whose wife had just collapsed in trying to finish our truck canopy in time for the trip. It certainly did not reach Louis and me, for we were in London. Certain documents, the jerricans and innumerable oddments had not arrived: it was important that they should be fetched. Now Louis had a car; it was only a little one but it was a car of great esteem. It was one of those cars which you step into from above and the doors just strengthen the body. It was, of course, an Austin 7 and a year or so older than Louis. All day long we sped about in London; bus drivers leant over us and smirked; taxi drivers just grinned, but we had a lot to do and concentrated on trying to beat them at the traffic lights. The documents were presented to us, the innumerable oddments were sold to us and we bought as many jerricans as the car could carry. Unfortunately, that wonderful object had to be left in London; so two tired individuals, swathed in jerricans, clanked their way in to Paddington station, caught a train for Oxford, and fell asleep.

If there are a few things to be done, then it is a good plan to make a list of them; if there are many things, then that list should be made longer; but if those things are seemingly endless, then no list will ever be made; for the threshold of the fantastic has been reached: any attempt by anyone is met with his own hollow laughter. Thus it was on the morning of our departure. In theory there was little enough; it was only just a matter of loading the truck, packing our personal kit and settling the few formalities which, by their nature, had to be left to that last morning. Deceptively little, but in fact so much.

I got up, put on a suit and went round to Balliol for hand-shaking. At this ceremony the Master reads out your tutor's report for the term. It is never the custom to be very attentive at these sessions; I was even less so than customary and wandered in and out dreamily, but woke up just a little on realising that I had done nothing about a G.B. plate. I bought one and went off to fetch the truck. A friend, impressed by my suit, asked if I was going anywhere special. I just had to tell him.

Back at Walton Street none of the others had arrived. There is little point in worrying that there is not enough time left to load a truck if you have no idea how long it takes to load one. So I began to collect my personal kit. We were going to need warm clothes for the English Channel in October, clothes for interviews in Tehran, clothes to keep you cool, old clothes and tough clothes. I referred to our letters of advice about clothes. 'It doesn't matter what you wear so long as your knees are covered'. 'A change of shirt every day will keep away prickly heat'. 'I just wore a large felt hat and a pair of stout boots.' Philip seemed to have faith in string vests. Louis thought everything would be all right if he took a suit; the other clothes didn't matter. Eric just talked about bush shirts and bush jackets in a Colonial Services Club tone of voice. I thought about it for a minute or so, but the whole subject seemed too big to grasp: I threw in three pairs of sandals, two shirts, some shorts and every handkerchief I possessed. I also put in my demobilization suit; I had never liked the thing and thought an amusing time might be had selling it in a bazaar. It was harder to think of other necessities. Obviously, enough toothbrushes should be taken to ensure that you don't have to share at any time during the trip, enough ink to write with and a pair of nail scissors. I could think of no more. I thought of books and then thought not: I wished to see what the East had to offer.

The others arrived and we began the loading. I rang various people up to come and see us off, and when they arrived they charmingly offered to help us load. It was an interesting sight that morning. Boxes, packages and rucksacks were appearing from the windows, the doors and the basement of No. 168. Eric had paced exactly 100 feet up the road in order to disentangle his measuring chain. Someone else was cutting our wire netting into two 25 yard lengths, so that it would be usable when we got stuck in the sand. The sand seemed a long way away: I lay underneath the truck wondering about it and pretending that I was mending the rear light. Could it be that there was a countryside consisting of nothing but sand?

One difficulty in loading for a month's journey is that everything seems to need a position where it is at hand. Nothing, except my suit and the miners' helmets, could be condemned as useless until our destination. Therefore a hierarchy of importance, an order of utility and usefulness was put into force which was to cause more banter than any single other factor during the whole trip. There is nothing amusing in getting out all the insect collecting stuff, the truck tool kit and your pyjamas everytime you want a cup of tea; similarly, the amusement in using the cine camera wanes if it is preceded by a rearrangement of countless pieces of equipment. There just did not seem enough surface area and none of us was likely to forget that fact. However, at Walton Street it was still a matter for jest. 'Do you think you'll want a spare shirt before you need the D.D.T.?' 'Surely Oxo cubes come before microscopes?'

But as we were in England, and more especially in Oxford,
chaos of this sort can occur without people stopping to watch
and cause more of it. I don't think any of us were asked where
we were going, but then none of us behaved as if we had nothing
to do except answer questions. To us the answer was inevitable:
where else but Persia? At last, by its very realisation, the wide
range of that October idea dawned upon us, but not for long, as
we were ready to go. Eric was there too to see us off; but only
Philip, Louis and I were about to leave, as he was following later
by air. Room was found for the three undergraduates who were
going to Genoa; room was found for their packs. Room was
found too for the great stack of documents which had to accompany us; for all were necessary and yet so few were vital.

I started the engine, yelled some suitable epithet at the
bystanders and drove off. We all yelled and shouted. 'Good
heavens, do all these other people not realise that we are driving
off to Persia? Let us yell and shout and tell them so.' So we made
much noise, for life at that moment was good.

CHAPTER II

Genoa to Persia

FOUR days later we arrived at Genoa. The port officials were perturbed that it was a truck, and not a car, which had to be loaded onto the *Esperia*. As this outburst was feared from the time when we first decided to go on the boat it had been our custom with forms and letters to refer to it as a vehicle. The payment had been made in England and the ticket entitled the truck to a passage; there was nothing for us to do except listen attentively to their protestations and then suggest that a suitable time had been reached for hoisting it on board. Eventually, fifteen minutes after the ship was supposed to have sailed, it was lifted up onto the deck and we all rushed up the gangway in pursuit.

The journey from England had been completed with a day to spare, although three days at Genoa had been foreseen when we left Oxford. Down to Dover it was easy enough; the English Customs were obliging, the French disinterested and our first night was spent near Bapaume. It was a night initially peaceful, but later on it rained and I was sick. Anyway, when camping out, there is not the same incentive to sleep late and we made a surprisingly early start. On to Dijon, where the engine failed again. In England a valve had become loose to make a tapping noise, but was soon cleared; however, in Dijon only coughing came from the engine. After two hours the carburettor had been dissected into its component parts; after six hours it was together again. The coughing was just the same and there was a certain relief that this should be so. Only when a garage man was fetched did it disappear and on the instant that he arrived. He had regarded us disdainfully right from the moment when he was told that 'Il y est un coff coff extraordinaire'.

That second night was spent in a ditch. It proved in the morning light to be surrounded by delightful Cézanne countryside: the mind is not quick to grasp the concept of reality at the beginning of another day and it was pleasing to live in a canvas for a little while. After Chambéry, we drove up to the French Customs house at Modane. Again they took little interest in us: this was exceptionally welcome as it was cold in the cloud which hung in the Mont Cenis pass. The Italians regarded us as another insoluble problem in their harassed existences. After an hour of discussion, they refused to examine our kit and demanded that we drove straightway to the Customs officials in Turin. We protested hotly, but ten Italian officials can be much more explosive in their vehemence. They made us pay 2,000 lire, marked our passports with a stamp four days out of date and pushed a smiling but bulky escort into the front seat. By disregarding his frequent and agitated misdirections we arrived safely in Turin and the night was passed in the Customs house yard. Our escort, delighted with the trip, thanked us for the ride and went off for the night to pay an unexpected visit to his family.

In the morning the officials arrived. Louis and I stamped in after them. Four hours later the officials disappeared for lunch and we trailed out of the building some minutes after it had become silent once more. It transpired that a deposit of 100,000 lire (£60) had to be paid on our goods. We refused, we requested a further escort to Genoa, we offered to pay for half a dozen escorts, but nothing except 'Centomila lire' was shouted back at us.

Leaving Philip with the lorry, Louis and I disturbed the Consul with a request to borrow the money if we deposited the same value of travellers' cheques with him: it was necessary to do this for we had no wish to be inundated with lire at Genoa. He was most helpful and kind. He produced the money; the officials were pacified and remembered, just in time, to charge us a further sum for re-sealing the boxes. These had already been sealed in Oxford and the extra payment was grudged; but it gave us our freedom and that, with our ship sailing on the next day, was not prized too lightly. Then our escort, who had been sleeping in some nearby shade, woke up and produced a display of tears when we refused to pay for his railway ticket back to the Mont Cenis pass.

His exhibition was so good that he was given his 2,000 lire and thanked gratefully for allowing us to witness such a remarkable feat.

Genoa was reached that evening after a pleasant and rapid drive along one of the autostradas. We found a place to sleep underneath a stony cliff by the sea and just next to the railway line. There were no trains, the night was warm and aromatic and the air was still: the world seemed at peace with itself. Only the flashing of the fire-flies vied with the reflections on the sea.

In the morning our three extra undergraduates went their three separate ways. Much later, we learnt that one had retired almost immediately to England with an exceptionally violent stomach disorder, that another was forced to live on generosity, for his wallet was stolen the very day of our departure; while the third, after painting in a small village called Rio Maggiore for two months, was harmlessly shot at by a zealous and over suspicious communist. Italy is a country where the Goddess of Fortune is peculiarly diligent.

For most of that day we sat in the Docks eating cherries and waiting for the *Esperia*. The *Conte Grande* was there already and filling up with Italian emigrants for Buenos Aires. Another ship catering for the fecundity of the people, the *Sebastiano Cabot*, was preparing to take a further load to Australia. There was also a Greek boat taking a heterogeneous cargo of individuals to Athens. A Turkish boat had stopped on its way from Istanbul to Marseilles. Around each of them was the fascinating turmoil associated with a ship in a dock and with its departure. The sudden shouts as a rope begins to tighten; the ebullience of the porters, and their warning cries as a crane swings its load; the sound of the derricks, of orders coming through megaphones and the agitation of the seagulls are all shown in greater contrast by the quiet, stolid complacence of the ship. Nothing is heard from its huge bulk save for the preparatory and the final hoot. Slowly it sheds itself from all the ungainly trappings of the port, slowly it moves away until its true shape can be seen. One or two more hoots, a change of direction, and it is outside the harbour wall and floating upon the clearer waters and the wider expanse of the sea. The vacancy of its berth then becomes apparent and the drama of its departure is emphasized by the sudden pointlessness of the long and naked quayside.

It was dark when the *Esperia* left Genoa. It was windy too. The deck class passengers began to look around for sheltered niches in which to spend the night; there were only thirty of us and a certain familiarity inevitably ensued: anyway, it seemed no time before the morning deck swabbing began. The first evening was spent at Naples; we went ashore, as did everyone else, and the two hours were quickly passed away under the influence of rather a lively wine called 'vino rosso di vulcano'. Back at the ship, it transpired that all the others had been doing exactly the same thing.

The *Esperia* is a new boat and was launched in 1949. Now she plies between the principal Mediterranean ports carrying passengers and cargo. On our trip, the first class passengers were almost entirely Arabs; that they were grossly rich did not need a searching glance. The second and third classes were more cosmopolitan; gold tie pins and gigantic wrist watches were less in evidence, but all three could look down with equal disdain upon the deck class. However, we were, as one of its fatter Signoras announced, 'Una classe molto distinta'. This was acknowledged by us, an Austrian and his daughter, two large Neapolitan families, a peculiar selection of old men and an English speaking Greek called Pericles. It was impossible to address him by his name without a strange feeling of elation.

Food constituted the biggest problem, for it was never enough. Even the old men harangued the cook. At every meal on every day the same routine arose; first the cook looked indignantly surprised at our criticisms, then he was scoffed at in English, Italian and Arabic until he, with a gesture of despair, threw up his hands and burrowed again into the kitchen to find some more spaghetti or cuttlefish or whatever was the order of the day. The rest of the time was spent in idleness. Louis painted a University crest on the door of the truck, which produced multi-lingual and obscure comments. We brewed tea, but the complex system of extracting petrol from the carburettor attracted the notice of the Captain; immediately he confiscated all the relevant gear and gave the crew a fire practice. They regarded us unkindly for a day or two.

Being at sea in the Mediterranean was great fun. The continual warmth in the air would make any night a worthy time and not just a cold and dark separation between two days; add this warmth to the horizon of sea with its roofing of stars and the time is very ripe for great imaginings concerning all that has gone on before on those waters. 'Siamo prigionieri, we cannot escape, we are at the mercy of the cook', we shouted, but imagination thrives on lack of food and complete hallucination comes with starvation.

The *Esperia* spent eight hours in Alexandria. We sat in and around the truck, for the ship swarmed with African dockers. I have never before seen such pilfering: bags were cut open, crates were bounced and then ransacked. Two Alexandrian policemen tried to prevent it all, but as this was impossible, contented themselves with emptying each man in turn. Out fell apples, almonds and cutlery. The sound of these cascades formed only a background to the vigorous protestations of both Arab parties. One of the dockers, with feet even larger and dirtier than those of his fellows, produced some peaches wrapped in a copy of the *New Yorker* from the depths of his voluminous trousers, and told us to call him Ali. It was at about this time that a compass completely disappeared from the cab of the truck: obviously we were nearing the East.

The dock itself contained many more policemen and thousands of Ali's companions. Pairs of horses pulling long carts were driven at a furious speed among the crowd. Large American cars hooted their way through and made slower progress. The drivers of the carts were lean and tall; those of the cars, short and fat: there seemed to be no exceptions to this rule. Neither paid any interest to our departure. Three miles out to sea the pilot was dropped; the smell of the harbour was lost a little earlier.

Asia first became visible in the early morning. Slowly Beirut emerged from the pattern of hills behind it. The deck class passengers were, after Alexandria, predominantly eastern and behaved much more excitedly when land was sighted. The differences between the Arab and Italian travellers were that the Arabs were carrying bedding equipment, they looked desperately miserable until land had been seen and they destroyed all the tidiness of the place.

The quayside was packed, the excitement and the shouting were terrific. Generally those on the land broke down and wept when they saw their loved ones, equally untidy and unkempt individuals, going through the same motions on the boat. There was a great rush to get off, there was also a big fight to get on: little progress was made by either group, but for us there was plenty of time. The hold had to be unloaded before the things on the deck would be touched; and our truck, as it presented the greatest problem, would be dealt with last. Our affairs were well smoothed over by a little man with a large British Legation band on his arm, and he speeded up the unloading of the truck. Although all our boxes had already been dubbed with two seals, the Lebanese considered that insufficient. They tied up the whole of the back of the truck with rope and then put a seal on that. Fortunately the rope was not too tight and later we were forced by circumstance to take advantage of the slackness, as all our kit was in the back. During our subsequent entrances, the seal proved inconvenient but did remain unbroken. Initially, it appeared invincible, the Lebanese were satisfied and said that it would keep us in bond until the Persian frontier. We thanked them and drove out of the dock.

Beirut was hot. It seemed hotter after Louis had backed the truck into a beautiful green Cadillac that happened to be gliding by. Actually its occupants were not as vociferous as they might have been, considering that there was a dent traversing one mudguard of the car. The affair cost us nine pounds, taught us a word or two of Arabic and to drive more carefully in a continent where the standards of driving are different and more competitive. But the *Esperia* had left us hungry and all was forgotten in an excellent chicken lunch given to us by Mr. McDermot of the Legation.

After the meal we bought more food, filled up with petrol and found the road to Damascus. This road wound up into the hills behind Beirut to a height of 6,000 feet; it was flanked by many trees, expensive houses belonging to the rich of Beirut and occasional glimpses of the whiteness of the town below. Then it dipped down into the broad valley of Litani and Orontes and the Mediterranean disappeared from view. Instead there were camels to be seen, long lines of them, and rows of olive trees. The road was tarmac, the truck was running well and we were filled with much contentment; at last there was only a length of land between us and the town of Kirman.

Up and on the other side of the valley was the Lebanon/Syria frontier. There everybody was affable; they thought the seal an excellent idea and clamped another onto the rope. By then it was night and night is for sleep; so a little further on we drove off the road and got out the beds. A jeep full of Syrian soldiers arrived and gave fierce demonstrations of the quantity of bandits in the neighbourhood. We gave them melon and played with their rifles until, much to our relief, they suddenly departed. The stars came out and we went to sleep. A short while later two more jeeps arrived and told us that our peril was too much for them to bear; they said we should follow them. I do not know where they went; for their little red light went much too quickly and we lost them. We drove on steadily and stopped on finding ourselves about to enter Damascus. The rest of the night was spent on a damp bit of ground just outside the town.

In the morning we drove into it. Louis left to find a bank and I went to buy more food. A skinny youth named Husain helped carry the stack of bread and fruit back to the truck: naturally he was displeased with whatever coin it was that I gave him. Louis returned with a dirty wad of paper notes which had come out of a clean white bank whose clerk had assured him that they were of value. The large amount of food was necessary because the next stage of the journey led us over the Syrian desert; and about that part of the trip we knew nothing save that the Nairn Bus Company runs regular services between Damascus and Baghdad and would be able to give us all the information. They told us of the two routes: the one south through Transjordan with road all the way and the other which is more direct and over the desert. Both meet just before Rutba Wells, an isolated town on the pipe line and 280 miles from Damascus. The Company's buses all travel over the desert and they advised us to go that way; for it was shorter, more interesting and obviated the necessity of entering Transjordan. They recommended that we journeyed only by day, a suggestion which received immediate agreement, and said that it was only important to follow the tracks, for they were bound to lead somewhere, even if it was just another lorry. They also told us that there had been signposts every five kilometres; although many of them had since been knocked over or removed a fair proportion remained. Their general opinion was that it was easy enough if the truck didn't break down: clearly that would alter the situation.

We filled up with forty gallons of petrol and four of water, and left Damascus in the afternoon. There was a good road until Abu-el-chamat, some thirty miles away; it was well surfaced, although nothing exists at the end of it except the Customs post and the way onto the desert. Many milestones bordered the road and informed us of the 500 miles that there were before Baghdad. These we thought impressive and took a photo of ourselves standing by one of them with the truck reverently situated in the background. It had to be there for, in our eyes, a great dignity had come over that vehicle and we beheld it with respect. Our awe nearly trespassed on superstition, upon a belief that mistrust in the machine would result in a break-down and, although words of great potency were to be hurled at it on various occasions, they were never thrown except when a town was nearby: 500 miles of desert is space enough to absorb a lot of rationality. Anyway there was nothing else to put in the background; the green land had been left behind: now it was brown and stretched away to be merged by the haze with the horizon of the sky.

At the Customs post there was the end of the road and scarcely any activity. One or two lorries were outside and thick with the dust of the desert, a strange red dust with a characteristic smell. The drivers were nonchalantly flicking it off the tyres in order to reveal the tyre numbers; for the authorities were trying to put a stop to the profitable business of changing old tyres in the country where the new ones happened to be cheapest. The lethargy amongst the Customs officials was caused, according to the drivers, by Ramadan, the fasting month of the Mohammedan year and a time when no food is eaten between sunrise and sunset. They were definitely very soporific, so much so that they never even looked at our truck; but then neither did they accept any of our fruit which they had washed for us at their pump.

The drivers pointed out the way to us, a way made obvious

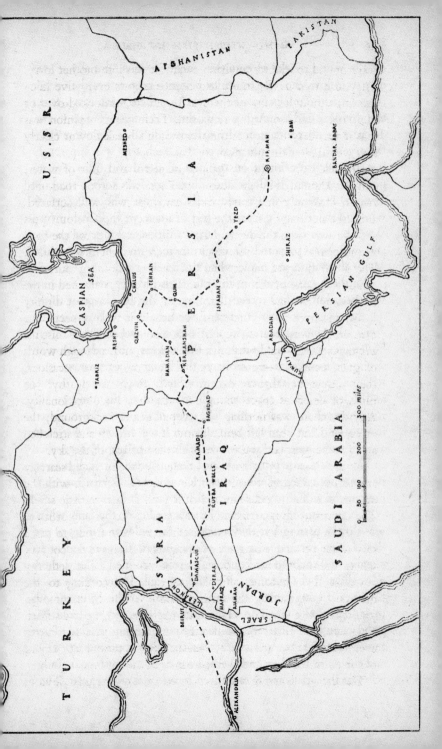

by the wheel marks of countless other vehicles. Initially it was
easy to follow, the only difficulty being to keep out of the deeper
ruts. Then the tracks became scarcer; for there were many forks
and divisions and the main way gradually diminished in its width.
There was no route generally acknowledged as the most satisfactory and the branches showed that each trip was apparently
just another experiment on the part of the driver. We saw no
point in ignorant boldness and always tried to keep a signpost
in sight. Naturally it was admitted that those who knew, those
who had made most tracks, 'the boys' in fact, were probably very
clever in their choice of route, but our mood was a generous one
and we were prepared to credit them with that superiority.
Many allowances are made when there is no road.

We three sat together in the cab. This did not make for con-
venience, but it was forced upon us by the bond arrangement
in the back. It was regretted because the plausibility of
companionship decreased in that imminent confinement. Two
hour shifts were taken in driving; this was for the sake of the man
sitting in the central position on the battery. For two uncomfortable hours he sat there doing nothing except watch the ruts
and holes and then experience the attempts, to his mind feeble,
of the driver to evade them. The seeds of discontent were sown
in that cab; for, through him, unwarranted criticisms began to
assert themselves. The seal on the back was to blame, but it had
to be; on such a trip it should not be permitted for each man to
be quite so aware of what the other is doing. Such immediate
judgement will always be resented.

The two outside people in the cab could see the land which
was slowly passing by; they could see the miles and miles of red
dust which formed that part of the desert, they looked at its
expanse and then listened once more to the engine: so long as the
noise did not change then all would be well. There were camels
to gaze at, young camels and camels that rolled on the ground with
their legs in the air. The vegetation was dry and scattered but
good enough for the area to be a camel breeding ground. Then
there were mirages to be seen; but the lakes appeared too blue,
and the palm trees around them, formed by the distorted elong-
ation of the small bushes, appeared too slender and regular. They

prompted Philip to talk scientifically about them and Louis to talk sceptically, for he said they were unconvincing. An argument developed and only ended by the appearance, straight ahead of us, of a large lake. With Louis continuing to denounce its reality, we drove up to it and paddled in the salty water. It was definitely strange that a lake should have been in that place; but it was stranger still how near we had to be to the water before we became convinced of its existence. However, it is not everyday that virtual images suddenly transform themselves into images of such pertinent reality.

That evening we had tea at a Syrian frontier post. It was a small collection of buildings with a well beneath and a flag above. Paradoxically, with no common language between us, the conversation never faltered; for great effort was made by each group to learn the names of the others and this caused sufficient chaos to have lasted for days. Everything was made harder and more disordered by a one legged individual who played incessantly upon his single-stranded home-made violin. He only ceased in order to climb onto the roof of a hut, point desperately at the horizon and bellow 'The Arab Legion is coming'. This was his only English sentence and he used it with a maximum of effect. Then they filled up our water bottles, told us the way and we left them standing beneath the flag. The sun was setting and the place where they had been became nothing but a red and fiery cloud; for the dust had risen up behind us once more as we drove on and on towards the east.

The kilometre posts became less frequent and each of those that still stood erect was perched upon by a large eagle. Post 251, 251 kilometres from Abu-el-chamat, was the first that was not so used and this was judged sufficient reason for us to sleep there. These eagles are purported to be the first arrivals at a dead body and always pluck out the eyes; with Zoroastrianism it is of significance whether the left eye is plucked out before the right; for then it is known whether the spirit of the dead one has gone to heaven or whether it has not. We tied a bunch of the eagle feathers collected from another post onto the radiator cap; a symbolic and effective measure. Only the Nairn bus disturbed our sleep, a creation of noise and light which came from the west and disappeared in the east. Its thundering form passed quite close to us as it drove through the night, over the uneven earth of the desert, over the land where there was no road; it went like a ghostly being, impervious to the land upon which it rode, disdainful of the irregularities, regardless of everything save its destination; and to that place it roared, relentlessly and powerfully, until the daylight came once more and made it lose its wilder aspect. Then it would assume the humbler form of a bus and find its way into the town of Baghdad. There, if it had been a sleeper, the passengers would wake up and leave their beds, quite oblivious that they had travelled in such a monstrous thing of light and sound as that which had roared past us in the night.

On the next day the diffuse maze of tracks was left behind; for we met the oil pipe line road shortly before Rutba Wells. A man asked for a lift along this road and we stopped to pick him up. A few miles further on, when he told us his journey had ended, there was no discernible change in the countryside, but he invited us to come and drink with him. We followed and, about a mile from the road, came to a low hut: several donkeys sat outside it and inside were three men; they got up and asked us to come in and sit down. A minute hut it was; for no one could stand upright and there was just room for all to sit inside. They offered us some dilute asses' milk of a most unsavoury appearance; we discovered ourselves accepting and grinned our thanks; its taste was not overwhelming, but there is always a bit of a tendency to grin when your face emerges from a bowl. Then tea was given and more grins were exchanged. One of them even produced a leg of meat from under the sack he was sitting on, but that did evoke a cautious restraint upon our part and we refused; instead, we took our leave. Who those men were or how they lived I have no idea; there was a sense of unlikeliness about them and I did not really consider that they existed nor, for that matter, did I believe in my own existence at that moment. The hard, dry earth crumpled in an unnatural way, the sun was too high and far too hot and there was no noise in the air. The furnishings of the land were, as in a dream, too scarce; nothing except their hut and our truck, nothing else but the earth and the sky. The re-starting of the engine broke the spell; anyway, such empty moments do not last even in a dream.

Rutba Wells is reputed to be the town that was dispatched by Aladdin when experimenting with the power of his lamp. The middle of the Syrian desert is the place where it chanced to arrive: the tale is a reasonable one and that lonely situation does not encourage the belief of the many more recent conjectures. There must, admittedly, be water nearby, for several hundred people live there. At one end is a passport office; at the other is a smart petrol pump: between them are many mud houses. In the daytime there is much inactivity, in the evening the whole population assembles and makes noise, in the early morning all is quiet again. Whatever the time, the few mangy dogs cringe listlessly in the street; their life has even less variety.

Our arrival was in the middle of the day and there were only the dogs. The passport office was empty, as were the neighbouring buildings, and we began knocking on doors. A small boy offered to go and get the passport officer out of his bed. He took an hour and we waited in the café, a room with walls made of large oil drums joined together by mud and kept cool by the many puddles on the floor. Our passports were stamped and we drove to the other end for petrol; the attendant was awake and filled up our tanks, but could only give us a little water. Ever since the man at Damascus had filled up our can with quite undrinkable, yellow, sandy water, there had been a shortage of it. Somehow, the mere appearance of a desert makes you aware of the value of water; mix that with the dry inactivity of sitting by a hot engine and thirst increases tenfold.

The land on the eastern side of Rutba Wells is even more barren and there is no scrub; therefore no camels, therefore no Bedouins. The road was straight, dead straight and we climbed over each other when changing places without even bothering to stop. 100 miles along it there was a tea house, just a hut with a man outside smoking a hookah and a boy with two Salukis: but tea and cold water were for sale. The man said nothing, the boy mechanically filled our glasses and everybody coughed from the fumes of the hubble-bubble. Conversation seemed valueless and there was none. We drank many glasses of tea before getting up to go. The man pocketed our money and the Salukis accompanied us back to the road; the boy lay down in the shade and waited for the next customer to come over the horizon. The hopeless tranquillity of the scene prompted a big discussion in the cab concerning the advantages of an industrious life: for once there was agreement of opinion; for once the beliefs were mutual, until thirst came over us again. Then the silence was not even disturbed by the rumbling of a hubble-bubble.

An hour or so after darkness had fallen we drove off the road and prepared for the night. There was no food, there was no water: there was, however, more unanimity on the quantity that should accompany us in the future and on our return. We discussed this point animatedly and waited for sleep: it did come eventually, but it took a long time.

We had a meal on the following day in the NAAFI canteen of the R.A.F. Station, Habbaniya. Our hunger would not allow us to pass such an obvious source of food. We waited at the Guardroom for permission to enter the camp and then drove along avenues of exotic trees and shrubs to receive permission from the adjutant to use the Canteen. It was a good meal, but the pleasure of it was spoilt by hearing of the war in Korea. It is a hateful feeling when you are suddenly informed that some further political boil has burst: perhaps the cleansing effect of the desert had made the news more sudden. The waitress was undistressed and said that she would have to start playing about with maps and flags all over again. Louis just shut his mind to it and made some remark about his old uniform. Philip began to debate on the probable causes and effects of the issue and both of them managed to prevent the waitress from making any further remark. The aircraftmen seemed completely unperturbed and ate their buns happily; they had come out for two years and knew they would be back home again after that time: until then they would have to wait whatever happened. Some of them never left the precincts of the camp in their overseas period and many agreed that Baghdad was really only worth one visit. It would take more than a war in Korea to shake them out of their indifference.

In the afternoon we drove over the Tigris and arrived in

Baghdad. The office for exit visas was closed by the time we had discovered it and, as the next day was a Friday and the Mohammedan day of rest, a clerk informed us that we would have to wait until the Saturday morning. It was therefore necessary to spend the two nights in Baghdad and we repaired to the Y.M.C.A., a comfortable place and within our means. It is a famous establishment and everyone we met who had been to Baghdad advised us to go and stay there. Without any knowledge of Arabic, we wondered how it should be found; but the four letters, pronounced enquiringly, achieved success every time. Mr. Lampard, its caretaker, waited until we had eaten and then took us for a drive through the city, pointing out the principal features and giving us a working knowledge of its layout.

That night we wandered lazily through its streets, no longer the ancient walled city which stood thirty years ago, but now, so the Iraqis say, the modern city of Ancient Babylon, the progressive city of the East. The old buildings are being pulled down to make room for new and double storied ones. Who is to say the value of antiquity against present day needs? In the last century the Sicilians utilized the stones and columns of two collapsed Greek temples when they made a harbour mole. The Suez canal contains stones from the Crusader castles which used to stand in Cyprus. The protective marble has long since been removed from the Pyramids. And now Ancient Baghdad is making way for the new: blaring loudspeakers and klaxon horns provide a fan-fare for the destruction of the things which used to be. But the bazaars have not been changed; the fantastic medley of life continues as it must always have done, with the climax being in the copper department, where prehensile toes grip the metal as it is loudly beaten into shape. All the copper men are said to be deaf; certainly they have reason to be and are similar in other ways: in their lack of facial expression and in the emaciation of their arms.

While we were in the Embassy and trying to get some further document I met a friend of mine recently down from Oxford. After giving us an excellent meal at his house he drove us to the Alwiya Club which arranges for the tastes of the English. There we spent a lazy afternoon falling into the swimming bath and being more appreciative than usual of the excellent qualities of water as a medium in which to pass the time. Someone saw a snake in the garden and put up a notice about it, but otherwise there was nothing to disturb our peaceful meanderings upon the surface of the pool.

That night we had supper with the Counsellor of the Embassy. We sat in chairs on the lawn under the tall date palms and the warm starry night, telling our better stories and producing our wittier repartee, so that the stillness of the air would be broken by loud friendly laughter and we would not have to think about the silence of the heavens.

Two days after our arrival we left the Y.M.C.A. A sudden lightheartedness afflicted us for no apparent reason and we drove merrily round to the Exit Visa Department, the Customs House, a further department at the airport, the British and the Persian Embassies in our efforts to deal with all the formalities now that another week had begun and the offices had opened once more. The Persian Ambassador was vexed that we should be going to his country; he told us to remember that Persia had suffered heavily during the two world wars and that we should not look at the economic state of the country but only at the butterflies. Quite how inspection of the latter was to be made without observation of the former was not made clear: time and diplomacy prevented us from discussing the topic with him.

The road north-east from Baghdad was straight and dull, except that we came steadily nearer to the mountainous border of Persia. After four hours we reached the Iraqi Customs. The dust was removed from the seals; they said that they were good and directed us along the road which led out of their country.

So we drove along the short stretch between the two Customs Houses and declared ourselves to have entered Persia. Someone said it in the cab, for it had to come; but it was not said loudly or with any emphasis. We had not crossed a mountain range to see a new land spread before us, nor had we come to green fields after miles and miles of desert; we had only driven for a few minutes away from the Iraqi Customs house, but we had arrived in the country of our destination, in Persia.

This, we felt, was of great importance. But it was nothing

more consequential than that some English students were about to go and live in one of its villages for a couple of months; there need be no trumpets to herald that event. Yet perhaps it was to be a test for, without any warning and without any formality, a village in the south of Persia was going to receive these four, to have them living in their midst, to have them as their uninvited guests. Why should this not be possible? We had read much about their country but no prejudice existed in any of us concerning the people and their ways; attitudes towards them and convictions about their lives had not been fashioned into any form at all; they were as a lump of clay ready to be moulded into shape. We had completed the first part by producing ourselves at the Customs house at Khosrovi: its fulfilment, the moulding of the clay, was up to Persia and the Persians.

CHAPTER III

Persia to Kirman

ON that evening each of us cared only that he wanted to look at Persia and the time was about to begin. Nevertheless, there were differences in us, in our methods of looking, and they could not be forgotten. The three individuals who got out of their truck at this Customs house were quite naturally objects of interest to those Persians who happened to be there. There was Philip, methodical and purposive, indignant only if his resolution of the moment was not being fulfilled: almost certainly he was first out of the truck with the documents in his hand. Then there was Louis, with half the resolution, but twice the indignation if things went wrong; half the energy, but twice the charm: certainly he did not have the documents in his hand and probably only his feet were outside while he flailed about with his arms to find a cigarette. As for my resolution or indignation, I know not; but I can guarantee I was still sitting in the cab without having moved a muscle, for I find it pleasant to assume attitudes of complete inactivity. These were the three who had come to meet the Persians.

Philip disappeared into the building; Louis found a cigarette and exclaimed, with an inordinate sense of relief, how good it was to have arrived. With all of us, our eyes became a little more open, our ears a little more receptive to the occurrences about us: we were now ready for these happenings, for the rising of the curtain. Let what might befall, we would observe it: let the players strut about and act accordingly. Louis and I settled back in our seats expectantly. Some prologue would probably describe the situation.

He came in the form of a harassed official who ran out of the Customs house with our documents fluttering in his hands.

Having gone twice round the truck, he counted Louis and me with his fingers as if there were many more of us and then hurried back into the building. The man had disturbed our complacency and we wandered in after him. It transpired that a telegram had been sent with instructions relating either to us or the four Austrian students who had just left: anyway the telegram had been lost and the instructions forgotten. 'There is nothing to be done until it is found', he protested, and began to look through all his papers. Unfortunately it was true and everything had to wait until the telegram appeared once more. Louis went out to cook some spaghetti and Philip and I joined him in eating it: then all of us waited for night and for sleep.

In the morning the whole yard was filled quite suddenly with lorries and the number of officials increased proportionately. They all in turn explained to us that the delay resulted from their efforts to be kind; for the telegram might not refer to the Austrians and might even be important: kindness is somewhat annulled when its presence has to be explained. Then, with the paper still unfound and for no reason other than that our truck was in the way, they dismissed us and told us to report to the Customs house in Tehran. So, hastily, a telegram was dispatched to our hosts there, saying that we would shortly be with them; this was an ineffectual move; but how were three strangers to know that the telegram would take a week and longer than a letter in the post?

All of that day we drove up onto the Persian plateau. Much of the country is over 6,000 feet above sea level and its western border with Iraq and Turkey is exceptionally mountainous. The drive was not along a road going steadily upwards; instead it twisted its way through steep valleys, down into wide green plains and then up again over some further range of hills. The surface of the road was atrocious, but the countryside provided more interest than had the desert and the battery box did not feel so hard. The monotonous barrenness of the sands had given way to fertile plains and hills of rock, the camels were replaced by donkeys and the Arab costume by the semi-European clothes of the Persian. Our cautious advisers had alleged that bandits lived in this part of Persia; we had made no preparations against their possible uprisings; for the first prerequisite of a bandit is that he carries considerably more weapons than his opponent. Therefore we deemed it useless to carry any. As the truck ground its way slowly up the passes or round steep bends or coursed down the equally tortuous route on the other side, there was no doubt in any of us that it was exceptionally suitable country for such men and their activities.

The pass before Hamadan was the steepest and the most suitable, the slope on the other side was more gentle and enabled us to reach the town just before all the light had left the sky. At Baghdad they had informed us of an American hospital in Hamadan which would certainly allow us to sleep in their grounds. After we had given a vigorous demonstration of Americans and hospitals to a small crowd near the centre of the town, our wishes were understood and a boy guided us to the place. There Dr. Frame and his wife would not dream of us sleeping outside; they provided beds and food and a steady flow of conversation about the Korean war. Down towards the town there was much noise coming from those for whom the beginning of the night meant the breaking of the fast of the day. The moon rose up from behind the hills, silhouetted their shapes and lit up the feasting scenes in the gardens of the town. Far away from their revelries and on a peak to the north was the rugged outline of Noah's wife, on her knees and bemoaning the loss of her fourth son.

From Hamadan the road becomes straighter and less interesting; before Qazvin the route is still through the mountains; after it there is only the wide dusty plain to be crossed. Tehran is situated at the foot of the hills which separate it from the Caspian sea. That plain before Tehran is desperately barren and the town itself comes as a surprise and as a relief: it is not an obvious situation for a large town and the site is unsuspected from the plain. We were grateful for its sudden arrival.

As was our wont we found ourselves carried by momentum into the very centre before having any idea of the direction in which we should be going. This time it was a town of wide main streets but with a few extremely dingy ones connecting them, of large white buildings with occasional rows of squalid dwellings. By every pavement ran the jube, a stream of water which had doubtless been clean at the top of the town but did not remain so for long. It differed in the squalid streets only in that its course was not restricted to one particular channel; it idled a way for itself wherever it chose to flow. Everywhere the traffic was noisy and boisterous, bus conductors leant out from their buses yelling the destinations, horses galloped by with their water carts, taxi drivers shouted at the pedestrians that they were free; the symphony of horns and bells formed, for the clamouring, a continuous background of sound. On the other side of the jube the pavement was occupied by veiled women and scabby beggars, by men with large crates strapped to their foreheads, by youths with smart suits who gazed at you loftily, and by the old men who, racked by the humility of old age and poverty, do not even lift their eyes from the ground. The jube flowed evenly past them all, except in the places where the small boys bathed and the women washed their clothes. In the side streets there was no pavement and no particular road: there the mixture was complete; there was the solid residue of living matter, and the jube flowed quietly beneath the lot. This was the town of Tehran, the town modern- ized by the Reza Shah and with an emulation of the West that shows up the character of the East. The rich man steps out of a car and may put his foot in the jube; the beggar sits down on the ground with his back to a clean, white wall.

A boy attached himself onto our door handle and gave us directions to the Oil Company offices. There a man appeared who offered to guide us to the house of our host, Mr. Northcroft, the representative of the Anglo-Iranian Oil Company in Tehran. The boy was detached and thanked; the road was followed which led up out of the town to Gulhek and towards the hills, where the air is cooler and the rich have built their summer homes. Just past the heavily wooded and sepulchral grounds of the Russian Embassy was our destination. We drove in and blew our horn proudly.

We had a very pleasant week as their guests. In England it had been imagined glibly that a day or two would be quite sufficient to deal with all the formalities in Tehran. But we had not known that public offices only opened in the mornings and the general speed with which our affairs were settled was discovered to be slower than all our imaginings. Nevertheless the week was most enjoyable.

In the mornings the three of us drove into the town and scattered into the various departments so that the maximum number of officials should be visited. Time was spent with the Customs, at the bank, in the Embassies and Legations. Letters of introduction were pressed forward. Travel Agencies were asked about transporting live animals. Other departments gave us permission to take out dead ones. Our presence in the country had to be displayed, noted and then confirmed. All in all, very many hours have to be spent in official departments when a party of students arrive on a scientific trip in a semi-westernized, mainly Eastern, politically strategic, pseudo police state. When the offices closed we assembled at the British Embassy and drove back to Gulhek for lunch.

On our third day in Tehran, Eric arrived by air. He talked volubly of the beauty of the Greek Islands at sunrise and of the mountain masses of Turkey, but I shall never credit transportation by air as travel. Every joy has been erased save that of arriving at another place.

In the late afternoon the parties began. As our presence in Tehran was not customary, as the human race is by nature polite to newcomers and as the English speaking members of the community had an abundance of parties anyway, it happened that all our evenings were spent at those gatherings. Louis put on his suit. Philip used to wear a blue shirt and a scarlet tie which gave to him alone a feeling of satisfaction. Eric had only flown from England and his clothes did not have a 'nomadic appearance', a description applied to mine. All the other guests were smart; we, after all, were only a temporary growth onto Tehran society. The briefness of our stay was an encouragement to make ourselves more rapidly acquainted with the routine of the occasions; they formed very pleasant interludes to the difficulties of the mornings. Food and drink were placed on all the tables and everybody arranged themselves nearby. The drink convinced us that the person in the next chair was not as dull as he, or she, first pretended to be. The food, the caviare and kabobs, were emphatic in their assertion that food is creditable just for its own sake, without reference to hunger or need. The evening passed rapidly until yet another Tehran party disintegrated as its members retired to their homes.

The weekend was an anniversary of the death of Husain, another religious occasion, and there was nothing that could be achieved in connection with our formalities. Instead, the North-crofts treated us to a weekend of luxury by lending us a Humber Pullman with a chauffeur and by instructing him to take us to the Caspian. To reach that sea it is necessary to go over the Elburz range, high mountains with plenty of trees and a good rainfall on the north side but drier and more barren on the side above Tehran.

The enclosed comfort of the Pullman was strange after the airy travel to which we had become accustomed. Except for the occasions when we walked, the countryside slipped by without sufficient intimacy having been reached with it; so different to the familiarity enforced by the truck. At the top the road passed through a long tunnel; on one side of it the sun was shining fiercely but a thick cloud greeted us when we drove out onto the other: truly the Elburz mountains divide the arid heat of Tehran from the Mediterranean climate of the Caspian. The descent to Chalus was almost entirely through cloud, yet there were occasional glimpses of a sea quite devoid of ships of any kind. In Chalus, one of the few places which served meals was an imposing and expensive hotel that had been commandeered by the Russians in the war; there we had a meal and sat on a veranda overlooking the sea, but there was nothing to be seen that was afloat on it. Further along the coast there was a Russo-Persian Caviare industry but their fleet was not visible. Caviare is such a valuable commodity that two sturgeon caught by the twenty or thirty boats is considered a satisfactory catch.

That evening we were driven along the coast road to Resht, the largest Persian town on the Caspian. There exists no tide on such a small area of sea and the beach was short; the road had been made to go very close to the shore. It was abnormal to have such a large expanse of water with so little activity associated with it. One or two gaunt gulls perched at its edge and sometimes a species of tern flew over the water; but otherwise there was nothing, nothing until the horizon put an end to it. On the other side of the road there were rice fields, until the ground became too steep; then there were trees that reached up to the craggy mountain tops.

The Consul at Resht had invited us to stay at his house, although our visit coincided with the date fixed for his inspection of the area. However, his servant made us comfortable and we slept on the balcony. On the next day the chauffeur disappeared to mend various parts of the car which had gone wrong. We made very little effort to inspect the town and its environs, for Resht is a town saturated with suspicion; its proximity to the U.S.S.R. and its consequent vulnerability makes each inhabitant avow that every visitor is there for unlawful purposes. All this part of Persia was occupied by the Russians in the latter period of the war; the Persians resented and objected to this occupation, but if you put your finger on a map at the bottom of the Caspian it is not hard to visualise the reason for the fear which hovers over them. As a horse must dislike pulling a heavy cart, so did we dislike the trailing crowds which followed along behind us.

Therefore that day was spent in the Consul's garden reading the Consul's books until he himself arrived in the evening to give us supper. Unfortunately there were arrangements in Tehran on the following day, and as soon as the car was ready the chauffeur had to be persuaded to take us back.

There was disagreement over this point. We debated whether it was profitable to see the country between Resht and Tehran, or to hurry on with the journey. The only reason that the former, the more rational and sensible, the more easy-going plan was not adopted was that there existed within us a desire to get to Kirman. This was not unreasonable in itself, as it had been our aim and destination for many months, but there had been times when this fixed idea had seemed to be the height of folly. We had driven swiftly through France and Italy, we had passed close to Baalbek, spent 60 minutes in Damascus, slept within 70 miles of Babylon and had not even bothered to look at the rock carvings at Bisitun which are so close to the road: instead we had looked intently ahead of us, for we could not allow ourselves to do otherwise. Any deviation would have weakened our purpose and who can say how long it would take to drive from England to Kirman if the aim was not definite and the fixed intention was not clear? Consequently, until that intention had been repulsed by our arrival in Kirman, the trip would only consist of rapid and jerky flashes of events, like a bubble in a mountain stream. We felt ourselves driven on and knew that this would be so until we had arrived there, until the stream had joined the placid waters in the plain.

Thus it was that we returned through the night and by a different route over the mountains, stopping at occasional cafés, but for the most part driving in the silence of the darkness and of the hills. We reached Qazvin and the plain of Tehran at dawn: it was the quantity and depth of the potholes which kept the chauffeur awake.

Two days later, at noon, we left Tehran and with us was our interpreter. Many months previously the Persian Government had made it clear that it was their intention to provide us with a student who would solve our language difficulties. They had informed us later that a young school teacher, by name Kemal Fazel, was eager and keen to accompany us. Then his eagerness faded and another was selected. During our time in Tehran many candidates arose and then withered away before even a meeting had been arranged. But Ahmed Saam had been more adamant; he had introduced himself to us all on the previous day and had presented us with a large sheet of paper on which was written 'Ahmed Saam, your servant'. When we met him again at the Embassy just before our departure he was sitting with his brother on an enormous pile of bedding and clutching what he called a camp bed. It was not so much a camp bed as a bed that had been taken to pieces. The bedding had to be taken, but luckily we possessed a real camp bed that had been bought for him. He was an active little man whose activity was mainly caused by his inability to keep calm in any situation: this could, of course, be applied to many people, but it applied in particular to Ahmed Saam. He spoke a sort of English, was 28 and a Kirmani, taught physics and chemistry, was one of a family of six, unmarried, without a father, and had a large quantity of black wavy hair. A brother ran a photographer's shop in Kirman and he invited all of us to go there and have our photos taken.

From Tehran to Kirman it is 700 miles. The road runs south from Tehran and is tarmac for the first 100 miles, as far as Qum. It was pleasant to bowl along again on a good road. The settling of formalities in Tehran had given a feeling that an obstacle had been passed, but also that nothing had been gained: there is no satisfaction in settling formalities which are not convincing in their necessity. A whole morning had been spent in acquiring permission to unseal the boxes and after the seals had been removed the officials took no interest in the things which the wire had safeguarded: formality for its own sake was far too frequently encountered and it was good to feel that those affairs had been left behind.

Qum possesses a beautiful mosque with four minarets and a golden dome, a dome that appears to intensify the rays of the sun; for its dazzling brightness is visible many miles from the town over which it rises. It was built by Shah Abbas, a contemporary of Queen Elizabeth's.

After Qum, the peculiar corrugations of the gravelled roads greeted us for the first time. They demanded a high speed to obtain the minimum vibration; but in spite of this and the efforts of the roadmen, who shovelled what had been flung to the side into the middle again, the business of eating a melon became even more of a problem. We ate food as we travelled; for in that way the distances were covered more rapidly. The big melon, ten inches or so across, was a lovely thing to eat, but the vibrations were most violent and our hair became unavoidably matted with the juices. We also ate tomatoes and bread of a flat, round type: upon these three things we survived for the period of the journey. Now that Eric and Ahmed had joined us it was impossible for all to sit in the cab; so the battery box was dismissed from our thoughts as a suitable seat and three places were made on the top of all our equipment. Ahmed's bedding and an enormous tent lent by the Northcrofts provided sufficient cushioning for the three to sit on up there, but dust made any position near the back quite untenable for them. The butterfly net, fixed to the top of the cab, collected insects and conveniently diverted the gaze of the bystanders who were all too wont to stare. So we lived for three days. The driver climbed out onto the roof every two hours while someone else held the truck on its course and then clambered into the seat. We stopped once a day for food and petrol and then in the evening, just before it became completely dark: Ahmed's bedding was thrown down to him, the camp beds were found and the warmth of the truck soon sent us to sleep.

Wherever there was habitation nearby, the countryside was spotted with the openings of qanats, the underground channels which supply the bulk of the water in Persia. Like molehills or bomb craters they speckled the land and stretched for many miles before disgorging their water onto the surface. For in the making of one of them the constructors dig many shafts along its length, partly for ventilation but mainly as passages for the removal of the excavated material. At the top of each shaft a mound is formed which gives the land above a qanat its characteristic appearance. These shafts are also used when repair work or removal of silt is being carried out, and as we drove along, we occasionally saw a large wooden wheel erected above one of them. By means of the wheel two men raise the little goat skin bag and then empty it of its contents. Down below, the excavators crawl along the channels and with short handled picks and shovels fill up the bag once more.

As there are shafts along the length of the qanat and as the water eventually flows out of its lower end, the depth of the shafts lessen towards the exit. The final shaft may be only 6 feet deep, but at the other end the water channel is often 300 feet from the surface of the land. An exceptional case is at Gunabad where the deepest well is 1,000 feet. In spite of the obvious labour and expense in excavating each shaft, it is generally considered economic to make a fresh one for every 150 feet of channel. The bad ventilation down in the channel and the difficulties of dragging the full bag along it to the base of the shaft make this necessary.

Yet, although 150 feet separated one gaping hole from the next, and one pile of mud from its neighbour, the medley of qanats that converged upon a town made the dotted lines become indistinct. As with birds before an island, the qanat wells warned you of the approach of a town; they are the ramifying tendrils which are responsible for its livelihood, the arteries of its existence and, as with arteries, their breakdown causes that existence to cease.

Herodotus, in describing the wars in Persia, writes of the simple procedure of filling in the wells of a town in order to destroy it. Nowadays, lines of qanat wells often lead to nothing more than a few old walls; the qanat has dried up and the people have been forced to move elsewhere. The extraction of water from a desert is not only a costly but a chancy business.

We stopped to have a look down some of these wells. Little stones, dislodged by our feet, rolled down the slope and then into the shaft: it was always too deep for the sound of the splash to be heard. Once a snake slid back into the stones which surrounded the mouth of the well; Louis threw a stone at it and then made steps for the truck: however, we had seen the qanats and drove on full of respect for the muqannis, the workers of the qanats. Throughout our time in Persia, although we heard many unkind words said about every other kind of Persian working man, no words were ever said against the muqanni. Ahmed was particularly vociferous in his denunciations about others and to him all carpet workers were cheats, all road workers lazy, all shepherds stupid, Government officials corrupt, landlords knaves and farmers ignorant; but he never said a word either for, or against, a muqanni. His silence on the subject and lack of indignation for their ways was, for Ahmed, tantamount to respect.

The next big town after Qum was Isfahan, a city which underwent great expansion under Shah Abbas at the beginning of the 17th century, when it was made the capital. The Imperial square and its associated buildings built at that time are still in good condition, but unfortunately we had to hurry on. Apart from confirming the story that Isfahan grows the finest melons in the land, we made a vow to spend more time there on the way back, when the work was done. Then we drove south once more and out of the town.

The road led over another high pass, through more desert, more expanse and more isolated villages until it entered Yezd. This town is flatter, its hills are further away, far less wealth has been spent upon it and the total result is less interesting. After Yezd and before Kirman, the road became so bad that it was necessary and infinitely more pleasant to drive along the salt-pan which stretched by the side of it for some twenty miles. It was the

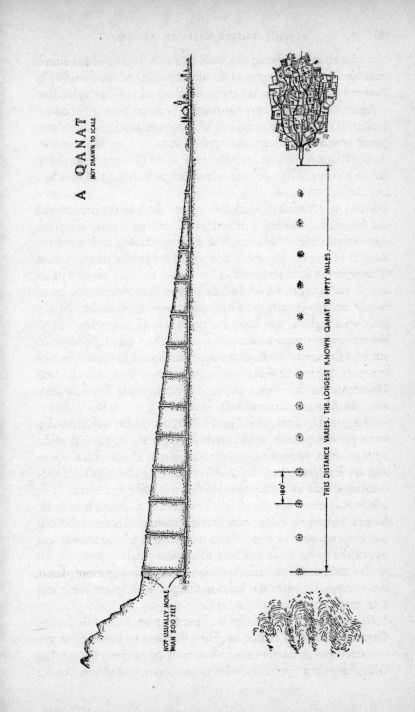

A QANAT
NOT DRAWN TO SCALE

NOT USUALLY MORE
THAN 300 FEET

160'

THIS DISTANCE VARIES. THE LONGEST KNOWN QANAT IS FIFTY MILES.

only one that we ever drove over and its smooth, firm surface made an agreeable change to the corrugations of the roads. We were not jerked about and there was no column of dust behind us as the truck hummed on over the last few miles to the plain of Kirman. Louis, vastly encouraged that we had seen only one species of plant in those twenty miles, began singing on the top of the truck and we all became a bit vocal at the thought of reaching our destination. The same thought struck Ahmed and he combed his hair.

When you have talked about a place for months beforehand and travelled 5,000 miles to reach it, a picture of that place has inevitably arisen. Moreover it is equally certain that however many miles are driven or words are used the picture is bound only to be a feeble representation of the real thing. Which one of us could have imagined that the hills behind the town should be so blue, that the greenness of the trees should be so beautifully contrasted with the rich brown of the clay walls and of the desert? We realised at once that Kirman is a delightful place. The lack of cars and the predominance of eastern things, its compactness and the confidence of all Kirmanis that it produces not only the best carpets but also the best opium, all help to make it of interest. Reza Shah, who made Tehran by deciding where main streets should go and knocking down all that was in the way, had also exerted his influence in Kirman: a wide street goes straight through the town with large roundabouts at either end, so large that the few lorries and all the other vehicles go round the roundabout in the shorter direction whichever it happens to be.

Into this town we drove on the evening of the 13th of July. Ahmed managed to prolong the question: "Where is the old British Consulate?" into a lengthy discussion before an answer was produced and the place had been found. An old man with one eye opened its gate to let us in; once again Philip jumped out, Louis looked for a cigarette and I did nothing: but this time there was nothing much to be done.

The Consulate was situated beneath the ruins of the old fort of Kirman, a fort that helped to guard the road to India. Now the fort decays and the Consulate has been taken over by the Oil Company, for a Consul is required no longer in Kirman. Shaikh al Islami, the Persian representative of the Oil Company for the area, lives there; speaking perfect English, he assured us of all possible help that he could give. Peter Wild, the doctor at the Church Missionary Society's hospital, had met us in the town when we were looking for the Consulate: there he had offered his help and had informed us of the presence of two other Englishmen at the hospital who could certainly assist us in many ways. Ahmed, catching onto the mood of things, reiterated that he was our servant and more so than before, now that we were in his birth-place: this reminded us and we hastily gave him permission to go and visit his family who all lived under the roof of his brother, Photo Saam.

These offers of assistance were most welcome and supported our desire to justify the journey. The truck had brought us there: it was necessary that the project should be fulfilled. The old fort had been built as a barricade against intervention by others; now it was crumbling but still existed. To what extent was a buttress to stand between us and the people of Kirman and its villages? We thought and talked about this for a while, speculated and then went to sleep. There was only one way to find out.

CHAPTER IV

The week in Kirman

I T was before the day had begun to get warm that a soldier
arrived with a message that the Major General of the town
wished to see us. He had lost no time and soon we were being
greeted by a stout man with a deep voice who spoke English.
The Army, he said, would do all that it could for us. Horses,
transport and escorts could be prepared. All that was in his power
could come to our aid. Each of us felt that some advantage should
be taken of his offers, not because there was great need of them
but in order to placate and subdue the intensity of his altruism.

The police lived in a different part of the same building and it
was necessary to register our arrival. A fat man sat behind a small
desk in a dark room and slowly distorted our names and addresses
into the Persian script. The Governor General lived in another and
more imposing building. Dr. Wild joined us there to smooth over
any difficulties that might arise. Shaikh al Islami also appeared.
Large rooms led into larger rooms with carpets of varying
excellence on the floor. Eventually a man ushered us all into his
presence. Just before a box containing twenty different types of
cigarettes was passed around and long before the tea arrived
Ahmed disturbed the peace of the scene by telling the Governor
that the Major General had already received us and had promised
us all that we would ever require. Now the Governor held the
senior post and should have had the privilege of seeing us first
and of granting our wishes. Dr. Wild and Shaikh al Islami
quietened Ahmed tactfully before telling the Governor that
whereas the Major General wished to please, he could naturally
not help us in as many ways as could he, the Governor General.
Then after admiring his carpets, some of which were most ugly,
everybody retreated towards the door; for it is not done to show
your back to a man who requires your respect.

For the rest of that day we unpacked and, out of deference to the Major General, sent round Ahmed with a request that a Jeep should be placed at our disposal on the following morning. The truck after all had to get us back to England. That evening Shaikh al Islami gave us supper and introduced us to his wife. She had a mass of black hair and bright blue eyes, a combination characteristic of the Northern borders of Persia which caused Louis to eulogise on its merits for the rest of the evening.

On the next day Louis was mysteriously ill, so only Philip, Eric and I went to look for the Jeep. All three of us were looking forward to driving one as a change from the Bedford. Down at the Army headquarters six soldiers instantly ushered us into a large Chevrolet ten-wheeler and in they clambered with their rifles and bedding. An officer came and, after going back to fetch two revolvers, asked us where we were going and how long we were going to stay there. Initially, we said, to Photo Saam. There Ahmed climbed aboard and was given instruction by us on the vital importance of understanding our messages before he delivered them. Notwithstanding the fact that we couldn't see out of the lorry and were going on a tour of inspection of the neighbourhood, the driver was told to go to Zangiabad, a village that looked suitable for our purposes from the map.

There was no road to Zangiabad. The driver took a course as straight as the qanat wells would allow. This involved going over all the little fields on the edge of the town, all dry without crops at that time of the year, but all with a surrounding wall of hard earth a foot high which had been to prevent the water from running away when the fields were irrigated. We three were flung about and discussed what type of village was most suitable. Eric wanted a village typical of those in this area and of a size that could be mapped by him in six weeks. I wanted to settle somewhere where there were plenty of accessible qanats and where the villagers were not liable to object if an Englishman spent his days paddling in them. This latter factor required a magnanimous landlord; for I wished to work not only in the drinking water of his village but also in his income. To a Mohammedan running water is a symbol of purity and cleanliness, while my intention was to look for the animals in the water. The magnanimity of the landlord would have to smooth over all antagonistic viewpoints. Actually there was no reason for me to announce that I was looking for the impurities in their water, but a favourable landlord was essential. Philip, although he had labelled himself as a Soil-chemist, not only intended to find out the relationships between the crops and the soil, but also wished to find out all facts on the economy of the village, on crop rotation and laws of land tenure. Therefore his village would have to be large enough to supply a sufficiency of fact. Louis wished to work in a village sufficiently large so that the botanical regions, brought about by habitation and the cultivation of the soil, would be distinguishable. He intended to make not only a general collection of plants, but to examine everything which grew for a short distance on one side of a transect through a village from desert to desert.

We had doubts whether this ideal village could be found and began to talk to the officer with the two revolvers. He was most amiable and said how glad he was to think that he was helping us. He explained that all the soldiers were necessary for our safety as Persia was in a state of unrest. Much discontent had fermented since the war and the bandits had taken to the hills again. Two soldiers had been shot three months ago and only forty miles from Kirman. Even the Governor's brother had been shot recently by some Bakhtiari tribesmen. He said how vital it was that each of us should always be accompanied by at least two soldiers and pointed to his subordinates sitting opposite us. Those of them who were on the bedding were asleep, those on the petrol cans were staring ahead of them vacantly. Each one had a red neck sticking out from the large neck hole of his uniform. They all had large peaked caps and heavily nailed boots.

Zangiabad was obviously not our ideal village. It rambled over far too large an area and big sections were withering away due, presumably, to the lack of water. One corner of it was being engulfed by sand blown from the centre of the Kirman plain. But it gave us an idea of a village. Eric walked round the fields with Ahmed asking questions of the farmers. Philip and I went with the officer to the qanats. One was being repaired and through the officer, for he spoke a little French, we asked the muqannis at the wheel about the fish. They admitted that fish were there and said they lived in every qanat. Birds live in the air and fish live in the water; it was never otherwise. I asked if anyone ever put them there and was told that they came automatically. They agreed that a fish's egg was quite large and would have difficulty in seeping into the qanat. They shouted down the shaft for some fish's eggs and up with the next load of mud came a tinful of snails. This story was acclaimed by every Persian, for it was argued that they couldn't be anything else. The little fish within the shell was always pointed out to me. They were equally emphatic that no other animals lived in the channels except bats and snakes, that as both these animals live on air alone and as the fish live entirely on water there was no need for any other form. To a Persian, Natural History is the essence of simplicity.

In this particular qanat three boys were working. It was too small for a man to crawl along and therefore unsuitable for my purposes. All the qanats of Zangiabad were the same; for the land beneath is soft and large tunnels cannot be made. In many places nars had to be used. These are oval bricks of baked clay and when placed end to end provide complete support for the channel. Many crack in the baking and the whole firing process is expensive, so they are not used unless they are absolutely necessary. If the roof does not collapse immediately the channel is made the landlord considers it cheaper to send down a boy on each occasion that a blockage occurs. Even the boys find it difficult to crawl up a channel supported by nars. These boys begin to work in a qanat when they are eight.

The officer was diligent and every aspect of the village was shown to us. The mill was a dark and dirty place, well below ground level, where a mill stone, driven by the pressure from a head of water, slowly turned and ground out the flour. The business of thrashing involved several pairs of cows which walked round and round on a heap of corn. They pulled a roller with wooden spikes which crushed out the corn. Boys with whips kept them moving. Winnowing was the old process of throwing up the thrashed material after the crushing had been completed. Rhythmically and easily the thrashings were tossed into the air. The steady and ponderous turning of the mill stone set the pace for all the activity of the village. The qanat wheel went no faster, nor did the cattle. The chaff drifted slowly over the land.

The drive back was in the darkness and more bumpy. Even the soldiers on the bedding were kept awake. But Ahmed slept. At Kirman we woke him up with a request to thank the officer and to say that we would be requiring only horses in the future.

For the first week in Kirman we drove around the area. It was necessary to find the suitable village. The basin of Kirman is about fifty miles from North to South and forty miles from East to West. It is bordered by the hills which are four or five thousand feet higher. The villages have grown up in positions where water is obtainable, where they are out of the way of the spring torrents and where the finer material which has been washed down from the hills is situated. The bulk of the villages in the Kirman plain were on its edge at the foot of the hills. Their size was variable and determined by the available quantity of water. Kirman itself receives its water from many qanats each twenty five miles long, which start in the South and give forth their water just south of the town.

The truck was emptied of all our equipment, the white canopy tied on the top and anything which might serve as a cushion was put on the floor. So we toured: through small villages like Neckar-kuh and Dorah Shah Dad, or larger like Koshariz and Zangar, to the coal mines of the Kuh-i-Badimu with an output of three tons a week, to Deh Shi, to Negar and to Asiabad. Never did we take any food; it was always produced for us. In a garden we would eat with some man we had never seen before, who had not known of our intended visit but who, on being asked for food, would insist that we ate with him. Payment for the meal would be proffered by us and refused by him; it was left to Ahmed's discretion whether the man was rich enough to be insulted by it or poor enough to be in real need of it; in which case it was thrust into one of the man's pockets. We ourselves found it impossible in the villages to distinguish between the rich and the poor save that the former received more deference from his fellows. They both wore shirts with no collars, pyjama trousers and the coat of an old suit. Ahmed said the landlords were distinguishable because of their selfishness. Even after eating a splendid meal from one of them and advising us not to pay for it he adhered to this opinion.

His prejudice was of a kind that is not tempered by experience.

From these landlords and peasants we extracted the facts concerning the villages. They were always ready to give and we to receive, but initially, before we could ask the questions ourselves, Ahmed was in the middle. He was town bred and did not credit the farmers with knowledge. Simple agricultural practice had to be explained to him by the Persian before any of it came through to us. The principle of letting fields go fallow or of the rotation of crops was a surprise to him; in consequence he asserted that the particular farmer was unique or mad. Ahmed could never admit that an illiterate man possessed knowledge that he, a literate, did not possess. Such is the view of all his associates who have lived in the town and have received an education.

The centre of the plain of Kirman is, except for small settlements, quite barren. The rest is hard desert and dry sand. This sand is a menace, for the winds blow it about. Initially, only the crops are ruined; but if the wind blows from the same direction for long enough, then a village may become submerged. Such remains can be seen scattered over the plain. This danger is recent, is increasing and the fault of the Kirmanis themselves. Under normal conditions most deserts will become static: small plants manage to grow and so help to bind the sand particles; then larger plants survive and the sand around them becomes harder and acts as a protective crust. Rain followed by sun increases the firmness of this surface layer and, if left to themselves, small areas of desert do not constitute an engulfing menace. Although the livelihood of the whole basin depends on the stability of the land, all sizeable plants are uprooted to be burnt as fuel. Camels, donkeys and an old Bedford lorry were being used to bring in this vegetation. Steadily the firmness is being lost: each year more of the desert begins to move. Great walls are built to arrest the advancing sand, but whenever there is a wind the sand increases its attack; the outlying fields are covered, the dust is spread over the town, the roads become blocked and have to be cleared. Nothing is done to prevent the problem. It is nobody's affair. "It is the will of Allah if great winds are sent." While every Persian is prepared to expound upon the large engineering schemes of the seven-year plan which will make Persia one of the greatest nations, nothing but a shrug of the shoulders results when a policy for neglect of the desert is suggested. The desert belongs to no one; ownership applies only to land which is cultivated. No responsibility is involved, only their future welfare and that problem is allowed to rest until the future.

Sometimes, in spite of the sand, it was quicker to return across the centre of the plain. Into the sandy region we drove at maximum speed, but its braking effect was tremendous. It was necessary to get down into the lower gears almost at once to have a chance of covering any but the smallest distance. Experience taught us a lot: not to worry about the skidding effects and to stop immediately you felt the truck was sinking in. There was no point in letting the back wheels half bury themselves for the sake of a few more feet. The wire netting was then used: we placed it just in front of the back wheel, around the front wheel and then straight in front of the truck. One person had to be at each back wheel, ready to push the wire under it when it began to spin round. The back wheel then gripped and the bulge originally around the front wheel of the truck had to be pushed in so that the back wheel did not land again on soft sand. It was then up to the driver to make all possible speed along the twenty five yards of wire netting in order that he should be carried a good distance when he hit the sand again. A further twenty five yards was considered satisfactory. The wire would then be dragged along and the process repeated: in this way and in fifty yard bursts the journey continued until a firm surface assured a more constant pace.

Slow as this method was, it was often faster than going by road; in a district where men travel by foot or by donkey roads are not considered important. In the winter, flood waters pour over them, leaving broad deep channels. The irrigation streams pass over them and are well ridged with steep banks to prevent any loss of water. The roads therefore become less noticeable as such, save that nothing is made to grow on them and their surface is slightly harder. To improve the road means to increase the hardships of the donkey and camel drivers who are resentful of the increasing competition of motor transport. We had noticed many unreasonably large holes in the road and once laughingly accused some camel drivers of having made them; they laughed too, but strangely. The poor truck bounded about on these roads; but more so when being handled by Eric and Philip. Eric had never driven before and Philip was just bad. After the fourth day it was noticed that five of the six leaves in the back spring had broken. Louis vigorously accused Philip, Eric apologised effusively but actually I believe it had been broken when I was once going too fast to avoid a pile of stones that had been placed on one of the good stretches of the road. Anyway Louis did most of the work in repairing it.

These camel drivers are an interesting people. They travel by night and let their camels graze by day. They have as little contact with other people as do the shepherds in the hills. Ahmed called them backward and automatically enhanced our opinion of them. Due to a great desire of mine to ride on a camel, we stopped at the first herd we saw and sauntered over to speak to the drivers who were sitting underneath a tree. They greeted us cordially and made us sit down with them. The camels sat nearby methodically chewing. The men continued with what they had been doing. One was spinning camel hair into wool, another was baking some bread and the third, the youngest, was making a camel hair rope. Somehow, by continuing with the task in hand, they gave us a feeling of being welcome. About once every five minutes they asked us a question. Each answer was pondered over and discussed. They thought it strange that there should be no camels in England and willingly let me ride on one. I sat on it and the indignant animal got up at once. I entreated her to gallop, but she would do no more than walk around the herd. I was told that she could never be made to leave her friends. This was too pathetic for me to continue riding and I returned her to the original position. Before I had time to make any of the weird sounds necessary to entreat a camel to sit, she had done so.

We were given a meal of hot doughy bread and tea. The conversation continued in its jerky fashion. The camels did nothing except ruminate and produce the fuel for tomorrow's fires. Towards the end of the meal the men began to laugh and even the camels hesitated in their chewing to listen. It transpired that my hat, a long, stocking-shaped thing from Germany, by being green, dubbed me as one of the descendants of Mohammed. This, to them, was so incongruous and unlikely that it caused them more merriment than I had heard for a long time. Afterwards I wore the hat, but less conspicuously, and looked fraternally upon all others with green hats: at least we had the green hat if not the ancestry in common. The religion of Mohammedanism is so well engrained in the poor people that it can withstand and survive the frequent jests that are made by all about it. It does survive; for the jokes are made about the religion and not at it: this difference is conclusive.

From each trip we returned to the sanctity of Kirman and the Consulate. Usually the food was cooked by us, but we had supper one evening with Dr. Wild. He and George Oddy, the electrician, gave us a lot of qanat information; but most of the talk was about the hospital. Peter Wild has himself suffered from many Asiatic diseases and apparently believes that his hours of work and hardships are no greater than are those of an English country doctor. He is much respected and has greatly improved the facilities of the hospital. Even an X-ray unit has been set up which had to be fetched from the ship at Bandar Abbas, a distance of 300 miles. This was quite a feat, for the road is very bad. The Oil Company does not send its petrol bowsers along it, but instead have contracted with private drivers to transport it in tins. Nevertheless, a piano had once been brought along that road. It was a proud possession, originally of the consulate and latterly of the hospital, for it had been carried all the way from Bandar Abbas on the heads of six porters. As with the X-ray unit, this was the best route for it to come by.

Many Kirmanis will not go near the hospital and many of those who do wait until they have to be carried there. The Persian is so used to the sight and experience of disease that the onset of a new one is not considered ominous until it has had serious consequences. A man may be blind before he reports his eye trouble. Nevertheless, much good work is done there in the curing of disease and Kirman and its villages provide plenty of scope for medical assistance. It has been said that at least one in every seven children has an eye infection.

Once we went to Negar with Dr. Wild; for he was friendly

with the landlord and wished to introduce us. Constantly people sidled up to him to ask for medicine. Little boys were produced with healing leaves on their head which, when removed, revealed large patches of ringworm. The children had a strange tolerance of these infections; flies walked undisturbed over their sore eyes. But as we were carrying no medicines everyone with a complaint was requested to go to the surgery. Some go, some don't. Nothing can be done for those that don't. The queue at the surgery is always long enough to occupy all his time.

However, I ate none of Peter Wild's food and heard little of the conversation; for in the moment of our arrival an internal uneasiness began to assert itself. I felt ill and drove rapidly back to the Consulate with a nose that was bleeding and a stomach that was heaving. There needn't have been such a hurry; for a whole hour passed before I was sick in one of the irrigation channels which flowed through the garden. These strange and sudden sicknesses of ours were increasing. With them arrived an unnatural indifference to disorders. The Persian attitude was becoming clearer.

On the next day all was well and Philip and I went to Bam. Shaikh al Islami had to go there on business and offered to take two of us there in his car. We left at two in the morning and drove south-east, past Mahun and on the road which leads to India. Bam is of interest in that it is the last big Persian town before Baluchistan and is considered to produce the best dates: Kirman is not hot enough for dates to be grown. We thought it would be revealing to look at another town and see what differences were made by a drop in altitude of four thousand feet. It took us five hours to get there along a road flanked by mountains gradually diminishing in stature. Bam itself is in a plain and looked much more desolate than any other town we had seen: it is dominated by its fort, a lofty construction and decaying only in parts. The fort used to form the first bastion of defence against the Afghan invaders.

While Shaikh al Islami settled his affairs Philip and I walked in the town. The tall palms leaned over the garden walls with their clusters of dates as yet much too yellow for picking, as the beginning of September is the time of the date harvest. The town was poor; great gaps in garden walls and the absence of new buildings showed that little money was circulating within it. The bazaar was tawdry and rather empty, nothing at all valuable was for sale. It was in the bazaar that two policemen stopped us. Naturally our passports, written in French and English, meant nothing to them; so we wrote down our names in their notebooks and walked on. Several other pairs of policemen stopped us and the process had to be repeated. Then suddenly they all realised that they had discovered nothing at all about the two foreigners and on bicycles a whole assembly of them caught up with us again. All relevant facts were explained very carefully and all of them stood around us solemnly writing what we said into their notebooks. Then, with the suppressed enjoyment of those who give autographs, we signed all their books and went on our way. Philip casually produced his camera out of his pocket, and they rushed on us again. The law forbidding cameras had been rescinded in 1941, but in Bam it takes a long time to die. We kept the camera by the facile diplomacy of taking their photographs.

Near the fort are many ruined buildings and old ice houses, conical structures which go far underground. In them was stored the snow brought from the mountains in winter and sold as ice in summer. In one of these the floor was covered with human bones. No one knew who had put them there. No one cared. Suspicion in that town centred around the living, not the dead.

The drive back from Bam was very beautiful indeed, with the Persian sunset doing its best to outshine all other sunsets in the world. It is a hilly district and all the hills and ranges varied only in the tone of their blue colour and in their shape. There was no depth to them, only outlines. The distances between the various silhouettes were impossible to visualise; for it was a time when only pattern and colour existed.

Except for Eric, we had now been very much in each other's company for a month. Petty bickering and childish spitefulness had begun; for the welfare of the individual had been too dependent upon the moods of his fellows. I had always felt that friendship is a thing which can be temporarily discarded; for loneliness occurs quite independently of the number of people in the vicinity: but companionship is a different matter. The companionship enforced by an expedition is indispensable and the only solution is to separate temporarily: a reunion will always be a success. Unless that physical parting takes place, there will be a split in the amiability and two sides will have been formed. Then the engagements cease to be so petty and become deeper, more harmful and exceedingly detrimental to the welfare of the expedition. To a certain extent Ahmed solved the difficulty; for he was a scapegoat and could be scoffed at by all who wished to do so. Occasionally it is recommended for a journey that someone is taken who is obviously going to be disliked by all, someone whose method of sniffing or chewing or coughing or talking or laughing is so noticeable and irritating that it will haunt the minds of the others. Then an aggressive but united conspiracy will ensue. But he is dead weight and few expeditions have room for such a punch ball to keep the others mentally fit. Ahmed was not one of these; for he was much too small and never rebounded in a satisfactory manner.

Something had to be done. With each of us, self-importance had assumed excessive proportions. Although the trip had only occurred because we were a group and as a group we would be most beneficial to each other, I felt as if I was flying over fascinating country in an aeroplane flown by a mad crew: we had to come down to earth and forget the failings of others. Unanimously it was decided that Philip and Eric should go to Neckar-kuh and Louis and I to Jupar.

CHAPTER V

The first week in Jupar

FROM all angles this was a satisfactory arrangement. Jupar had an excellent qanat and was suitable botanically. Neckar-kuh was a village so small that Philip and Eric would be able to make a complete survey of its economy, of every change in the soil and learn all that they wished about the place: after this decision we felt happier. Philip and Eric were to have Ahmed and the truck.

Luckily we had already been introduced to one of the Jupar landlords, a young and dapper individual called Izzatullah Khan; he offered to drive us there in his jeep. Louis and I threw friendly goodbyes to the other two before bouncing away in the general direction of Jupar. This village was 30 miles due south of Kirman, being on the edge of the mountains which enclose the basin; our route lay across the centre of the plain and after a very little while Jupar began to appear, at first only as a streak of green upon the brown land and then as a host of trees surrounding a small blue topped mosque. Behind it the Kuh-i-jupar rose with sudden directness to 13,000 feet.

There seemed a crowd around us even before we stopped; boys were sent scurrying away to find the Kadkhoda and other dignitaries of the village, who appeared rapidly in various stages of disintegration and perspiration. Louis and I tried out our Persian on the people who chanced to be standing in front of us. Although Ahmed had been borrowed for the day, he was to return that evening in the jeep: some knowledge of the language was now most necessary. We spoke our sentences with much deliberation and thought: 'Jupar is a village in Iran'. 'There is no road to Kirman.' 'Tonight we go to sleep.' The villagers listened attentively and nodded wisely. Everything we did was watched by all

eyes; I blew my nose and felt it was necessary to make a big
thing of it, for the attention was so great; Louis idled with his toe
upon the ground and all eyes lowered themselves to see what he
had drawn. We introduced ourselves: 'This is Louis, I am Tony',
and from that moment forward everything was different; Mr.
Louis and Mr. Tony had been welcomed into the village of Jupar.

The landlord arranged a house, acquired three carpets, ordered
some food, instructed the bailiff to look after our needs and
produced a servant for us with the name of Mirza. This landlord
gushed forth much kindness; but it was fortunate for us that he
was helpful and we liked him, Izzatullah Khan, by the end of the
day.

He and Ahmed left in the evening; I looked up the word for
tea, demanded it and Mirza made some. Some six hours later I
was still demanding it and Mirza was still making more. Sometimes when Louis and I are feeling weary, sometimes when life
has moments to spare we try to recall the number of people who
came to visit us that evening. When the jeep had gone and long
before the chickens had ventured back onto the road, the first of
the visitors arrived. 'More tea please Mirza'. They asked what
they could do to help us and were greatly disappointed if no task
could be allotted to them. We asked them what their job was and
then tried to think of some way in which they could help. The
evening wore on; fifteen people promised to collect scorpions
for me and invitations to supper poured in. Some asked questions,
some just looked. We told them that there were many villages
around Oxford and that all had roads leading to them. They
discovered that there was one wife amongst the four of us and
answered that in Persia it was contrary, as one man could have
four wives: as Eric wasn't there to attack the alleged duplicity of
his wife, it didn't really matter. Anyway, nothing mattered that
night; the conversation drifted on and the moon came out.
'Have you got a moon in England?' The moon had just appeared
from behind the mountains and lit up their shape; it lit up the
square houses of the village with the plane trees hovering over
them; it lit up also the prostrate forms of Louis and me with the
attendant throng around us. Its shadow crept round and soon its
light fell upon Mirza blowing at the charcoal of the samovar in an

effort to make yet another cup of tea. The last of the guests drifted away, Mirza went to close the door behind them and came back to find us asleep. Our stay in Jupar had begun.

On the evening of the first day we were taken on a tour of inspection of Jupar. About fifty people decided to be our guides; any wish of ours was immediately granted and the more wishes we uttered the greater was the satisfaction of our hosts. A motley procession wandered around the village. It drifted into the mosque and then down below the ground to see the grinding of the corn. I was shown the fishes in the qanat and told that on one day a year the largest fish wore a golden crown which it borrows from the treasure that lies at the head of every qanat. I was told that for five days in every twenty-one the outflow of water is less and that this is caused by the breathing of the mountains. They said that hedgehogs lived on sunlight and that crocodiles lived in the desert, that the porcupine was immortal and that fish only live on their eggs. It was obviously a night for credulity; I looked up at the stars and they all winked back at me. Finally, the whole gathering climbed up a little hill that appears suddenly on one side of Jupar. Although it is only 100 ft. high, it dominates the village and the surrounding desert. There we all sat upon the ground with the two of us in a place where everyone could see us. The sun had set and all the earth was blue. Lamps were beginning to appear in the village and people were sitting outside enjoying the warmth of the evening. The dome of the mosque was black against the sky. The trees waved silently. A car was being driven along the India road.

An interpreter had been found and an old man told us of the history of Jupar. 'Many years ago there was no Jupar in the whole world', he began; and my eyes looked over the land. 'One of the soldiers guarding the road to India, in that fort over there, thought that there would be water near this place. Many people believed this, because at one time there was a small stream in the summer time. They used to call it Ja-i-parsal, "the place of last year"; but they changed the name to Jupar. The soldier, who was a poor man, managed to persuade a rich man to build a qanat. That qanat is still flowing and still gives water; but the fort fell down many years ago.' I looked at the ruins of the fort which only just stood out on the horizon; so much time had passed since that fort had guarded the trade route from India, the route of Alexander and the way witnessed at Kirman by Marco Polo. 'This rich man called it the Gauhariz qanat, the qanat of flowing jewels'. He pointed towards it and we all turned to look in that direction although, being dark, there was nothing to be seen except the peaks of the Kuh-i-Jupar. By this time all the light had gone from the sky and it was the hour for everybody to eat; the assembly stumbled down to the village. Then Louis and I bade good night to our guides: it is a slow business shaking hands with fifty people.

I wished to be shown around the qanat system of Jupar. If I was to do any work in the qanats, it was primarily necessary to find out just what their internal aspect was like. The bailiff presented me with a muqanni. I collected Abu Ali, a boy of twelve or so with a great character and a few words of English. He brought with him his brother-in-law, a medical student called Mahmud, who talked incessantly and someone else whose name I never learnt. Leaving our shoes at the entrance, we stepped into the water and into the qanat. At the beginning it was about six feet wide and six feet high, with the water reaching up to our knees. Abu Ali began chanting eerily and got great satisfaction from the echoes. Mahmud continued to talk; he said that he knew English only from medical text-books but, which was true, knew nothing of its pronunciation. He constantly asked for medical sentences so that he could puzzle out what they meant: he was apparently oblivious of his environment. I, very definitely, was not. Sometimes the roof was less than four feet high, in other places it was many yards above. Occasionally there were great caverns where many roof falls had occurred and also, as a relief, would come the light from one of the shafts to the surface. There are many reasons for the irregularities: a blockage may have necessitated a new detour, the thin portions might have been an attempt at economy; the deep parts are proof of the everlasting search for more water when its level in the channel begins to drop. So, sometimes scraping our shoulders, sometimes bumping our heads and always stubbing our toes, this small party waded on towards the source. Abu Ali continued to chant, Mahmud to talk; and only by their efforts were we not enveloped by the silence which threatened all the while to close in on us.

A muqanni leads a risky life and may meet his death in one of many ways: he may slip when climbing down the well, he may be concussed by a stone that is dislodged above him or be crushed by an ordinary roof collapse. He is likely to be asphyxiated in the deeper wells, as there is little circulation of air; he may be poisoned by gases that occasionally seep into a qanat or be bitten by one of the snakes which has fallen into the water and has not been able to climb out again. Also, many cases of drowning occur in a qanat: a blockage may have occurred below a muqanni, in which case the water will accumulate on his side; or, if he is clearing such a blockage from the lower side, then the sudden onrush of liberated water is quite capable of drowning him. This all results in making him a very superstitious man: a bad dream or a sneeze occurring within his family is considered sufficient warning of danger and he will not go down any qanat that day. No qanat owner will force him to or deny him his wage: there is reason why the qanats are often called 'the murderers'.

Gauhariz qanat has many branches flowing down to its single exit. Every now and then we would come to a junction; sometimes one of the channels would be dry but more often they contained water. Whichever it was Abu Ali would shout up it and listen to the tubular noise which it produced: Mahmud would take this opportunity to demand another sentence from me. I started writing down which route we had taken but the muqanni saw my map and protested. 'Lazim nist', he said, 'it is not necessary'. And then followed one of the most confident assertions that I have ever heard. It seems that if you are lost and on dry land, then you should walk until you find water; if you have a lamp, then see which way the water is flowing and follow it; if you have no lamp (and are not suffering from paroxysms of fear) walk in the water until the light from a well shaft appears; even if it is night there will be stars at the top of the shaft. He finished the formula at that point with the presumption that a well shaft many metres deep presented no difficulty: I continued with my map, but surreptitiously.

As no branch of Gauhariz stretched for more than three miles

THE CROSS SECTIONAL SHAPES OF THE CHANNELS

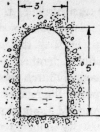

A NEW CHANNEL

CHANNEL THROUGH
BAD GROUND
SUPPORTED BY NARS

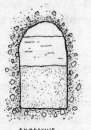

EXCESSIVE
DEPOSITION OF SILT

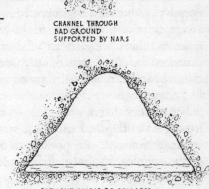

OLD AND LIABLE TO COLLAPSE

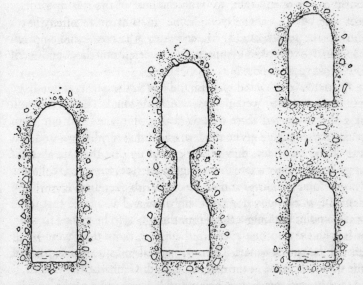

DIFFERENT RESULTS OF THE SEARCH FOR MORE WATER. EITHER THE FLOOR IS
LOWERED OR FRESH CHANNELS ARE MADE BENEATH THE ORIGINAL ONES.

it was after a couple of hours that we reached the end. There was
no well from this point to the surface; only 150 ft. of desert. The
channel was far narrower than it had been all the way along;
we crouched on our haunches and got in each other's way: it was
not a pleasant spot down there. I flicked my torch about but the
beam rested either on solid wall and roof or the muddy water and
ourselves. Abu Ali had stopped singing, Mahmud had stopped
asking questions, the other friend and the muqanni were even
quieter; I think we were all subdued by the place; it was not a
situation for arrogance of any sort. I asked Mahmud what
claustrophobia meant and crawled away backwards the way we
had come.

For most of that day we plunged about in those qanats: always
it was exhausting and usually it was cold; but certain channels
felt quite warm. It was possible to float down them, either face
downwards or upwards; you would then push yourself along
from the bottom or the roof. It was possible if an occasional
submerged and jagged rock was not a deterrent: the fish would
bump into you whichever way up you were; the bumpings and
their numbers increased as we neared the exit. It was good to get
out into the open again, to lie in the heat of the sun, and to see
nothing but sky above you. Some goats were regarding with
disdain the foully muddy water which was now exuding from
the qanat; we looked sympathetic, collected our shoes and went
off to eat some food.

I had now discovered that fish did live in the qanats and in large
numbers, but they were neither white nor blind. The Persians still
said that they got there automatically; this view did not seem
particularly tenable in the modern scientific world. I was told that
they lived on water, they ate air or simply that they ate all their
eggs, leaving only a few to propagate the race; they said that there
was no food problem for not one of the fish ever died. Everybody
denied that anybody had put them there and all agreed that there
was no point in doing a thing if nothing was to be gained from it.
It is true that no one ever ate them, yet there they were in all
except the saltiest qanats. The only natural and stream-like parts of
the qanat occurred at the exit; here, with Gauhariz, the water ran
for a short distance before being divided according to the owner-

ship laws and flowing into the highest gardens of the village. The laws are complex for the qanat owners but the complexity does ensure that today's owner receives the money due to him, either because an ancestor of his built the qanat, or because some other relative of his had craftily arranged a marriage so that neither he, nor his descendants, should ever be short of water and money. The water flows into the first and highest garden. The owner of a garden pays for water according to the size of his garden; for it is assumed that he will take all the water necessary to irrigate every square inch of that garden. However, so far as the fish are concerned the stream is too polluted a dwelling place just as soon as it flows through the hole in the wall: no fish were seen to penetrate very far into a Persian garden. Therefore the fish, and there were many hundreds of them in Gauhariz, have only a short natural stretch which is bounded on one side by darkness and on the other by pollution.

The stream flows on through the village, sometimes dividing and occasionally being joined again. A division may be made to flow over one of its previous branches or out into the street to serve as a public washing place. These deviations are all resultant of deaths and marriages in the past and all culminate in producing the simplest distribution of infection known to man; down they flow with the streams becoming smaller, dirtier and more insanitary; down to the poor part of the town, until finally the streams are no more: the clear stream of the qanat of the flowing jewels is then not even a muddy trickle. That part of the village is poor and squalid, for the flow of water cannot be relied upon; perhaps at one time the qanat output was bigger, perhaps optimism about its future was larger or faith in the merciful bounty of Allah greater; whichever it was which caused those houses and gardens to be built they are always there and always crumbling away. Somewhere before the end of the village, and long before the decrepit area, a reservoir for water is made; into this the water flows at night, for little irrigation goes on during that time. This practice ensures that no water flows right out of the village; it damps whatever hopes there may still be in the hearts of the decrepit ones and provides a breeding place for mosquitoes, the like of which they could never find elsewhere.

This stream is the life of the village; without it the village would be as dust. Although mainly used for irrigation it also provides all the drinking water; and the first duty of a Persian's day is to go and collect this water from the mouth of the qanat before too many other Persians have paddled in it or the animals have come down to drink from it. Drinking water is free; not because of any benevolence on the part of the owners but because of the impossibility of charging for it. As it is, there is much disregard for the private ownership of the qanat; a second duty of the Persian's day is to cover up the traces of any robbing of water he may have made during the night; for a man who has no money, who has a stream flowing near his garden and who has an unscrupulous bent, in short a Persian peasant, the gurgling of that stream provides too great a temptation. So when the Kadkhoda, the bailiff of the village, blows out his lamp and retires to bed a good many shovels are grabbed by a good many unseen hands: it may be necessary to remove a large chunk from the bottom of your own or a neighbour's wall, but it does not take long for it has been removed so many, so very many times before: whatever has to be done is done quickly and efficiency comes with practice. There is never any question of the water not flowing correctly; with the passage of time the unlawful channel has become too deep.

Once, when I was returning late at night from a walk into the mountains along a route that I knew quite well, I suddenly found myself wading through a small stream that had never been there before; the odd thing was that it flowed straight under a garden door. I couldn't think up the Persian for 'There is a stream flowing under your garden door' and, anyway, it was late; so I strode on. I was soon splashing down a path which had previously, as I remembered it, been a dry and dusty way; many streams had dried up but more had been born in the night. It chanced that I should pass that way again the next morning and there was the dust I knew, the dust of ageless time, the dust as old as the desert itself. Sometimes, of course, the diverter is so fatigued by the night's work that he falls asleep when the warmth of the day begins to seep into his system; then it is that the stream continues on its unnatural course. Its owner will hastily put things right, but the tell-tale dampness will be there for the Kadkhoda to see, even if the owner hadn't gone bounding off to find him. All three then argue until the heat of the day becomes too oppressive: the argument swells to a climax and finally all is forgotten under the beneficence of sleep.

Part of my interest centred in the mountains which rose behind Jupar. If these mountains contain streams that are perpetually flowing and are stocked with fish, then I could understand how the fish colony in a qanat was initiated: for in the spring, when the snow melts and the water cascades down into the plain, great rivers are formed and much land is flooded. Then it would be possible for the fish, or their eggs, to be rushed down with the water and be swept into the well of a qanat. These floods are a serious menace to the qanats; for if water pours down a well shaft collapses may be caused. The muqanni does all he can to prevent this: he builds mounds of earth around the shafts or covers them over completely. Special water men live at that time of year near the threatened parts; their job is to encourage the flood water to flow along the channels that have been prepared to receive it. Not always do they succeed: on occasions water pours down the shafts to cause devastation all along the qanat. When this occurs it is only too easy to understand how fish come to be in the qanats; but only if there are mountain streams which never dry up throughout the year.

Louis wished to see what plants grew up there: I wished to find the streams. The governor had told us that three Army horses were at our disposal in Jupar if we ever wished to use them; Mirza professed a knowledge of horses, Abu Ali of donkeys. It was decided that Mirza should come to look after the horses when the way became too steep; that Abu Ali should come on a donkey with the oats and water for the day. We chartered the horses for sunrise.

Immediately the sun had appeared one of the Gendarmes came in protesting at our lateness; and five minutes later Louis and I were nervously patting three young stallions on the neck. The Gendarme told us that they were not allowed to get too close to one another, that if we didn't give them water at mid-day they would drop down and die, and they must definitely be restrained from galloping. With these three points well in mind, we collected Abu Ali, loaded his donkey with all the oats and water that three horses could ever want in a day and balanced him on the top. He had with him a large topi which nearly rested on his shoulders, a very long and ancient double-barrelled shot gun slung across his back and a broken-down umbrella which not only kept the sun off him but doubled the speed of the donkey whenever it was erected. Mirza got on one of the smaller stallions, for he was a smaller man, and rode off in the direction we had to go. Louis and I both got on at the same time: our horses rushed at each other and glared face to face. No one around made any effort to move, save for the Gendarme who could be seen backing away; I quietly put aside any thought of doing Biology on that day. Our horses became frightened by the vociferous instructions which were being bandied about by all to all. Suddenly they galloped off after the others with both of us sitting just behind the saddle; it was a strong rein and I held on: it was a strong horse and he didn't deign to notice. When we caught up with Mirza and the donkey, baser desires in my horse overcame the desire for speed, and we stopped violently with the two front legs astride the horse of Mirza. Abu Ali hit him on the nose with his gun; Mirza turned round and punched him in the face and I took the opportunity to get back into the saddle, for I had been catapulted over it. Very soon, encouraged by the thumpings on his nose, he mastered himself and we thundered off once more along the narrow twisting lanes of the village.   Later on, some donkeys confronted us round one of the corners and equally suddenly we stopped. This caused us to be surrounded in dust and such confusion amongst those donkeys that the braying they set up was prodigious and quite unnerved my horse: he remained motionless. By the time the dust had settled there was not a donkey to be seen, only some tiny foot prints well spaced apart.

Louis's horse was comparatively impotent and behaved in a more respectable manner; he was put fifty yards in front and similar distances were arranged between the rest of us. Of course there were occasions when this routine was disrupted, with all the usual consequences, more hits on the nose from Abu Ali's gun and more thundering of hooves.

We rode away south of Jupar, past the qanat wells and up the broad valley which cuts into the hills. At the beginning our shadows stretched along the ground; they were good shadows, with exaggerated nodding of the horses' heads, the rounded shoulders of the riders and the flicking of the great long tails. As the sun rose higher the mind became drowsier. The shorter shadows danced disturbingly over the larger stones of the dry river bed. It was all uphill, but there was no lack of vigour in the horses: they gazed around them fiercely and stumbled on any stone which chanced to get in their way. After three hours or so the broad valley became narrower, making the cliffs towering above seem even more precipitous than we had originally supposed. Behind us the valley broadened out into the wide basin-shaped plain of Kirman; a small sand storm was blowing in one corner. The bus was just visible in the middle and stuck in the sand where it always gets stuck, but where we were nothing was happening. There was no breeze blowing around us, there were no trees to wave their branches; even the sun seemed still.

At last, when the stones were too large and too numerous, we stopped. Mirza made some tea and we all ate bread and cheese. It was that flat round type of Persian bread which always brings away so much of the clay from the floor of the kiln. The cheese was goats' cheese, acrid and pungent, a cheese on which the flies would never settle. The horses kicked restlessly at the stones. Some crows flew over quite silently.

For all that day we walked in those mountains. Louis dug up plants and put them away in his press. To me they were all the type of plant that is bound to be beneath you when you sit on the ground without looking; they all had spikes and thorns and pointed leaves. To Louis they were phenomenally difficult to put in his press, but interesting in that, botanically, he was in quite another world. To Abu Ali they were as nothing; all day long he stuffed gunpowder, stones and little bits of rag into the effective barrel of his gun and then fired it off where he thought the echo would be good. The whole day was punctuated with these devastating explosions. I walked around looking for water and for signs of water, but found no traces. The few insects that were lying about on the hot stones were swished into my net, then from the killing bottle into a box with a label: 'Insects. Jupar hills. 10,000 ft. Dry rock.' No more description was necessary, for there was nothing more to describe; the breathless silence did not concern the insects.

The return journey was less eventful. During our absence my horse had bitten through its rein and had run away; Mirza had caught it again and I never understood quite how. I joined the rein together, but it was difficult to reach the knotted remains from the saddle; however, it probably gave the horse a feeling of subservience although it gave me no support in times of stress. The evening was pleasant and our shadows lengthened on the other side. Darkness came as we entered Jupar once again; the horses were handed back to the Gendarmerie. Stiffly, slowly and bowleggedly Louis and I slouched back to our rooms.

At first I was inclined to put a notice on our door saying that we would pay for animals brought alive to our house. Then it was pointed out to me that the notices which were already on the door related to the paying of taxes and the smoking of opium. My informer hinted that among the villagers there was an aversion to the reading of those notices; also, few of them were capable of reading. Instead, I noised it abroad that money would be paid for animals, with a price varying according to the species of the animal. At first a grotesque array of mutilated creatures was produced for me. Things that had once been healthy lizards and scorpions, but had since been ground under the heel of their captor: I refused to pay and said that all creatures must be alive and well. The first wave was followed by a second of boastful animal catchers who wished to know the prices of all animals; only then could they decide which they were going to catch. So a list was drawn up: vultures, bears, mountain goats and cobras were at the high price end; small snakes, monitors, bats and jerboas were in the middle; while scorpions, lizards and insects earned only a little money for their captors. After three days, in various boxes around the garden we had two pure white hedgehogs, one tortoise, three scorpions, one tarantula and three large lizards.

By this move not only did we receive animals but at every meal time people drifted in to see us; either they brought us an animal or they brought us tales about animals: one told me that when his brother came from India a year ago he saw a herd of bears; another, that a tiger had recently been shot near the Caspian. I thanked them, handed them a cup of tea and begged them to tell me more. Once an old and crinkled man told me a crocodile had been in his garden; at least, that is what the dictionary said. It is a far cry from Jupar to the valley of the Nile. He said that he tried to catch it but it disappeared; he was not sure whether it escaped down a hole or up a tree. I was even less sure what it might have done and gave him an extra large cup of tea. Although I carried out a strict policy of no money for mutilated specimens, they still arrived. 'Why are the heads of these snakes cut off?' 'In order that we might bring them here.' 'I prefer them with their heads on.' 'If we did not cut their heads off, we would not be able to bring them here.' Eventually they leave without money: I am left with a decapitated snake and without any gain; however, they were food for the hedgehogs and did save me splashing about in the stream at night for their normal diet of toads.

One of the nicest points about living in Jupar was that we had so many evenings out. Plenty of people were surprisingly ready to invite a couple of dirty Englishmen to supper and the dirty ones were always ready to accept. The system at all these parties was the same. It was then and gave you the feeling that it would always be. When the sun has set and the moths are flying and waiting for the hurricane lamps to be lit, then is the time to knock at the door of your host. In a country where wood is scarce and expensive a great thick door is a sign of wealth; some houses seem to have no other possession than an enormous door. The opening of the door always takes a long time; for many transverse beams give support to it and have to be removed. All this time there is apparent suspicion in the mind of the host, for he speaks no word: the only sounds come from the bars and bolts of the door. Then, suddenly, the door is flung open and his immediate volubility and welcome more than make up for his previous silence. He asks you to sit on his carpet and apologises for its poor quality; you have to protest at his modesty and point out its good features. He lights the hurricane lamp and it gushes away to make the world a brighter place. He may spoil the scene by switching on a wireless: wirelesses come into the same category as the wooden doors; they are, principally, possessions with their true functions being comparatively unimportant. They are distinctive only in that they all manage to be tuned into more than two stations for any given setting. The cicadas dislike the competition and chirp in disharmony.

At the beginning of the evening everyone is sitting very correctly, bolt upright and in the true cross-legged manner; conversation is formal and stereotyped. Melons and grapes appear before you: these are eaten slowly and without enthusiasm. They are not the meal: they serve only to pass the time, the couple of hours before the meal arrives. At first we were inclined to eat vigorously of the fruit, with the result that the meal caused complete stupefaction; later, by enormous efforts of will, only half a melon and a pound or two of grapes were eaten before leaving just a little appetite for the meal itself. The formal atmosphere of the party gradually breaks down and the women of the family peering over the hedge take an increasing interest in the proceedings. I can never sit cross-legged for long and slowly sink through that long range of positions ending inevitably with the whole body flat on its back. Most of these intermediate positions are characteristic of the fidgety habits exhibited by an opium smoker: this fact never fails to be pointed out by our hosts. The stars twinkle restlessly: it has been said that there are more stars above Kirman than anywhere else in the world. It was said at one supper party in Jupar that 'Jupar is high because the stars are near.' This surely puts everything in its right perspective.

Eventually the meal comes. The bare feet of the women walk up and down the table cloth which they have laid before you: the food is set down by your side: the whole vast meal has appeared. Its main constituent is rice and your host is quick to ensure that your plate is piled high with it; this cannot be eaten without leaving a ring of rice on the table cloth, a ring that remains to show the generosity of your host and the greatness of the quantity which the guest must have consumed: both are considered admirable. With the rice is eaten chicken, herbs, sultanas, mast (youghurt) and bread. The rice is mixed with them just, and only just, before it is pushed into the mouth. The original mound of rice has various gravies poured over it. Remarks of appreciation are always hazarded when the mouth is overflowing with food: this lends weight to the remark and the larger the mouthful the better it is; but if you can overeat yourself to such an extent that the fact becomes plain to everyone else, then all is as it should be.

However, all is enlivened by the production of the Arak bottle; it is swathed in a wet bandana to keep it cool, a terrible anomaly; for Arak is one of the hottest drinks that has ever burnt its way down my throat. It comes into line with the Italian Grappa and the Greek Ouzo and with any spirit that has been distilled solely in order to produce a drink that is as fiery as possible without any reference to flavour. Mast is always thrown down after it; this is supposed to nullify the ill effects and apparently succeeds: certainly no intoxication comes after it, so the whole source of enjoyment must come from that hot searing pain which lasts in your throat for two or three seconds, giving the feeling that a scar will probably remain for two or three years. There is also a wine, a far more palatable and delightful drink; sweet, perhaps and syrupy, but it is a wine and does not scald the flesh. As all alcohol is forbidden by Moslem law, those who drink it achieve the secondary satisfaction of breaking this law.

Finally the party begins to disintegrate and it is time to go. Desperate politeness is observed. 'Will you please order me to leave?' 'No, I order you to stay.' 'No, please order me to leave.' A servant comes with a lamp and you, after walking backwards out of the house to show deference to your host, turn to follow the lamp through the narrow streets which are at night time so much, so very much, more treacherous: one more Persian supper has been eaten. Thus it is that, feeling rather pleased with ourselves, stopping every now and then to pick up another toad for the insatiable hedgehogs, we find our way home again.

It was necessary to spend the first few days at Jupar in an atmosphere of pleasant ineffectuality. It was true that we had been to the mountains and down Gauhariz, but they could be considered by the villagers as further aspects of our initial conducted tour. We could not immediately begin work and sever ourselves from their attentions, for the people had to be made aware of us: we had to show acknowledgement of the fact that we were the intruders. In Persia polite formalities are lengthy: when two of them meet in the street they shake hands and make many enquiries concerning the health, prosperity and welfare of the family. This polite and protracted preface to every conversation occurs even when two have met purposely in order to discuss a particular subject. It was right, therefore, that we should obey the rules: we had met Persia in its street, in its narrow twisting lane bounded by the high walls, and sufficient correct enquiries had to be made before there was any question of settling down to the project in view.

CHAPTER VI

Jupar 2

O<small>N</small> the fourth day, when Louis went out with his plant press, he was greeted kindly but not excessively. The introductory period had been completed. Therefore he went on his way, which involved idling over the land in a desultory manner until he saw some further plant species to be picked and pressed. With desert plants this process of picking and pressing is made harder by their tenacity in gripping the soil, and by their resistance to an enforced change in shape: their roots are strong and very grasping; their stems are hard and tough. An advantage of the arid climate was that no difficulty arose in drying what had been picked, for this is usually the principal snag in plant collecting: the quicker the plant resembles hay the sooner the botanist is satisfied.

In spring parts of the desert become covered with flowers, tender plants not adapted to summer heat but only to the rapid production of many drought-resistant seeds. The plant itself has a short life immediately after the annual five inches of rain has fallen; but they cover the land and make a pleasant variation to the three normal colours, the brown of the earth, the green of the trees and the blue of the sky. Even Ahmed talked of the beauty of the flowers in spring.

Louis did his collecting before the day became too hot; he always slept on the roof and woke up early with the sun and the flies. The heat was of a kind that permitted work outside but the work had to be reasonably energetic in order to prevent the onset of somnolence. Chasing lizards and walking in the hills was infinitely preferable to the wearisome search for flowers. Also the slow gait and sunken head of a searcher gives him such a dejected appearance that he must be affected by it. I left later: until the day became hot I never felt inclined to go down the qanats. Anyway, at breakfast there was a spate of animal catchers who had to be seen to: scorpions and lizards on the ends of pieces of string, leeches in bottles, mice in tins and bats in handkerchiefs. Breakfast was always protracted and never dull. I kept a large box of very small change and handed it out according to the excellence of the capture.

It was two miles to the entrance of Gauhariz qanat and the hot walk made it pleasant to step in to the water and wade up its channels. Unfortunately, the business of progression in them was always very slow; the varying shapes gave relief as to posture, but always necessitated a rearrangement of everything which was being carried. For the most part the rucksack was put on back to front while my rounded back scraped along the roof. In one hand was the lamp and in the other were more nets; for the rucksack was of necessity a small one. The lamp was a primitive affair, lent by a muqanni and consisting of a wick leading into a tinful of paraffin: it was effective until it was dropped in the water or a sudden wind blew it out. I never understood these gusts, for they were practically instantaneous. One moment the flame was being blown out and the next I was left in quiescent darkness; an absence of light made more intense by its suddenness and a silence made more impressive by the immediate cessation of my paddling and of the thunderous noise which accompanied it. Naturally I carried matches all over me in order that some of them should remain dry, for the blackness was very complete and the light most comforting.

In various channels and situations in the qanat I used the nets. They were conical, with a small tube at the end, and most satisfactory; if there was not much mud on the bottom, it was possible to pull them along and collect the contents from the tube. But usually, as the stream only flowed at half a mile an hour, there was plenty of mud and the net and tube would be rapidly choked by it: in these places I left the nets for a time, hoping that some animals would be washed down into them. The contents of the tubes were put into jars which had been wrapped in wet cloths to keep them cool. The temperature in Gauhariz was 65° Fahrenheit; outside it was 90°: the animals could not survive this increase. I also caught the fish with a butterfly net; this was easy, for they became disturbed by the lamp and swam recklessly up and down the stream: when they swam down they were caught. It is hard to understand why the Persians don't eat them; I should have thought that a man who considered roast porcupine meat a delicacy would be most enthusiastic over a fried fish: anyway, the fish caught by the butterfly net were always eaten at our supper. The stomachs, which had been removed, were examined for their contents, as the food chain, the diet of the animals within the qanat, formed part of the study. Generally, after five or six hours I became cold and left the place.

For the rest of the day it was necessary to inspect the catch and put the minute crustacea and insect larvae found in them into formalin. This had to be done quickly; for once the cold water from the jars had been poured into a flat dish for easier examination, its temperature began to rise: the activity of the animals decreased when the water became too warm. Also, the protracted breakfast and the slow passage in the qanats meant that most of the day had passed. The long summer evenings did not exist in that latitude and the sun set early. If you set up a lamp in order to work for a longer period the large moths blundered foolishly into the light and into the dishes of water. This was not a worry, for the onset of darkness always induced in us a sudden drowsiness: the fierce light of the day had given way to soporific warmth. We never found any difficulty in sleeping; that is, until the flies woke us up in the morning.

There was a man named Husain-i-Hakim in Jupar. He had told me that he possessed much knowledge on all subjects and especially on the qanats. Hakim means Doctor and his job is to vaccinate people when epidemics are in the vicinity. In the healthier times of the year he has little to do; he spent these days hunting in the area and living pleasantly upon the money gained during the unhealthy seasons. He willingly agreed to guide Louis and me to a spring in the mountains, the existence of which had been reported by one of the villagers. It was in the early morning that he met us with a donkey on which he had laden tea-pots and cups, two rifles and a lot of food: he had also brought Abu Ali. The sun was just rising when the four of us left the village.

Initially, the conversation was all about a leopard he had shot two months before; Abu Ali continually interjected and scoffed at the more exaggerated parts of the story. Later on, the subject was brought round to qanats and how they are made.

Qanat is a word of Assyrian or Akkadian origin and came via the Hebrew and Aramaic languages to be used in Persia. But this type of water channel is definitely Persian in origin and was originally called kariz; somehow the word qanat has ousted the word kariz, which is now used only in Afghanistan. Polybius makes the first reference to them in describing the wars of 209 B.C. But although the word qanat may have originated well prior to this date, it is not known when it acquired its present meaning. It is probable that qanats are as old as the towns in those parts of Persia where water does not flow either on or just beneath the surface.

The real principle behind all qanats is that if a man constructs one then he owns the land which its water irrigates: this dictum is very old and still applies. Only if there are other qanats in the vicinity, or if the land has been enclosed, does it not hold; then some arrangement has to be made between the qanat owners so that no water is unused and there is sufficient land to be made productive. Of course, the land necessary for each owner depends on the amount of water which flows from his qanat. Gauhariz irrigates an area of two square miles and there are five channels, each three miles long and leading from a depth of 150 ft. The two square miles contain a lot of houses but there are very many gardens for which rent must be paid. Once a qanat is made, provided that the water table it has penetrated does not sink, a high income is assured: the limiting factor is the difficulty in building such a qanat.

The man who believes he has enough money calls for the water-finding experts. They arrive and inspect the neighbourhood. Partly by intuition and partly by intelligence in connection with the lie of the land, the proximity of any springs and the abundance of plants in the summer, they estimate where there will be water beneath the surface. Their decision is never discussed with the landlord, for the secret is a jealous one: instead, they point to a spot, collect their money and go.

Then surveyors are called for. They dig a well at this spot and

continue downwards until water is reached; if no water is arrived
at before a depth of 300 ft. has been dug, then the well is abandoned and a fresh party of diviners is summoned. However, if
water is found, then the well is deepened until a depth of two
metres accumulates overnight: this quantity not only makes further
deepening unpractical but shows that there is a sufficiency of water
at that level. The depth of the well, this mother well, is measured
with a piece of string and it is calculated where the water will
flow out onto the surface; naturally there has to be lower ground
in the vicinity to make this possible. The surveyors measure the
fall in the ground until it is equal to the depth of the well in this
way: a pole is placed a certain distance away from the mother well
in the direction of the lower ground; another piece of string is
stretched taut between this pole and the top of the well; by
adjusting the height of the string at the pole end and by dropping
some water on the centre of it they believe it is possible to make
the string horizontal; that is when the water on the string has no
tendency to flow in either direction. The height of the string on the
pole is then noted and this is measured off on the original string
which had marked the depth of the well. A knot is tied in that
string and the remainder of it refers to the further fall in ground
which is necessary before the level of the well bottom has been
reached. Only a few surveyors use a spirit level to affirm that the
string is horizontal. This process is continued until the whole
length of string is dotted with their knots. The surveyors then
point significantly to the ground: at that spot water will appear:
the rock can be struck in the wilderness.

Before the surveyors leave they dig wells at intervals of 300
yards along the route they have surveyed; by reference to the
knotted string they dig them to the correct depth. Their purpose
is to assist the muqannis, who will later do the excavating, by
enabling them to dig correctly and at the depth intended by the
original survey. In a distance of 25 miles a small but continual
error will have far reaching effects; the surveyors have prevented
it. These men then collect their money and go.

It is the muqannis who perform the final task of digging the
channel up to the mother well. If they started at the spot indicated
by the surveyors, the flow would be sluggish; therefore they start

a little further down, with this distance varying according to the estimated output of water; it is the shortest when the output will be large. Then they dig the channel: guided by the surveyors' wells, they excavate their way. Every fifty yards a well is made to the surface for the removal of the material and for ventilation. The channel is kept straight by the simple procedure of placing two lamps in it behind them several yards apart; if, on looking back, they see that the first is superimposed on the second then the channel is straight. That this system is faulty is shown by the fact that there are always sharp kinks just short of the wells; for they have been dug before the channel reaches them: the kink has been made to rectify the error.

THE CONSTRUCTION OF A QANAT

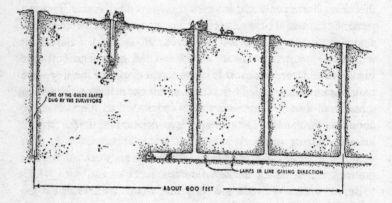

ONE OF THE GUIDE SHAFTS
DUG BY THE SURVEYORS

LAMPS IN LINE GIVING DIRECTION

ABOUT 600 FEET

When they reach the water-bearing strata, seepage begins into the channel, but all the water flows away down the path they have made. The water which has accumulated in the mother well is removed before the channel reaches it; when this occurs their task is finished. Water flows steadily out of the other end of the qanat and is welcomed by the excited landlord; In sha'llah, by the grace of Allah, an income is assured for life. Either he sells the water or farms the land which it irrigates; the latter is considered more profitable but the former is not unsatisfactory: Shaikh-al-

Islami had to pay £200 a year for the privilege of having a qanat stream flow through his garden.

All conversation with Husain-i-Hakim and all interruptions by Abu Ali ceased when we reached the mountains. The donkey became obstreperous and had to be left tied to a tree. Husain strapped his food, guns and tea pots about him and strode ahead. Quite a way up the valley there was the spring: somehow I was expecting a rushing stream of clear liquid, certainly not just one damp stone and a minute pool covered with pond skaters. This didn't deter Husain from scooping up some of the water and making tea from it; strangely enough, when the tea was placed before us it did not deter us from drinking just as much as he gave us. Husain carried a complete set of cups and saucers; even on his hunting trips he carried a samovar: I wondered curiously how much he would have brought had we intended to spend the night. At this juncture he took off his shoes and socks and went to sleep.

These actions provoked Louis and me to go collecting. It was a steep valley with rocks made smooth by the cascading water of winter and spring; they were difficult to climb and I slid about helplessly. Louis was infinitely better at the game and collected plants from hazardous spots. The principal events of the day were that Husain nearly sat on a snake, Abu Ali got stung on the toe by a hornet and Louis had a temporary attack of constipation lasting about six hours. More shall be written concerning Louis and his health in due course.

We left the spring to return in the evening. At least I had satisfied myself that it did not contain a stock of fish with which to supply the new qanats when winter floods overwhelmed the area. Husain showed us the place where the women and animals were hidden when robbing bands were in the district; it consisted of deep shelters with stone roofs and underground pathways: all of it was well concealed from the eyes of anyone down in the plain. As the place was obviously disused, this caused us to comment on the fact and then Husain to make comprehensive generalisations on the recent economic advancements of Persia and how the country would be still better if only she had her oil. This cry was a constant refrain: 'Give us our oil and then there is nothing which we will not be able to do'. Not a single person did we ever meet who did not sing it: the crisis was likely to come. But on that evening Husain's tirade was deflected; for we passed the Zoroastrian tower where the Parsees place their dead. Kirman and Yezd are the biggest strongholds of this religion in Persia. Husain is a Mohammedan and he laughed at their ways for the rest of the journey to Jupar.

Philip and Eric arrived after a week. They had stayed at various little villages and, having satisfied themselves as to their means of existence, wished to examine the larger village of Jupar. According to the Kadkhoda it had 4,000 people living in it; this seemed far too large a figure, for we always regarded the place as a definite village. It looked like a village and could never have been called a town. However, it suited their purposes and Eric started to make his map: it was to cover a big area starting with the desert edge below the village, embracing the smaller qanats which entered Jupar from the side and taking in all the surrounding fields. The Gauhariz system and its mountain border were to be at the southern end: altogether a length of seven miles. Every morning he set off swathed in his equipment: the range finder, a plane table, red and white poles, field glasses, a large camera, protractors and rulers and at least three water bottles. Every morning he returned after a very short time to collect his India rubber and clanked out of the door again. He did a lot to impress the villagers of the earnestness of our venture: all day long he stood on the top of some promontory and surveyed the land around him. A small circle of boys was always at his feet and he had only to give the smallest sign of hunger for one of them to dash away and bring him a melon: his static conspicuousness enabled him to fare better than all of us in the receiving of food. Eric was never hard to find and began to provide landmarks for our conversation. '100 yards past the place where Eric wore his hat.' 'It was just south of the hill which Eric didn't stand on.' He was of inestimable value to the expedition.

Philip had contrived not to bring all the things which Louis and I considered he was absolutely certain to bring; so great was our certainty that we never even sent him a list of the things; therefore Louis returned to Kirman, though mainly to ask Dr. Wild if diarrhoea which continued for a fortnight was a regular occurrence. Philip went too, because he had blood group work to do in the hospital and just in case Louis had to stay there. Two days later Philip arrived back again in Jupar; he was late because a sand storm had made him hopelessly lost in the plain; then three of the cylinders had oiled up. Louis had been left in Kirman with amoebic dysentery.

So it was that Philip and I spent the afternoon cleaning the sparking plugs before starting on a health purge. Initially, I carried thirty gallons of water in an effort to clean the privy but failed. Something had to be done; for Louis had picked up the animal and it was likely that the rest of us should do so too. The removal of the entamoeba means vigorous treatment with emetine and this enforces a ten-day stay in bed: it was most necessary that the rest of us did not follow his example; but a solution did not present itself. Our drinking water was fetched by Mirza in the early morning; this we did not boil, for we considered it free from disease. Our washing water had come the entire length of the village. We washed in it but hastily, and our washing was more a vestige of an old custom than a desire for cleanliness. I got clean enough in the waters of the qanats. However, the food eaten at another man's house or the tea he gave us to drink had to be hazarded; at least the food had been cooked and the tea water boiled, but a really poor man gave as his best just water with a little sugar in it: this couldn't be refused and nothing could come between you and that which he proffered.

Even our own food was not clean. The flat bread had been handled by many people and in the day time the flies were always there. It was possible to dip plates and fruit into permanganate solution, but Mirza tended to consider this a strange English custom, as if it were a grace before a meal: he may have dipped the fruit in, but he did it perfunctorily and the ceremony became as abbreviated as present day baptism. There was so much opportunity for the catching of disease that our attitude towards it became more fatalistic and less intelligent. When Louis went it was more than likely that we had caught it too; therefore the stable door had already been left open. But a few policies did evolve: they were, to drink suspected water only on an empty stomach; to eat Mast as much as possible for it is an excellent disinfectant, and to have a meal of Sulphaguanidine tablets once a week; these cannot kill the entamoebae but severely hinder the existence of all other forms of intestinal life.

Philip's work was mainly associated with the soil. He sealed up tubes of it to be examined in Oxford and then intended to correlate the type of soil with the crops grown. Amongst the farmers there was a steady determination in method which assisted him, for few experiments by them were ventured upon: life was far too hazardous to risk a lessening of the crop. Similarly, no man specialised; and however small the holding, it was in all respects a miniature of a larger place. At Neckar-kuh, for instance, there were six men: three worked on carpets, two were peasants and the other did nothing; he was, according to Ahmed, 'lazy and without efficiency'. These two peasants looked after 2 cows, 3 ewes, 2 goats, 2 donkeys and ten hens. They grew many vegetables, grass, caraway seeds, lucerne, wheat, barley, millet and maize. There were apple, pomegranate, walnut, fig, pear, mulberry and pistachio trees. Even the castor oil bean is grown, in fact anything and everything to ensure maximum protection against all forms of elemental catastrophe. They can do nothing against drought or dust storms, nor against foxes, for they have no firearms, nor against porcupines, except to grow more valuable crops nearer the house. They can do nothing except try everything and this they do with avidity.

However, Philip certainly did no work in the latter part of his fourth day in Jupar. It was the day of the pseudo-porcupine hunt. An old man with an enormous wart on his nose came and told us he had found a large animal: my dictionary was ineffectual concerning animal names and I began to draw some. It was while I was drawing a porcupine, easily represented by a small face and a mass of quills, that he stopped me. Now we had not come from Oxford prepared to catch porcupines and could think of no suitable implement amongst our stock; therefore the old man and his two silent followers were invited into our rooms to pick upon anything which they might consider necessary for the chase. They decided upon 1 shovel, 100 ft. of nylon rope, 1 small carpet, a four gallon petrol tin with the top cut off, 1 ice-axe and a 6 foot pole rather like a scout pole. Philip and I—Eric was out—became intrigued, but then we had never caught a porcupine before. We set off through the village feeling very gay, with all the while the old man looking gloatingly at his ice-axe. Out into the desert we went along a line of qanat holes; then suddenly the old man began a shuffling run and held the ice-axe high in the air. He finished this charge standing over a disused well hole and shouting that it was still there. True enough, about 25 ft. down and on a ledge was his porcupine: it was the strangest porcupine that I had ever seen, for it had the body and tail of a lizard, a flattish head, a thin forked tongue, a loud hiss and was at least three feet long. A Varanus in fact, a type of lizard, but it had the appearance of a Rhinegold dragon.

The pit it was in had been a qanat well, but it had become too wide and collapses in the qanat had been caused by it. As with similar wells it had been partly filled in from the top: sufficient for the channel to be excavated again. Now a pit was left thirty feet deep and half as wide; it was unclimbable even for this creature, which was obviously the crocodile that had already been spoken of by the villagers. One of the silent companions began throwing stones at it so that it started to ooze back into its hole with a snake like movement. We looked helplessly at the implements we had brought. The old man grinned and the two others grinned: we grinned back and did not estimate the help they were going to give us very highly. I let Philip down on the rope on the far side of the hole and then asked the three to hold the rope while I went down; they held it for a bit and then forgot about it so that I landed abruptly in a cloud of dust. The three peered over the edge and told us that it spat poison. This was disquieting but untrue. In order to confound it we took off our shirts and suddenly smothered the animal in them, pulling it out of the hole as we did so; its stertorous breathing was muffled, for its mouth vigorously gripped the sleeve of Philip's shirt. We shouted for the petrol tin, rolled him up in the two shirts and stuck him into it. At first the three above were far too excited to think of holding on to the rope, but at last they considered the problem of extracting us from the pit. The noise from the tin was eerie and attracted much attention as we returned to Jupar. Our backs were both bright red long before we reached even the outskirts of the village, but we had with us a most wonderful animal. The three padded along proudly behind us.

It took us two hours to make a cage and while this was being done the three heroes of the hour described the chase to all who wished to hear: we supplied them with grapes and tea while they entertained the crowd. Then the shirts were unrolled, the animal transferred into the cage and received more attention than it had ever known before. Visitors poured in steadily. They were a considerable nuisance, but at least the fact that we were in search of animals was becoming more widely known. A villager proclaimed that it was a 'Buz Majjeh', a goat sucker, and lived on their milk. I did not believe this and gave it a mixed diet of grass, egg, partridge lights and a small lizard in order to discover what was its normal fare in life. We were all very fond of this creature and were reminded of its presence by a loud hiss every time we went to the privy.

The buz majjeh brought us in many more acquaintances. Fat, thin, unshaven or bearded, they were all our neighbours in the village. Among them were some who worked on carpets. That many such people were in Jupar was well known; for wherever you went there sounded, behind the braying of the donkeys, the deep thumping of the carpet makers. They invited us to inspect their work. We showed them the buz majjeh and accepted.

Certain things were particular about the rooms in which the carpets were made. As in most houses there were no windows, but they differed in having a hole or glass panel in the roof. On either side, for they are mostly made in pairs, are the carpets. On each of these sides there is one beam above and one below; both projected into holes in the walls. Arranged vertically between them are the many warp threads which form the foundation. The tension of the warp is obtained by having bars passing through the beams which can be turned and then locked in position. As the carpet is made it is occasionally wound onto the lower main beam of the loom.

Behind the carpet sit those who are making it, usually women and children but sometimes men. The children in the villages start work when they are five or six years old, although this is against the law. All the weavers squat on another beam

which rests on the floor: again this is against the law for the
weavers' seat must be raised above the floor to a specified height.
They work for about 9 hours a day and receive a very low wage
in comparison with other trades. Admittedly, the boys who mix
clay for the potter or assist the tinsmiths in the bazaar are probably
paid still less, but the hand-made carpet industry only really
flourishes where no alternative employment is available. Certainly,
where factory employment is available the weaving masters
would lose their labour. Although there are many laws in carpet
making which are not adhered to, I do not think that there is any
benevolence behind the lethargy in enforcing them; it is merely
that laws always appear to be less rigidly applied in the villages
of any land.

One row of knots is done at a time. Each knot is twisted around
two threads and the remaining length of wool cut with a knife.
The women make the knots amazingly quickly, the children take
a little longer. The pattern is called by someone sitting in between
the carpets who sings it to them in a strange, chanting voice.
His words are repeated by one of the four who are following him;
four because the two sides of the carpet are symmetrical and there
are two carpets. During this chanting only the knots which mark
the end of a colour are filled in, the remainder being completed
when he has ceased. At the finish of a row the knots have to be
thumped down into position causing the characteristic noise. This
has to be done evenly to ensure that the line is straight.

Most of the carpets being made in Jupar were three yards wide
and, when completed, five yards long. This is not the commonest
size for carpets, but it just happened that a lot of them were being
made at the time we were there. They take five weavers about
half a year to make. The Jupar carpets were of the 80.40 type
which have something like 16 knots to the inch. With this size a
weaver can make 8,000 knots in one day, although a record of
19,000, said to have been done by an Armenian woman, is quoted.

But the carpet industry is in a bad position today. Fewer
weavers are being employed by the Government carpet company
and fewer carpets are being bought. Britain, although it is still
the most important entrepôt for oriental carpets, has not imported
for the home trade since 1940. Various other European countries

buy carpets, either directly from Persia or through London, but they are considerably more expensive today than they have ever been since the carpet industry expanded to meet the western demand. We even heard it prophesied that the industry would be finished in ten years. Others say this is unlikely and that business will improve; but it is noteworthy that the prophecy has been uttered only 40 years after the first decade of the 20th century when there occurred the tremendous acceleration in the carpet trade.

Now, little money is being invested in the industry. In this the carpets are not unique for no great sums are being spent on building qanats or on improving the old method of building them. The wheel with which the mud is brought to the surface has a wooden axle that turns in two wooden supports. These make it most difficult to turn. The 2 men at the top find it hard work to pull up a bag that certainly doesn't weigh more than 80 lbs. With such a large wheel it should be an easy process. Their wooden one is so cumbersome an affair that the business of manipulating it is the limiting factor in the time taken to make a qanat. If only it had an iron axle with iron supports one man could work it and far more rapidly. Such an expenditure is not contemplated by any landlord when a wooden axle costs much less. Instead, their money is made, changed into some material and valuable form and retained. They are not making the hay while the sun shines but before the rain comes. The different viewpoint is governed by fear that the tide of their fortunes may shortly be reversed against them. The difference is admitted but the fear is not. Only when the difference is untrue will the fear have gone.

As the villagers grow everything in order that total disaster shall not occur, the landlords make preparations to evade the results should such an event take place. The lack of faith in what may befall is the same. The fear of the muqannis in the qanat is just as real, but there is no such outlet save that of superstition. The courage in any man varies curiously from day to day and to the muqanni this is a warning. I blame it on recent events, but it certainly occurs. Quite suddenly one is filled with the most morbid doubts and unreasonable fears.

Down in the qanats they only arose when I had nothing much

to do, when perhaps I was waiting for the nets to collect something. Then I became aware of the elongated tomb of the qanat and all senses increased in their sensitivity so that any hint of danger would be detected. Unless these thoughts disappeared, to be replaced by others, the nets did not remain there for as long as I had originally planned. Sometimes there was a reason for this sudden sharpening of attention, and then, when the harmless nature of what had occurred had been observed, the tension was relaxed: it may only have been a shouted greeting from a man at the top of the shaft when he had seen me pass beneath him, or a snake swimming past in the water; even a piece of camel thorn which had floated quietly and suddenly into my notice produced the same effect.

On the first visit a bat was flying in the qanat. While these squeaking creatures are pleasant flying in and out of trees on a summer evening, different proportions are assumed when they fly straight towards you in a channel four feet high: this one was about eight inches across the wings. Later on I became less conscious of them. They flew up and down after being disturbed and when they managed to fly past me I knew that something had just happened nearby, but exactly what had happened I was never quite sure. Once there was an awful 'flumpf' as a mass of earth fell from the roof into the water behind me. I hurried back to see if the channel was blocked and a few feet away another invisible mass plopped into the water. I left the site hurriedly and inspected it on the way back. There was a nasty scar on the roof but that was all: the echo of the channel increases the sound of the fall alarmingly but to nothing like the same extent as one's own imagination. I well understood the superstition of a muqanni.

On occasion I met people in the qanat. They were either working or walking to their place of work: their excavating and talking could be heard many wells away. On one day, the steady picking of a muqanni was coming out of the darkness; I walked on; for there was just room to pass and the nets were along that route. I held my little guttering lamp in front of me but I knew that I should see his lamp before I saw him. My lamp was never expected to throw a beam; six feet was its range. I walked nearer, the picking became louder but there was still no light from his

lamp: I walked faster, for there should have been a light; I desired
reassurance. Suddenly, right in front of my face, appeared another
face: it was hairy and grotesque and its two blind eyes stared
straight into mine. The picking had stopped. My lamp had singed
the hairs on his arm. I think I said 'Salaam', but I squeezed past
him quickly, scraping my back badly on the roof of the channel.
There was silence. I hurried away to let him begin picking again;
for there is great silence in the world when even a death watch
beetle hesitates.

The duties of a muqanni finish where the qanat flows onto the
surface: he has nothing to do with the stream. Where Gauhariz
flowed out there was quite a large pool; from there the drinking
water was collected and it also formed a public washing place.
Then came a shallower area where the sheep could walk in and
drink. Finally there was a long, wide section with bricks covering
the bottom and sides. The water flowed quite evenly over this
area before encountering the division, the maqsam. Five similar
channels led from the maqsam and each was believed to exude
the same quantity of water. In former times there had been only
five owners but in the 400 years which had passed since the qanat
had been built marriages, agreements and inheritances had
disrupted the simple maqsam of the past. The ownership of
Gauhariz and similar old waterways was now very complex.

This was even truer for land ownership. Equal shares for sons
and half shares for daughters has led to a vast mix up. Ahmed kept
on informing us of his, or members of his family's ownership
of a field or a few trees in a village through which we were
passing. Naturally this same disruption extends over distance.
Muhammad Reza Saam owned a few fields 30 miles south of
Kirman, some pistachio trees 80 miles north-west and an orchard
in Shiraz, 300 miles away. Not one of these properties was large
or particularly remunerative. Such small holdings necessitate
that the towns and villages are divided by statute into similar
minute areas.

Primarily Persia is divided into provinces each under a
Governor General. Kirman is one. Each province is composed of
a township and bakhshs or clusters of villages. Each bakhsh takes
the name of the principal village. Over the bakhsh is a Bakhshdar

who has a few civil servants and Gendarmes to help him. While the bakhsh of Zangiabad had 3,000 people, the village of Zangiabad had only 50; the remaining villages were even smaller and their names were not taken for the whole group. Over each knot of villages is the Kadkhoda, who is not a civil servant but is chosen by the landowners and approved by the Governor. The landowners pay him a regular wage, but he also receives money from the villagers when he has assisted them in lawsuits and other difficulties. Each village, and their size may be judged by the fact that in all Zangiabad there was only one with a population of 50, is divided into sixths and these sixths into sixteenths. Thus each village, perhaps like Neckar-kuh with 2 working peasants, is divided into 96ths. Only in this way can the laws of inheritance be carried out.

Share-cropping by the peasants is the usual method adopted by the landlord for the management of his land. The peasants work in groups and with a leader. Each year they draw lots for the fields, selected by the landlord or his agent, that are to be cultivated. Naturally no lots are drawn for the fallow fields. As there is little chance that the same group of peasants will draw a lot for the same fields when they next come into rotation, there is no incentive to improve them. Each group farms the field that they have drawn and then leave it. Only when the landlord makes an arrangement whereby one peasant often receives the same land is a raising of fertility considered.

Financially the landlord of a Persian village is in a definite but quite incalculable position. A few figures are certain. For instance, in the villages on the edge of the plain the landlord takes 70% of the cereals; but if he provides draught animals 80% and all the straw. With opium, 50%; unless he provides manure and extra labour at the time of ploughing, in which case it is 72%. He has many rights but it is not considered correct if he uses all of them. On any day he can take fruit for himself but he is not expected to do this too regularly. Hospitality always has to be granted to him and his guests. The peasant has no bitterness towards him. He is accepted as a necessary burden and naturally no efforts are made to increase this weight; no more trees are planted by the peasant, for 'if we did they would become the property of the landlord'.

For his part, the landlord has to pay the taxes, look after the peasants, pay for the water and generally for the seed. The peasant houses should be repaired, money should be lent to them in bad years to avoid persecution by the professional money lenders and petty disputes should be settled by him: he should be the guide in their affairs. The landlord is generally left with about 30% of each year's crop as net profit: thus he fares well. The peasant fares according to the wishes of his landlord and such a system can easily be criticized. The instability of the country does not encourage the benevolence even of a far-sighted landlord. But selfishness exists only in so far as the unwritten laws permit it and the landlords accept their definite duties mutely, for the system is also their inheritance. They never fail, for instance, to give a sheep to a man who has shot a leopard.

The landlords were kind to us; most because it was their nature and some because they had heard of the Governor's friendly attitude. This cut both ways; for not only were we assured of their assistance but of their curiosity. This inquisitiveness resulted either in a visit to our house accompanied by loud offers of help or in some invitation. However, Muhammad Reza Saam, a scholarly old gentleman living near Jupar in Shahabad, invited us to go on a gazelle hunt. Now I had no desire to turn one of these beautiful animals into a quivering heap of bloody flesh; but the invitation was there and no evasion was possible. Anyway, it solved an idiotic discussion we had been having on which day should be chosen as a holiday: Friday was the Moslem day of rest; Saturday was the fortieth anniversary of the first democratic government in Persia. Then came Sunday and August bank holiday. One quite senseless source of amusement with us was the insertion of Friday in a sentence where Sunday should be: 'A lie in bed as it is Friday,' 'Friday lunch' and 'that tired feeling on Saturday morning' were all bound to bring helpless applause. The invitation was for August bank holiday. Only Philip and I were to go; for Eric was temporarily ill and Louis was still in Kirman.

We got up while it was still dark and a bleary eyed soldier gave us the horses. Muhammad's son, Abdul Samdi, arrived on a splendid white horse and we all set off into the desert. The excessive energy was taken out of the horses by making them

gallop: the air was cool and fresh and nothing moved save us and
the little cloud of dust behind us. The hollow sound made by the
hooves was quick and sharp: it did not disturb the silence of the
land.

After three hours we reached the butts, small walls of stones
behind which it was necessary to crouch. Our shot guns were of
the hammer type and loaded from the muzzle: into them was
stuffed cordite, a small piece of cloth and a large amount of buckshot. Samdi told us not to shoot at anything more than a hundred
yards away; in Persia anything mechanical is stretched to its
utmost. A servant of Samdi's named Darvish was instructed to go
and find some gazelle. The scheme was that he should drive these
animals up the dry gulleys which confronted each of the butts; for
a gazelle when pursued will naturally take the least conspicuous
path. So Darvish galloped away while we sat behind our stones.
The sun rose higher and the increasing heat made us extremely
aware of our own conspicuousness. Everything became hot; the
stones through which we peered, the gun barrels in our hands
and the air which went down to our lungs. The rays of the sun
beat mercilessly upon us.

Darvish could just be seen, but the shimmering land made him
unclear: no gazelles came springing up the gulleys. Much later
he came galloping up. He said he had pursued one small herd, but
on reaching the entrance to the gulleys they had shied away: as
this herd was apparently the remnant of a larger herd, it was likely
that they should show a certain reluctance to go along the same
path as had previously proved fatal to so many of them. The
second drive, about three miles further on, was more successful;
for we saw the gazelles: they came trotting up to within 100 yards
of our positions before they in their turn saw us. I was not displeased: with such a quantity of buckshot a hit was liable to be
made wherever I chanced to aim.

We breakfasted by a qanat stream and went to sleep for the
middle of the day. The return journey was pleasant: the horses
were curiously tired and walked slowly. When they came to one
of these gulleys formed by the winter floods they galloped down
in order to scale the other side with the minimum of effort. Each
time they were just as surprised to discover the bottom of the

slope had many large stones, as have all dry river valleys; therefore a sudden and uncalculated jump had to be made: the rider, as on all similar occasions, contented himself with remaining in the saddle.

Our route back was not through the desert but along the line of villages flanking the hills to the east of Jupar. Outside one house was a stuffed leopard. Samdi said it had been shot recently by an old man of 75 who makes his home in the mountains. He is believed to be completely carnivorous, living solely upon ibexes, mountain goats and similar forms. Once or twice a year he shoots a large carnivore, some leopard or panther, that has probably come over from the wilder regions nearer India. With its skin he descends from the mountains and collects one sheep from each of the fifty villages which are in that area. The raids of a leopard would be most severe and against such attacks the majority of villages are helpless. The old man then sells this herd, collects perhaps £200, spends all this money on bullets and cartridges, and retires once more into the hills. Unless the villagers go into the mountains themselves, no one ever sees him except when a leopard skin is over his shoulder and a flock of sheep is before him. Assuredly this man has worked out for himself a satisfactory way of life: for two accurate shots a year the land below supplies him with all that he needs. As the sheep-rewarding tradition is considered to be of great antiquity, there has probably always been a man living in the mountains. I wondered what makes a man sever himself from the land and disappear into the hills and if he finds any enjoyment at all in his occasional visits. The earth and its affairs must seem most petty to him.

On the next day rain came to Jupar, the last flick of the monsoon as it spent itself inland. There had been no rain in the summer for seven years and on the last occasion great floods were caused. I was down in the qanats when it started and was perplexed by the large number of stones which came hurtling down the well shafts: I had to make silly little darts to pass underneath them. With the rain had come a wind that made deep booming notes over these shafts. I felt suddenly extremely cold in the vast organ-pipe system and listened to the different notes. The wind must have been very gusty, for the wells did not all boom together; also the noise took a long time to reach me from the wells further away; the channels magnified and distorted whatever sounds came down to them. My lamp was blown out and it was useless trying to relight it; so I squatted in the water and waited for the wind to finish. The storm was brief, its echoes died away and there was silence once more in the channels. I lit the lamp and went downstream, accompanied by much camel thorn which had been blown into the shafts. Outside all was still: only the clearness of the air testified that something had happened.

At home, if what was generally the Finance Controller's office may be called such, Eric and Philip were bitterly complaining. They had been caught in the rain. Naturally they had seen it coming, but the idea of a refreshing shower was not distasteful to them. The first drop had landed neatly in the centre of Eric's map and had presented itself, not as a small film of pure, clear liquid, but as 'a disgusting great blotch of mud'. The remaining drops had filled their hair with sand and their eyes with grit while the precious map was rushed to the house. It rained a little that night and Eric was forced to come down from the roof. The rain did not cause any floods, for it was insufficient. With the corn all out in heaps and waiting to be thrashed it could have been disastrous; but it was not and no one would starve. Nothing resulted from it save for the very clear sky; this lasted for some days and completely ruined all sense of distance. How could it be that the old fort of Kirman was thirty miles away?

Early the next morning a boy brought a snake in a box. It was a solid looking box with no lid. The boy said it was all nailed together to prevent the long, thin snake from getting out. He had brought along several grubby companions and a certain amount of our prestige was at stake; I stood around in my pyjamas and thought a bit. We had some meat-safe gauze and with this a cage was made: it had a little door which hinged on wire and was a considerably better job than would have resulted had the work not been blessed with this all-seeing, all-critical throng. I was just receiving all their suggestions about the matter of transferring the snake, and glad to hear them criticizing one another, when the box was neatly opened by a man who smashed it in one blow with a shovel. The snake promptly appeared but hesitated long enough for somebody else to catch it by the tail. By shaking the snake he successfully prevented the fulfilment of any aggressive intentions on its part. The cage was placed on the ground, the snake's head was hung near it, and as the animal crawled into it, the rest of its body was lowered by the man who held its tail. The door was closed, everybody admired the hissing form and I gave the boy his money, with an irregular subsidy for the man who had grabbed it.

It was an African sand snake, nearly four feet long, but had no markings and was pale in colour. It almost died in the morning by being left in the sun: at lunch-time it was lying on its back with its mouth wide open. When the cage was turned upside-down it remained in the same position: after being put in the shade and having had some water poured over it, the snake slowly revived. I had little idea with what to feed it and put in a small frog and a large insect; but that evening both of them were alive and frightening the snake. Thenceforth, when we walked down to the bottom of the garden the snake as well as the buz majjeh hissed fiercely. Some day, perhaps, I will become accustomed to the reptilian hiss, but at Jupar, when that noise came out of the darkness and from a cage made of meat-safe gauze, I felt the day was a long way off.

Mirza took a great pride in all our animals and showed them off to visitors. Regularly he took the three hedgehogs for walks in the garden. One of them was very young and correspondingly small; it received his special attention. The day following the snake capture, he filled half its cage with earth, much to my annoyance and the disgust of the insect, the frog and the snake. He insisted that snakes ate earth but gave it less each day after I had reprimanded him for, he said, its appetite was waning. However, Mirza was an intelligent individual, for he understood our attempts in his language. He cared little for hygiene or cleanliness, but was related to a considerable number of people in the village. Thus he wielded influence which was probably more satisfactory than the mere cleaning of plates.

One day he invited us to come and see a carpet cut down. A relative of his had thought that it might interest us. Once again we ducked into a carpet room, but this time it was silent and the pattern was complete. The carpet was still held tight with most of it wound around the bottom beam. In order that all the tension is not restricted to a certain part during the cutting down, many people sever the threads which hold it, until it drops onto the floor. Those who had made this carpet took no interest in the business; they were only there on that day because we were, their eyes were never on the carpet. I gaze fondly on any piece of work which has taken me longer than a minute or so, but this carpet to them was only a time card, a record of hours put in. The last few knots were not made excitedly; they were made just as methodically as the other five million. Two of the weavers carried this carpet outside and spread it on the ground. It was possible to see the whole of it for the first time and also where the muddy feet of winter had rested. There was still no interest shown by them. Elsewhere we found that most Persians attached great importance to their carpets, but the weavers themselves looked upon them as a means of income, things made to walk upon; scrubbed clean when dirty and replaced when worn.

However, a carpet that has just been cut down is not a thing of beauty: no more does it represent the oriental carpet than does a shaggy sheep represent clean, white wool: both have to be clipped. With a curved pair of shears the greater part of the pile is removed. Only when this shearing has taken place can the detail of the pattern and the brightness of the colours be seen. The finer the carpet the shorter the pile can be cut and the shorter the pile the clearer is the pattern. Many of the first carpets which arrived in the western world were not new and unused; they were old and cheap and second hand. From this arose the assertion that Persian carpets in order to be good should have dull colours. This news was treated in the East in a most straightforward manner. The new carpets were put in the street and all the village walked over them; the bright sunlight bleached them and they were ready for sale. Later came the usage of certain chemicals which faded all their colours to a dull and even hue. To the connoisseurs they were the real Persian carpets. Nowadays this view still lingers; for bright new carpets are believed to have had the wool dyed chemically, and whatever the colour may be, it is considered better if made by vegetable dyes, although some of these dyes produce a brighter colour than the corresponding chemical one.

The Persians accept the situation, for it is they who have to sell the carpets and they collect the vegetable dyes. Perhaps chemical dyes are used too, but they are able to say that vegetable dyes have been used in the making of the carpet. Otherwise chemicals are used; for it is believed that if a colour is good it does not matter how it arose. The real connoisseur could distinguish them by knowing the resultant colours of all the vegetable dyes, but now it is considered safer to rely upon certain chemical tests. Certainly we believed that we would never forget the Kirman red, a delightful deep claret colour. Even lying in the dust it looked fine and over it we said good-bye to the desultory weavers.

That evening was the most wonderful of all evenings that I saw in Jupar. The sky was clear, the visibility seemed perfect and the mountains were brought so near that it appeared possible to scale them in a trice. It was lovely to breathe in the air and take a delight in everything that could be seen. I wandered dreamily in the desert to the north of the village looking for animals, but knowing full well that nothing existed on that side of it. The daily bus, the Kadkhoda's bus, went by me on its way to Kirman and all, especially those sitting on the roof, shouted their salaams. A large goatherd sauntered across pretending, with the imagination only a goatherd can possess, that the pasture there was delightful, and not just some isolated pieces of camel thorn. The whole herd was kept in perfect order by a youth armed with a sling. Stones were constantly hurled at its flanks, scattering those inwards that were straying too far. The goats always reacted correctly to the stones that fell near them: they gave little jumps and ran towards the others. This boy had on a ragged pair of shorts, half a shirt tied round his neck and no shoes. As he ran his clothes flapped around him; it was absolutely right that he should be dressed in such a way. David had been a goatherd and this youth was the same: this part of their lives was probably identical. I had always been cynically incredulous about the slaying of Goliath and asked this youth to smite a sunflower which stood a short distance away. True the sunflower did not fall down dead, but it straightway received a blow from a stone not even round or smooth. This boy gave me the sling and laughed at my brutish efforts. Then he rounded up his herd with great whoopings and slingings till they slowly turned for home, with the peace of the land only disturbed by little puffs marking where the stones had fallen. I was left feeling that I did not fit into the scene and not even sure which scene it was that I didn't fit into. The distant speck of the bus stuck in the sand reminded me of the present and of supper.

The whole country tends to live a little in the past. New carpet designs are rare. New methods of building qanats are not contemplated. Even the taxes are paid according to what has been. In our area they were resultant of an estimation of the land productivity made sixteen years before: only a reassessment by a Government inspector, and he probably has to come from Tehran, could alter those taxes. Any flood, sand drift or drought may have made them quite unreasonable, but not only does money have to be spent to encourage the inspector to come, but his fare has to be paid too. Therefore it is usually cheaper to pay according to the old rates and to hope for a reassessment. Due to this sixteen-year-old estimation and the changes which have occurred during that time, the landlords at Mahun paid taxes varying from two to fifty per cent of their income: those of them who have had bad luck in their land always receive this second blow at the hand of the tax-collector. I imagine that when the next assessment takes place effort will be made by the landlord to exhibit fields poor in appearance and apparently poor in their fertility. Such a time interval between assessments enables them to make good the loss of that one year of sacrifice and after that year they will not be burdened by having to pay their rightful taxes.

There is also direct ten per cent taxation upon house property, business and land ownership. Assessment on property and business profit is made at the beginning of the year and long before any actual profit can be realised. There is a tendency at this time for the tax payer to consider that he has been unjustly treated: he could appeal to the local Finance Officer or even to the Bakshdar, but this takes money: as with disease it is thought better to become immune to that which has smitten you.

Up till 1950 the ten per cent tax was given to the tax collectors in money. Then a new regulation was started which enforced actual grain to be given for the profits on wheat and barley. Presumably the Government wished to have a grain reserve itself, quite independent of the reserves which every landlord has stored up for himself.

Difficult as a country like Persia is to tax, the Government have placed a tax on most things and the actual difficulties are left to the collector. Wine and spirits, wherever they are made, are taxed. There is a slaughterhouse tax, a brick kiln tax, a tax on sheep and goats. Everything has to be inspected by the collector, who then has to extract the money: the difference between the estimated tax and the tax actually collected must be prodigious. In an illiterate village like Jupar where few figures are kept, the collector has little proof of what has occurred: such a village sees few merits in literacy.

CHAPTER VII

Jupar 3

IT had always been our intention to leave the intrigues of the village for a few days and spend the time in the mountains. Louis was still not back, which meant that there would only be four of us and probably for three days. I did a small calculation and Mirza went off to buy 75 eggs, 18 lbs. of bread, 6 lbs. of rice, 3 large water melons and 18 lbs. of grapes. He was also asked to arrange for two donkeys and a driver. He returned, but only with 65 eggs; he said if we cared to wait another day the chickens would lay some more: we decided not to wait as the food he had bought already made quite a presentable array. With Mirza there was no difficulty in the acquisition of food; every morning he was told what to buy and every evening he told us how much it had cost. Apart from the things we had ordered for the mountains, we ate cheese, tomatoes, mast, eggs, fruit, a few potatoes and an occasional chicken. Dates came only in the latter part of the stay. Most food was cheap and cost us less than 2/6d. per day per man. Mirza's evening reckoning was always great fun: it occurred just after supper and was announced by Ahmed who said: 'You may now listen to Mirza's bill'. Then would come the list: 'Eggs, 11 rials; mast, 4 rials; grapes, 18 rials; tarantula, 1 rial; samovar charcoal, 2 rials; cheese, 6 rials; wire for snake cage, 2 rials; 3 scorpions, 6 rials; and so on. Always there was this mixture, and never, as he read them out, was there any change in the intonation of his voice.

We left Mirza behind to look after the animals. For the first day we strolled along behind the donkeys: these poor creatures have wretched lives and are for ever aware of the large stick wielded by their drivers. When one of them strayed from the path there was an exclamation of complete surprise from its tormentor and the animal was thwacked back into position again. I resented this excessive brutishness and more so when it came from his son, a lad who made all the same noises as his father in a far higher key, who wore a thick pair of pyjamas, too short by a foot or so, a little peaked cap and enormous shoes.

We walked eastward from Jupar initially and parallel with the hills. Immediately south of Jupar the ways were too steep, as we had seen on the day at the spring. To the west of the village we had been with the horses, but the Kuh-i-Jupar, the highest peak and 13,000 ft., was to the east and it was that area which we wished to visit. The sun was at its highest when we reached Khanu, a village in a slight valley and invisible until suddenly the whole of it was spread below us with the first field only fifty feet away: Ahmed swallowed his pride and expressed surprise. The valley it is in stretches away down to the plain, 2,000 ft. below was Mahun, but Kirman, 40 miles away, was hidden in a haze. A large plane tree dominated Khanu and under this we sat. Unfortunately, on this day it was my turn to be afflicted internally: always one of us was affected in this way. I was directed to a minute dwelling right in the centre of all the terraced fields: I walked nonchalantly down to it and entered quickly. The walls were very low but you could make yourself invisible. I quickly left the place only to return again before I had reached the tree. Chasing out two sheep and being deaf to the remarks of all the peasants in the fields, I disappeared once more. The sheep peered in at intervals to see if all was well. All was not; I felt ill for two hours or so and then recovered.

We turned up the next valley after Khanu and reached Baharistan, the 'country of the spring' and the home of two small families. They had built for themselves two houses and made a little terracing beside the tiny stream which gave them their life: tall plane trees provided shelter for the houses. The steep sides of the valley had shielded the spot from the warmth of the sun for the last part of the day; so as soon as the meal was over everybody got into their sleeping bags. The night was very cold, but at the first hint of day there was similar adroitness in getting out of them. Eric and I climbed up the other side of the valley, which was then in the sunlight, and sat enjoying its warmth.

Philip did not, partly because he believed he was more impervious to cold and partly because he is less tolerant of the most temporary starvation. To us his appetite verged on gluttony and to him our desire for warmth was just a lack of stamina; to all of us it should have been nothing but a sign of the simple fact that human beings tend to require variety in companionship. However, at the time our grievances were most real; there was not the resistance within us to consider them otherwise.

Baharistan was 8,000 ft. high and the Kuh-i-Jupar 13,000 ft. The valley we were in led up to a small plateau about 2,000 ft. below the mountain of Jupar and the donkeys couldn't go that way: therefore we asked their driver what was the name of the village at the head of the next valley to the east. He said Karan Sara Sang and we arranged to meet him there: he was to take the donkeys and Ahmed, who is not well adapted to a mountain environment, down the valley of Baharistan and up the next to Karan Sara Sang. Confident that such an arrangement could not possibly go wrong, we set off up the path to the plateau.

Above Baharistan the valley was good for walking but not for cultivation; therefore the water, which came from a spring at the head of it, was made to come down in a narrow channel to the village: even with this precaution against seepage and evaporation there was considerably less at the bottom. At the top end the valley ended abruptly: it became necessary to scramble up whatever was judged to be a path. Higher up all paths were made by mountain goats; they were narrow, more definite than the lower tracks and led us over steep slopes of scree. Philip had most fearsome thoughts about landslides, but in spite of the angle at which everything was set there was no tendency for it to shift: all of us skidded down in places but none for very far.

The piles of scree leant against the mountain sides up to the level of the plateau at 11,000 ft. The ground there was covered with scrub and I saw more birds than I had ever seen down on the plain. There were few insects, many spiders and some black and yellow tarantulas. Tracks of goats and ibexes and, once, the pad mark of a big cat showed that life was abundant but merely well concealed. A large eagle flew over to frighten the crows, which in their turn were frightening birds the shape of woodpeckers that flew like ducks. There were wrens, pigeons and a type of linnet. At the top of the valley there had been sand martins; but for the most part the birds, although numerous, were unrecognizable, as they were all slight distortions of birds that we knew.

It was easy to see the valley in which Karan Sara Sang was believed to be, for all the country miles to the north of us was spread out in relief. Baharistan could be seen and every other speck of green in all the other valleys that stretched northwards. With four hours of daylight left we set off down to the village of our rendezvous and ran down the scree, down out of the scrub area, out of the region of the birds and into the valley beyond. The sun was then behind the hills and sent jagged shafts of light over our heads, but we had reached the place: some women working in the fields said that the name of the village was Chashme Kuchek. We gave a flowery description of Ahmed and the other two but they denied ever having seen such people. Karan Sara Sang was said to be four farsakhs, four hours walk, over the hills: the valley we were in was the wrong one. As the highest village was scarcely inhabited we walked down to the second, a more impressive settlement called Torgekhan. On the way down much righteous reasoning, assisted by lack of any opposition, proved that Ahmed and the driver were in the wrong, for they had misled us: they had rightly gone to Karan Sara Sang, but it was two valleys away from Baharistan.

By good fortune a stout man who stood beneath a hurricane lamp was the landlord: he ordered food for us and while we ate it he sat contemplating the scene and spoke only to tell us to eat more. Although we had come down to 8,000 ft. it was mighty cold: I began performing convulsive shivers which, when the food was finished, the landlord suddenly noticed. He accepted the fact that our beds were at Karan Sara Sang without comment and produced some blankets: he put one on the ground, instructed us to lie on it and threw the rest on top of us. He then returned to the hurricane lamp and resumed his interrupted conversation. We, after some muttered comments against those who had warned us against the perils of prickly heat, shivered and went to sleep.

In the morning Philip went off to Karan Sara Sang. Eric and I collected insects and warmed ourselves in the sun. Without any form of programme we got very lethargic: by the time that Philip returned we were both well asleep and awoke only when Ahmed had begun to snore. As the Persian Government had entrusted us to his care, he had naturally been most worried by our failure to arrive at the meeting place. When Philip had finally appeared, then Ahmed had come running out of the village to meet him: he had never run before in the remembrance of any of us. He was genuinely distressed and explained how little he had been able to sleep because he believed us to be lost in the mountains: his eyes were indeed red from the long wakeful hours of the night. We were all touched by his behaviour and from that day our attitude changed towards him, even after we had discovered that very many mice had also prevented the driver and his son from getting any sleep.

There was no time to return to Jupar that day; for it was nearly over when we met again. Instead, we ate melons under the trees of the landlord's garden. His mute acceptance of our affairs continued until he saw my knife; it was long, pointed and rather useless except for eating melons; but it gave this man much pleasure and he played with it for the rest of the day. As the old man had admired the ice-axe, so did the cleanliness of metal seem to attract this landlord. There being no local source of iron it was naturally a rarity; even keys and locks were made of wood. The blacksmith at Jupar had fashioned all his wares out of broken tools and pieces of worn out vehicles: knife blades from files and files from lorry springs were his principal conversions. Bars of iron were hammered and then cut into nails. Everything he made had already served another purpose. The old man and the landlord were admiring things which had never been other than what they were. Although books referred to deposits of high grade iron ore at Kirman, these reports were unfounded: traces of iron were present in some of the rocks, but in any area this is generally the case. Such tales take a long time to die, but it would be interesting to know the manner of their birth.

On the next day we walked back to Jupar. Philip said he couldn't stand the pace of the donkeys and walked on ahead. I talked instead to Eric, a man tolerant of the views of he who happens to be nearest to him. This is an attribute which does not always please either a tolerant or an intolerant companion. If he was a publican he would probably be a good one, and if he was a policeman he would be just as likely to be a good one. However, he will be neither of these; for he has been granted a colonial job in Kenya. His principal disadvantage at Jupar, a point relatively insignificant elsewhere, was his marked ability for letting my animals escape.

Ahmed was talking to the donkey driver. He still made a disgusting noise when he ate, frequently spat after great internal preliminaries, always put in as big a mouthful as his jaw would allow and spoke without any reference to the quantity of food that was in his mouth. He had a knack of getting himself or one of us into some diabolically embarrassing situation; but he tried to help us and tried with great energy. This, we felt in our occasional rational moments, was more important.

Louis was still in hospital and inevitably a certain amount of outside sympathy was extended to him. Before he went, his dysentery had made him irritating and slightly unwholesome; he had asserted his knowledge in a particularly brutal manner, with insufficient charm to overweigh the brutality. But when he was not suffering from dysentery, he attempted, in whatever he did, to do it fully and play the role of the part. While he was repairing the lorry, he assumed an artificially strong and gruff expression, quite different in appearance from the suave Louis in Tehran. The incoherent mumblings of a botanist accompanied him when he carried his plant press and he looked all right on a horse. But he became ill and badly so. His sickness changed all other more likeable moods and he was left only as a patient. Our sympathy towards him during that phase began on the day that he left us for Kirman.

Philip was the youngest of the party and the initiator of the expedition. These two facts did not coincide neatly. He was Louis' favourite target and encouraged him by his indifference. As he had been on expeditions before he was aware that patience among their members decreased with time and his indifferent aloofness arose from this fact. It was not believed by the rest of us to be the answer.

For my part, I was disgusted at my own lack of tolerance; that I should be capable of being so irritated. If a friend annoys me, then he is soon forgiven; for once again I notice his better qualities. If a child is tiresome, then forgiveness comes quickly; for the child is so full of potentialities that a momentary noise is excusable. If I do something petty or stupid myself, then an excuse rapidly appears to account for my stupidity; but if a fly annoys me, merely in its righteous quest for food, merely by leading the life it is intended to lead and buzzes incessantly into my notice, then I am really annoyed; for no good is there, no finer qualities, no great potentialities, no excuse for stupidity of my own, with the result that I am extremely displeased by its activities. Thus it was that my associates seemed to generate my annoyance. Its occurrence was temporary, but its proportions were large. As with courage, the stock we have of patience can be expended: after this time the triviality of the things that annoy us is fantastic.

Eight hours after leaving Torgekhan we reached Jupar. Five minutes later those who had caught animals during our absence began to descend upon the house. I felt extremely weary and put these catches into temporary cages. A snake was put into one of Eric's map cases, a blindworm in a jam jar and the scorpions into anything that would hold them. Unfortunately, this policy didn't pay; for a cat managed to eat 14 lizards that evening and Eric let a bat out of his field glasses case. I began to set a large trap for the cat, and while I was doing so, it came and drank from our bowl of permanganate normally used for disinfecting fruit; it drank a lot, which gave us scope for a successful prophecy that it would never appear again.

The scorpions were caught in large numbers, because they came into the houses at night. They could also be caught by digging up their small desert holes or even by placing damp bricks on the ground: their partiality to crawling under these has made them the sacred animal of brickmakers. The blindworm was not poisonous, but is said by the Persians to be the most deadly of all the snakes. It is called Jaffir's snake, after a fable in which Jaffir is the hero: he once found one of them and was kind to it by putting it in the straw his donkey was carrying. Time passed and the snake threatened to bite Jaffir and his donkey; Jaffir protested, but the snake replied: 'My revenge for your best is my worst' and he prepared to bite them. At that moment a fox appeared and by guile persuaded the snake to fall into a pit; then the snake protested, but the fox buried him saying: 'You threatened your worst. This is the best way you can die.' It is a strange and callous fable, presumably intended to point out that evil is not always revenge for evil, but a thing in itself which can be given birth in any offender.

That evening a boy came in very silently and presented me with a large scorpion. He was crying gently, and whimpered that the thing had stung him on the finger. This finger was held tightly in the other hand and was quite blue. The book said 'permanganate', so I cut the place open, squeezed something out of it, and then bathed his finger in the liquid. The boy continued to sob, and as I was intent on cleaning the wound, it was a while before I noticed that two women had come into the garden. They said nothing and I asked them if the boy belonged to them. They nodded and pulled their chadahs, the cloaks which cover their heads and reach to the ground, tighter over their faces and said no word. Only their eyes were visible and these stared unflinchingly at me out of the darkness. I continued with the finger and finally bandaged it up. He had stopped crying by then, but the gaze from the women continued with nothing being said by anyone. It took me longer than it should have done, but the women could not help, for I was a stranger and a man. The silence was a portent of the great gulf that existed between us, between the man who was cleaning the wound of a child and the staring eyes of the woman to whom that child belonged. I gave him a pill to make him sleep and the women took him away through the door and closed it quietly. They left me to myself and with a feeling of inestimable guilt.

I was grateful to the next visitor, who clattered through the door in the usual way to shatter the stillness which had been there. He presented me with a bleeding porcupine's head. It had been shot in the act of stealing grapes and the rest of it, he said, had been eaten for supper. It was a shame about the rest, but I accepted the skull and spent the next day boiling the flesh off it; the garden was filled with a putrefying smell. Such a smell is rarely met with in a country where there are so many carrion feeders of all kinds that decay does not have time to set in. Two days previously a dead donkey had been thrown off the street, for it was dead and in the way; the next day most of the meat had gone, and on the third day, only the skull remained: nothing but a skull to mark the place where a donkey had been. Even the smell did not linger in our garden.

I amused myself by going down a porcupine's hole one day. There were several of them scattered about, south of the village; so, selecting one which was well made, I disappeared inside. This hole started about six feet below the level of the ground, as it was at the bottom of a narrow cutting which the porcupine had made. The hole was not so steep, but went gently downhill for ten feet: there was no possibility of crawling along it with the knees beneath the body, but it was quite large enough for me to worm along it. This hole led into a dome shaped cavern about four feet high and six feet wide: I had no idea that the porcupines lived so well. The place was clean and on the floor were the quills, black and white and sharp. From this chamber many smaller holes led off, holes that were no larger than the animal itself, and not passable for me: the lamp only lit them up for a little way and they were all straight for the distance that could be seen. There was no way of telling whether any of them were occupied, but there would only have been one inhabited, for the porcupine leads a solitary life: the male does not remain in the dwelling of the female with whom he has mated: she rears the family and he looks after himself. Each night he leaves his home and goes to steal the fruit and plants on which he lives. As every garden has a water channel leading into it under the wall, the entering presents no difficulty; then he returns to one of his homes, for he has several, to pass the day. The snags in his life are that his maraudings make many enemies and that his flesh is much admired; otherwise his contentment might be absolute. In the middle of the day, when he is lying in his hole and the peasant is asleep under a tree, there is peace between them: it is a shame that the conflict will be resumed when these two sleeping forms wake up.

The snags in the lives of those whom he robs are far more numerous. With less reason for contentment the village peasant, by his familiarity with the hardships and apparent indifference to them, often gives the semblance of a satisfied being. That he is not is made more obvious by the number of opium smokers: forty per cent of the adult male population has been stated as a figure of the number of smokers. Opium is easily obtainable for those who wish to render themselves less responsive and more insensitive. The law states that all opium grown should be sold to the Government but the law is not enforced. Ethically there are many arguments why it should be enforced, economically the landlord considers it a suitable crop and the Government finds itself unable to prevent illegal distribution.

From a landlord's viewpoint such a crop has the disadvantages that the net income is less than for wheat and barley and it is easy for the peasants to steal some of the hardened sap before it is collected. Opium is advantageous in that it requires less water than other crops and something else may be grown on the same land in the same year: this subsequent crop will be affected by any manuring that was done for the opium. The landlord takes from half to three-quarters of the yield, according to the labour and manure he has supplied. The peasants share is opium or its money equivalent.

From the Government's viewpoint the export of opium is profitable; but it is very harmful within the state. Legislation started in 1910, when a monopoly was decreed on Shirek of Soukteh, the residue left in the pipes after smoking and the most dangerous opium derivative used in Persia. A gradual centralisation was envisaged so that, if successful, the use of opium, except for medicinal purposes, would have ended after seven years. The 1914-18 war weakened the Government and made it impossible to enforce the laws. In 1924 it was estimated that one third of the opium crop was sold illegally and not through the administration of the government. The quantity to be collected from each landowner was assessed by Government inspectors from the appearance of the crop in the field. Presumably the large amounts disappeared during the collection. At that time the sap has oozed out from the scratches which have been made on the poppy seed case and is scraped off into a bowl. The contents of this bowl will eventually be taken to be weighed; but not before many people have had an opportunity to buy and sell some of its contents.

In 1928 Reza Shah made all trade in all opium a Government monopoly. The landowner could still grow as much of it as he wished, but he had to sell all the produce to the Government. Initially there was little of the crop sold to the inspectors; for the high tax imposed on the resale of opium meant that the illegal sale, which bypassed the Government, was being encouraged. Then in 1931 the tax was greatly reduced and the selling to the monopoly rapidly increased. It is generally accepted that the monopoly control before the war brought a larger percentage of the opium into Government warehouses.

By the time of the second world war the British no longer took a large part in the distribution of Persian opium around the world: instead the Japanese had taken over. Consequently, after 1941 the quantity exported suddenly decreased; but it is believed that the growing of opium was still extensive. Various laws were decreed during the war in an attempt to discourage the growing of opium, but the Government could not enforce them. However, they did show the trend of opinion, for the monopoly laws of 1928 had not been aimed at a decrease in cultivation. It is unfortunate that the new programmes for the gradual withdrawal of opium had not been put forward at a time when the Government had power.

In 1947 a law was passed which forbade the growing of opium, but this was repealed shortly afterwards. Then in 1950 the expense of the inspectors was not considered to be justified by the small quantity of tax and opium which they managed to collect. Therefore, in that year there were no assessors. The landlords, in order to placate the Finance officer who was certain to have seen their fields of poppies, had decided to bring in a small quantity, so they could have some defence against his possible accusations. In Jupar these men were quite solemnly taking their portions to be weighed at our home, the Finance House; 6 manns were handed in out of an estimated 700: 39lb. out of 4,585.

As most officials in the Kirman villages seem to smoke it, there is no attempt made in any of the villages by any smoker to disguise the fact. Those who do not have the habit admit they are comforted by the knowledge that it is obtainable should they ever wish it. Even mothers dose their restless children with it. Now the contraband trade has arisen and greatly assists in the internal distribution. The donkey driver with whom we had gone to the mountains had once been prosperous but had been ruined by confiscation and imprisonment after being caught with a load of the drug. The hard penalties inflicted upon those who are caught have been answered by an increased reluctance to be caught. Some enforcement officers are said to have encountered 150 armed horsemen guarding a caravan. Six months before a Gendarme patrol near Kirman had been badly shot up.

The export, both direct and indirect, of opium from Persia can prejudice the well-being of other countries. But as an opium addict will die if the drug is suddenly taken away from him, so would there be a drastic increase of poverty in the land if the growing of it was successfully forbidden. The process of its withdrawal must be gradual, as had been surmised in 1910. Forty years later the process is so gradual as to be unnoticeable.

In the carpet industry there are the same reasonable laws which are not enforced due to the unpleasantness that would be caused. The antagonism in the opium trade is just the same: a violent contradiction of that which is and that which ought to be. Nothing is encouraged by the corresponding antagonism in religion. With a religion that encourages marriage at 9 for girls and 14 for boys and a state that ordains 16 and 18 to be the youngest ages there is inevitably friction between the two. But in the villages it is neither the state nor the religion that decides the marriage age: the girl is married as quickly as possible and the man as soon as he can support a wife. As with the opium, as with the carpet laws, it is poverty that makes the decision for them.

Ahmed, usually so forthcoming, was reticent about his sincere religious beliefs. After drinking arak or clouting a donkey he would reply unflinchingly, in response to our questioning, that in his religion such acts were not allowed. Once he said that, as there were so many commandments, you had to decide which ones you were going to follow. He never laid out a prayer mat, but was perfectly prepared to give a demonstration of the ceremony: his offer was never accepted. There are five times for prayer in the day and all work should cease then. The Arabic words of the prayers used on these occasions are quite meaningless to the bulk of those who recite them; yet they are mumbled determinedly.

'There is no God but Allah' is understood by all. Ahmed said that was enough; perhaps he was right.

Five times a day the people are reminded of their duties from the mosque. There is a singsong call emitted extremely loudly by a man especially selected for the task. This sound was peculiarly melodious and wavered over the village rather charmingly.

One night the calling was seriously disrupted by great shouts and whoops of joy. It all emanated from the bus which was just coming up the road from Kirman. The noisy ones poured out of its door and chief among them was my main lizard catcher, a man with an endearing smile, no job but an ability to catch lizards with a butterfly net. He greeted me vigorously and described breath-lessly the success of the feast, of his very own marriage feast. I asked him where his wife was. This was accepted as a huge joke and its success continued for some ten minutes. It was then repeated by another and was about to have a further run when a man, who had announced that more refreshment was ready, ushered them up the street.

I had to resort to Ahmed and cut him short when he began to laugh at my question, which had already caused far more gaiety than the choicest of remarks deserved. He explained that the marriage feast was an entirely masculine affair, that it took place on any day after the marriage and when money could be found to pay for it, that its date bore no relation to the date of the marriage, to the proven fertility of the wife or to the birth of a child. It was just an occasion of festivity and is called a marriage feast because it is paid for by the bridegroom's father.

Ahmed argued that a marriage should obviously be celebrated, but as the ceremony is such a dull affair it should never be on that day. Certainly the service is simple: they are married by a priest in the house of the bride's father and only a few important relatives attend the marriage, which is always in the evening. There is no feast. Theoretically, this is the first occasion on which the man sees the face of his wife; up till then he has only seen her veiled appearance and the vivid descriptive pictures drawn by her father. It was two years before the lizard catcher decided to celebrate the event.

The lizard man was a pleasant individual who came to visit us every day, just to see if we were all right. Often we went hunting lizards together, while he pushed his bicycle at my side: he never rode it, but it was always there. He would walk along, talking of other things, until a lizard sprinted away; then he dropped the bike, grabbed the butterfly net and yelled at the lizard to stop; with great leaps he pursued it until it became entangled in the net. The conversation was afterwards resumed without comment.

Then there was Esau, the hairy one, with as much brain as a sledge hammer. He never spoke, just grinned and shook hands by enveloping the other person's fist in his own; he had a chest like a gorilla and the most gentle of temperaments. He always came with the Kadkhoda, another regular enquirer after our welfare, who always asked us to teach him 'Good morning' and 'Good evening': after a month the lesson finished, for he had made no progress. Naturally he was knowledgeable about the affairs of his village, but to nothing like the extent he said he was. His chief merit was that he brought Esau along with him.

Among other respected acquaintances was the chief animal hunter of Jupar. This was the description he gave of himself when he first came into the garden to welcome us. The title remained, but after a month he had only brought in one small lizard. Then there was Chauffeur who drove the bus to Kirman, and Sim-bacheh, the wire boy, who supplied us with wire to make the cages. These and many more became well known to us in Jupar. On the bad list was Ma'shallah, the son of the Kadkhoda, who came in undoubtedly just to use our lavatory which was, as we poured one bucket of water down it once a week, without dispute the best in the village.

Occasionally some old women brought us animals. As the fear of being considered a loose woman is so great, the selection which came in openly to see us were those upon whom such an accusation could no longer be thrust with any sincerity. Their skin was cracked into the smallest of fragments, their hair was usually dyed with henna and their voices were harsh: when they talked among themselves they cackled loudly. As it is the man who lives a life that is less restricted, he is likely to be more interesting than the woman whom he subdues and suppresses, whose existence is servile and closeted.

1. *Approaching Damascus (above); 'at last there was only a length of road between us and Kirman'.*

2. *Persian roadmen (below) who 'shovelled what had been flung to the side into the middle again'.*

3. The ruins of an old ice-house (above) in Kirman where winter's snow had formerly been stored to cool summer's drinks.

4. In Bam much time was spent looking at our passports (below).

5. *The more that fuel was uprooted, the sandier grew the plains (right).*

6. *Louis replacing the broken back spring of our Bedford (left).*

7. *Stuck in sand near Kirman (right). The man in the suit is Ahmed.*

8. *We learned about qanats, and boys peered at us down the shorter well-shafts (above).*

9. *Philip Beckett, with the hat (below), had bought our lorry from a large ex-W.D. dump.*

10. *Reinforcing nars (above) were used in those channels that needed such support.*

11. *There was a collapsed part of Gauhariz where the sun shone in to make a warm and pleasant place (below).*

12 to 16. Roof-building with bricks of dried mud. Jupar villagers (left) and (below, clockwise) a shepherd, a potter, a shoe-repairer and the blacksmith.

17 to 21. A settlement at the foot of the Kuh-i-Jupar (right): (below, clockwise) a sower of corn, a spinner, the miller whose daughter's name was Esmat, and a soldier.

22 to 24. *Excursions from Jupar were always rewarding, whether to collect the 'pseudo-porcupine' (above), to search one of the few streams in the hills (below, left), or to be high up (below, right), where 'the breathless silence did not concern the insects'.*

25 to 28. *Some of the Gauhariz channels. A few were neat, as if they had just been made, and some had become ragged, but water flowed through most of them.*

29, 30. A qanat from above resembles bomb-craters or even mole-hills, but it was easy to understand down below why they were often called 'the murderers'. The 12-second exposure has given that lamp an imposing brightness.

31, 32. At the maqsam a qanat's water is most carefully divided according to ownership. A muqanni (left) emerges from a well-shaft, assisted by other muqannis with a windlass.

33, 34. Winnowing (above) in one of the fields beyond the village. Many of the houses within Jupar contained carpet looms (right), the carpet-makers usually being women and children.

35, 36. (Opposite) Philip digging one of his holes at Sagutch, and the mosque at Mahun. Its school-rooms served as the expedition's home for a week.

37. (Left) The tenants of Baharistan.

38. Mirza (right), the former charcoal-merchant who became our cook.

39. (Left) A grandmother, mother and child in Jupar.

40. *(Right) Trees only grew in Jupar because of the Gauhariz qanat.*

41. *(Left) Each village was a muddle of small streets between high mud walls.*

42. *Sagutch was different (right) by following a natural stream from the nearby hills.*

43. On the way home (above), with the lorry emptied of most of its load.

44. The valley of Ab-i-Zezar (below), in the Zagros mountains, where both new species of blind fish were found.

The status of the wives in the house was very lowly. In spite of the many evenings spent with the scholarly Muhammad Reza Saam, no action of his enabled us to distinguish between his wife and the servants. Although Mirza's wife cooked our rice and washed our clothes, she was never seen by any of us. But the wife does wield a certain authority, as was shown by Husain, who possessed two wives. One evening I went with Mirza to visit him. As he had three houses and was in the third, it was quite late when we knocked and he came to the door in his pyjamas. He did not object to the visit and gave me the answers to my questions. His wife then appeared in the background and asked Husain if his guests wanted tea; I hurriedly refused and said that they were probably both getting cold. Husain denied this and Mirza whispered that each wife saw so little of him that they were never cold; it was not worth while thinking up the necessary sentence to spoil this misunderstanding and we gracefully retired. Mirza was much amused by the affair and explained that Husain spent two nights a week with his older wife, only one night with his younger and four nights in the third house by himself; this routine had continued in an unbroken fashion for the fifteen years since its initiation at the second marriage. The boisterous Mirza admitted that, although sex is by instinct pleasurable, dutiful sex must be unbearable.

Ahmed was in a position which none of the villagers could ever attain, for he spoke English: this acquired for him their respect. If they had understood his English the respect would have been less; for Ahmed, determined to be of every assistance, had brought with him a dictionary; this book made things very hard for him. Apart from glaring errors, with which the book was punctuated, most of the 'a's were considered to be indefinite articles. For instance, the Persian for satisfaction had opposite it: a satisf, a ction. Consequently, when one of these deformities was used by Ahmed, we had to ask for other meanings of the same word and piece the whole together. But the respect was there and we did not grudge him that; that is, until the day when he made a greater error of his own. He said a man could find a bear for me; I was delighted, offered a sum and the man was despatched. One day later, Ahmed asked me about bears in England and during the conversation it transpired that boar had been his intended word. Instantly another man was despatched with cancelling instructions. Such an animal would not have been worth sending back to England, and although it would have been good to have had ham every day, the Moslem environment detracted from this idea. However, no boar did arrive; for, as was the custom, only the least boastful produced anything

Nothing was known of what the people thought of us as individuals. Probably our differences from them were so great that our apparent similarity overwhelmed our own peculiarities. I was sometimes called the old man because of a grotesque beard I happened to have at the time. They never mastered any more names than Mr. Louis and Mr. Tony. That there were usually four of us didn't matter to them; the two names sufficed. I think it was right that they looked upon us as a unit, for after all we should have been.

But all of us who lived in the village were similar in our outlook on Kirman. Even when we ourselves had only been in Jupar for four weeks, the distant town was looked upon as if it contained a maze of excitement and gaiety; quite definitely it did not, but the feeling was strong. At Baharistan we had had it for Jupar. The Kirmanis have it for Tehran. The Tehranis cast soulful glances towards America. Everybody in the land envies the dwelling place of another and we became infected with it. Each man thinks his location gives him just reason for grievance and he kicks at the dust with his feet to show the wretchedness of his plight. Any discussion on this topic instantly led to the Oil Company and its affairs, to the wealth of Persia and to her hardship in that she possesses none of it. 'There is gold beneath our feet' is a recent saying of alleged antiquity. Even those crops which were normal give farmers cause to complain, for there had been better crops in the past. They didn't refer to good years, only bad years and ordinary years. With a high infant mortality each Persian should consider himself fortunate that he has become adult; but his life is lived in the atmosphere of ill fortune engendered by himself. As he knows that everyone meets with death, that prospect is viewed less bitterly.

The only funeral I saw was a discouraging occasion; there was no sign of affection by any of those taking part. Either this occurred because they had cared so little for him in his life or because they cared not for him in his death. The body was wrapped in various cloths and carried in a wooden framework by about six men: the lack of formality and the reluctance of those standing in the road to get out of the way made it difficult to see who were the bearers. When the procession passed the mosque, feeble dirges were uttered by this motley crowd and answered with a greater spirit by a priest on its parapet. The wooden frame was placed on the grave after the body had been removed from most of its wrappings and had been laid with its face towards Mecca. The frame was left there for a few days, as otherwise there are only some stones to mark the place; the dry dust of the desert quickly effaces the new appearance of the grave.

This particular individual had been a sixteen year old boy, who had committed suicide on account of the constant persecutions of his elder brother. When this became known the brother was arrested and taken to the Kadkhoda to whom he paid £8. A court in Kirman would decide his fate and the Kadkhoda would try to help him. But long before that happened, his brother's grave would be indistinguishable from all the other piles of stones on that side of Jupar, from those which the children have made and those which were placed to lengthen the memories.

They are sorry for themselves in their life and find little sorrow for those who are dead; there is sufficient unhappiness upon the surface of the land for them to remember the silent ones who are beneath the dust to the east of the village. Such were the affairs of the burials of those who dwelt in that place.

However, we were suddenly to become even more acquainted with its people, for one afternoon the Buz Majjeh escaped. Mirza had been exercising the hedgehogs at the time and did not notice its departure. I returned from the qanats to find the garden full of people aimlessly looking for it; it had been a great favourite with them and they were as distressed as I about its loss. Conflicting opinions ranged as to whether it had taken to the trees, to water or into the ground, and everywhere was searched. People poured over our wall to inspect the fig trees in the next garden, the stream was inspected to its source at the mouth of the qanat, all gardens around were disturbed by the violent onrush of the searchers; our own garden became packed. For the rest of that day the chaos continued and was put to an end with darkness: only then could we relax; for, although a casual inspection of our rooms would have assured even the most diligent that a lizard nearly four feet long was not within, the curiosity of the villagers had at last a chance to be satisfied. Of all the suggestions proffered as to its possible new abode, there was only unanimity in that it might be in one of our rooms. For five days that creature was unseen; then, on the sixth it was found in a hole in a wall and recaptured by Eric and Mirza.

During its absence my unhappiness was partly appeased by a jerboa hunt. As all manner of traps had been unsuccessful, Abdul Saam chartered a few of his servants to dig some out for me. These creatures were about three inches long with large ears, a long tail ending in a tuft, and large hopping back legs. The digging was done with characteristic aplomb; for soon a cloud of dust had arisen and the ground could no longer be seen. Water was suggested, and with similar thoroughness a large barrelful was poured into the hole; this was overmuch for the jerboas and two came prancing out. One was instantly killed by a dog, hitherto unobserved, that happened to be standing by, and the other was caught with great dexterity as it entered another hole. Everybody shook hands and then threw clods of earth at the dog: I thanked them and returned to put the live one in a cage and to skin the dead one. It was not until two days later that Eric inadvertently let the former escape.

After five weeks in Jupar, Philip and I decided to go and stay in Mahun, a larger place and with different types of qanats. Eric wished to stay in Jupar for a further ten days to finish his map; Louis was about to return from Kirman and intended to work awhile in Jupar before going with me to spend some time in Negar. Eric and Philip would then be in the hills, in the Kuh-i-badimu. Those were our plans.

Tentative as they were, they forced me to realise that I had only one more day in Jupar. It had always been my intention to discover if any life entered the qanat where the water seeped in through the sides. As the seepage area was usually fairly lengthy it was obvious that the extreme left hand channel of Gauhari

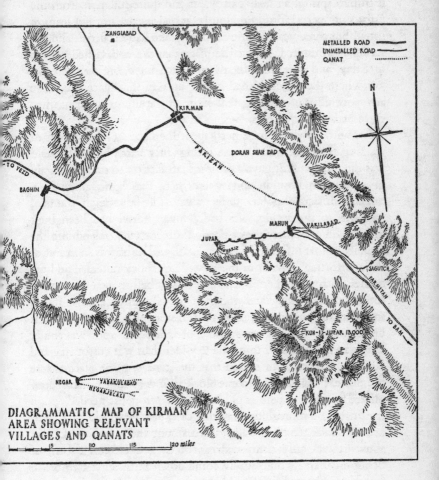

METALLED ROAD
UNMETALLED ROAD
QANAT

ZANGIABAD

KIRMAN

DORAH SHAH DAD

TO YEZD

BAGHIN

MAHUN   VAKILABAD

JUPAR

SAGUTCH

KUH-I-JUPAR 13,000

NEGAR   YAKAKULABAD

DIAGRAMMATIC MAP OF KIRMAN
AREA SHOWING RELEVANT
VILLAGES AND QANATS

5   10   15   20 miles

was the most suitable; for there the bulk of the water surged in as if from a spring, an inrush of water and quite different from the usual slow permeation. Previously, it had been a normal seepage qanat, but three years before an earthquake had occurred, and the spring had resulted. It was the place that we had visited on the first day, and ever since then I had been intending to put a net just where the water gushed in, for only in that place was there any possibility of proving that some of the life in the qanat was there because it had been washed into it.

So, with only the finest net I spent the necessary two hours in walking the three miles to the spring; fifty yards before the end was the final well. It gave a pleasant satisfaction to stand up again in an upright position and where there was light, although it came from a small point 150 feet away. The last stretch, the final 40 yards to the spring, was badly made, for it had been built through an extremely rocky portion: great stones bulged into the channel so that it formed a twisted path and sight was soon lost of the comforting light from the well. The echoes increased and the tunnel became smaller. Then there was a bell shaped space with the channel dividing and going on both sides of a large round stone; it was not possible to sit on this stone, but it could be leant upon and gave a strange measure of relief. The roof was wide; the stone had forced it to be made wider than was customary and safe; the muqannis all agreed that the stone was the place where the channel would first become blocked. A very large sum had been offered to anyone who could remove the stone; it needed rough treatment and some sledge hammer or explosive would have to be used to crack it into movable pieces: but the round wide roof above it was only composed of compressed erosion debris, of firm gravel and would surely come down at the first tremor: in fact there appeared no plausible reason why it had not come down with the earthquake or in the years that had followed. Beyond the stone the channel continued until it ended blankly and emphatically. Although that solid and final wall was known to be just in that place, it had an unexpected quality; it represented a realisation of all the mental pictures which had never been allowed to form themselves, of what a collapse would look like. The way was impassable: the picture had been formed.

I put my net over the stream of water which spurted into the channel. The noise was terrific, with the effervescent echoes of the bubbling water, the little stones being rolled thunderously along by it and one's own breathing magnified out of all proportion. As through a stethoscope the thumping heart could be heard, but against a bewildering background of sound. The force of that surge of water and the underlying pressure which must have evoked its inrush contrasted strongly with the unstrengthened channel and the frailty of those who had made it. I listened to the sounds and thought about the frailty as I watched my net billowing from side to side in the spring.

The net caught only one insect larva, but it only remained there for fifteen minutes; for me that was enough and I went downstream. The 15 minutes had been long ones; for there was nothing to do but look at the net, listen to the water and ponder on the thickness of the walls. The net tugged at the string which held it; the water hurried away downstream. It was just a quarter of an hour before I was filled with a similar eagerness to leave the spot. Only near the exit of Gauhariz, where the water flowed more easily and without any noise, did I too lose my eagerness and forget the dominating urgency. So, as solace, I stopped to look for animals beneath the stones in the stream, made attempts to catch the bats which hung from the roof with a 1lb. jam jar and thought up a story about an opium ring whose activity and extinction occurred within a qanat system.

Then, once more I followed the mud downstream and reached my shoes and my shirt. This point of exit was not the final opening, but was in a collapsed well about a hundred yards from it; it was easy to walk down to the water through a small tunnel by the side of this well and it saved me going through the first hundred yards: therefore I used it, for time was saved and a less conspicuous place was formed for the discarded shirt and shoes. But it was a place of religious association and existed directly under a small building which marked the spot where a descendant of Mohammed had been killed. Often people prayed on the spot above and occasionally came below to bless the water; the short cut to the qanat stream had been made for this purpose. This I did not know, until one day I floundered round the final corner to observe a prostrate woman with many candles before her. Naturally I stopped; but as she made no move, I silently collected my clothes from her side and left by the other exit. Thus, on all future occasions, in order to try and respect their customs, I blew my lamp out before reaching the final part and silently waded to it: unfortunately this practice once gave four soldiers, who had gone there to evade the heat of the midday sun, a severe surprise when a silent figure suddenly loomed up out of the darkness. The mad woman of Jupar was once in this place and let out a fearful yell the moment she saw me; she screeched her words and flapped around for all the time I took to arrange my bottles and the rucksack; luckily no person was near to hear this sacrificial incantation. However, on the last day no one was there and I was glad to sit awhile and watch the slow peaceful stream of water which floated past the light. Its tempestuousness had been left three miles up the channel: now it was only the Gauhariz qanat, the qanat of the flowing jewels.

Shortly before Philip, Ahmed and I left Jupar, a knotted handkerchief was handed to me; as it might have contained anything from scorpions to butterflies, I opened it cautiously but without feeling the shape of the creature within. Suddenly, out popped a small squirrel-like dormouse, somewhat the size of the jerboa; it bit me on the finger and then ran up my neck to jump into the branches of one of the slender trees which grew in the garden. At all times when anything was happening there were a good many people in the garden and some of these began to climb the trees. I too climbed up and the dormouse went higher and higher; various other trees leant about under unaccustomed burdens and the number of directing orders which issued up from below was prodigious. As it remained at the tips of the branches, everybody shook their trees until the poor creature was forced lower down. Then a peasant, with that same lack of tenderness that he and his kind meted out to all animals, grabbed it, but in doing so pulled off its tail. As with some lizards, this is an adaptation to assist escape; but we all slithered down our trees and poured invective on the man. I had not done this before in Jupar and felt ashamed when I became cooler and had retired into the room to kill the animal with chloroform. The invective was not looked upon harshly outside; some had been delighted with my brutal control of the Persian language, which had so forcibly been exhibited; everybody thought that the man had been careless and, with this universal condemnation, he did not have occasion to point out that it was he, after all, who had caught it.

CHAPTER VIII

Mahun

THIS small crowd saw us off and we drove out of the village. It was only twenty miles to Mahun, but the road was not good; about halfway we rested and looked back at Jupar. The small blue mosque stood out from the brownness of the houses which it dominated: it was not very old and the blue tiles were not valuable, but in its setting it was as it should have been. 150 years before, a rich man named Mohammed had been called for by his overlords in Isfahan. This troubled him and he made a vow with his God that if they did not punish him then he would build a mosque in the village of his birth: it is not recounted whether he deserved to be punished; only that he received no punishment and the mosque was built. He had tiled it with dark and light blue tiles; these were not expensive, but reputedly all that he could afford. Mosques are covered so that the reflection of the glory of Allah shall be as bright as it can be made: consequently, one finds that in Kermanshah there is a covering of beaten down petrol tins. Like the tubicolous worms which make their dwellings out of the material on which they chance to live, the Persians have used that which was at hand. These four-gallon tins in which petrol is delivered to the inland and southern regions of Persia are multifarious in the uses to which they are put; they are beaten into trays, into watering cans, into drain pipes, shop counters, and window sills and soldered into any shape that is desired: they are to the Persians what telegraph wires are to the migrating swallows, they appear as a necessary part of their livelihood. Being the prime source of metal in that region they are much sought after, but nowhere are they elevated to such a position as on the mosque at Kermanshah.

The mosque at Mahun was a larger building with several

cupolas, but only one was tiled and in an entrancing light mottled blue. Certain pilgrimages are regularly made to Mahun and, as a lot of land has been left to assist in its upkeep, there was considerable wealth associated with it. Two pairs of minarets flanked the main part of the mosque; they had been built at different times and were slightly different in style and height: both were extremely slender. As with Jupar, the mosque at Mahun transformed what would otherwise have been a collection of brown walls and houses into an organised and beautiful whole.

We drove on again and arrived in the town. The school teacher, Mahdevi, had previously offered to look after our needs there. He was a charming man and spoke excellent English, for he had been educated at the English school in Kirman; this school had been closed by the Reza Shah before the war, but Mahdevi never ceased recounting its virtues. As it was then August and the Mahun school was on holiday, he offered the school rooms as a place for us to live in. They were in a building just next to the mosque and had a garden that must surely have been the most resplendent in the town. It was very large, with long borders of flowers flanking the many pools and streams. The garden gate was at the end of a broad path and about 75 yards from our room. All visitors knocked loudly on the gate and, on receiving the welcoming shout, entered, closed it, and then had to walk the long distance to the schoolroom before they were greeted by us. The portentousness of this ceremony was most imposing and raised our undignified appearances to a different status.

If ever we felt that the collecting of insects and the skinning of animals were a little distasteful, in such a place we could lift our eyes and the vision of the British Museum of Natural History would fade rapidly from our minds. Instead of that tower was a dome, instead of those buttresses were minarets and instead of the gawking masses were the prostrate forms of the true believers; all of this was seen, not in a puddle in Cromwell Road but in a pleasant pond bordered by petunias. Mahdevi had previously made the bold statement that he would arrange for us the best place in Mahun: he had done so, but then Mahdevi was unique among Persians.

Unfortunately Mahun was a town and Jupar had been only a village. Therefore there were considerably more civil servants living in it; many more people whom the Governor General could instruct to help us: they had all been instructed and descended upon us on the first morning. They were most polite to us and we tried to show gratefulness. The Bakhshdar came, well dressed, dark in his complexion and smooth in his manners. The Kadkhoda too; stout, with a fleshy face and a manner of closing his eyes and lowering his head every time a remark was made that might conceivably have contained a compliment for him; his hands he clasped tightly together. The Finance man, small, without a tie, but with a pleasing smile; he nodded while his superiors talked. The Inspector of Education had few powers, but announced himself altruistically. Landlords appeared, quite unmistakably landlords the full 75 yards away—so different from Jupar; and all the time Mahdevi was there and worried that for two of our days in Mahun he would have to be away in Kirman. This civil procession appeared every morning at breakfast-time, until we learnt to have our food a little earlier, but by that time they had done their duty; for they had made themselves acquainted with us, as were the instructions, and we knew where to find them should we need more help. Their duty, however, had been more than fulfilled the moment they produced Azraq to be our servant: he was an excellent man.

On the first day I took Azraq in the truck to show me the qanat system of Mahun. The water came either from little qanats near the town or in two streams which flowed next to each other from a point fifteen miles east of the town, along the road to Bam and to India. At this point one of the streams, still separate from the other, came out of a qanat six miles long. The second one came from the mountains as a normal stream, but was said to originate from a spring, about two days' walk away. No village had been built where the qanat came onto the surface and the stream flowed down from the mountains; for it was an area that became regularly flooded in the spring; the water surged through the valley, down to the plain of Kirman and successfully prevented the construction of any buildings or the accumulation of sufficient soil. Mahun, which is just at the edge of the plain and at the end of the pass, is on slightly higher ground and the waters of springtime rush by to the north of it.

The qanat had been named Farmitan, 'strong in body', and was five miles long. Azraq said it was very old and in bad repair; moreover, he doubted if we could reach the end, as the many collapses had deformed the regularity of the channel. With Azraq leading and me holding the lamp, the two of us sauntered into the entrance; gaily we wandered along, bent in the customary qanat posture, and gaily we crawled along on our hands and knees. Then the tunnel decreased in size and it became necessary to propel ourselves along by our elbows until suddenly, round a corner, the water level reached up to the roof and we could go no further. Azraq held his breath and crawled away in the water to try and reach some air; he went up backwards so that all haste could be made on the return journey should air not be found. I thought that he had succeeded, as it was quite a time before his walrus-like face surfaced again in front of me: he had found none. I made a similar abortive attempt by trying to float up on my back. I thought then that any space of air could be detected and utilized by my nose: as it was necessary to go up head first, I spent rather longer than intended on the return journey and frantically paddled faster to acquire more speed; this timorous procedure resulted in my kicking Azraq in the face and knocking out the lamp.

We climbed down the wells higher up and tried again to pass along the channel, but the result was always the same; no room, no air and a doused lamp. So we left Farmitan in order to investigate the shorter ones, about one mile long, which approached the town from the north-east. We went down the one called Vakilabad and shuffled along it. This particular qanat was directly in the path of the flood water and any life in it could easily have come from the torrents of the previous year. The material through which it was dug was loosely packed and any contact with the sides and roofs brought down a shower of pebbles: it was not at all dangerous, but the whole place seemed far too fragile, for the flood water had made it so. Seventy years ago it had been built by Vakil, an official of Kirman, but it would not last for another seventy; such qanats are made only for relatively short returns; they cost little as they are short, serve their purpose for a hundred years and then are made again. Vakilabad, although decaying badly after so short a time, had not been a fruitless enterprise.

The third type of qanat in that district existed on the edge of the plain: each one was long and deep and supplied Kirman with water. They had their beginnings, their mother wells, on the outskirts of Mahun, while their exits were on the borders of Kirman, 25 miles away. Their wells were all covered over and this practice was very necessary, by reason of the dust storms of the plain and the shifting of the sands. Azraq uncovered the one called Farizan after the name of the area which it irrigated. Much sand showered into it, when the covering bricks were taken away, and fell down into the darkness; no answering splash could be heard. The well was round and straight and 300 feet below the top was the water. I threw a brick down, but again there was no splash; for, unlike a normal and solitary well, much of the sound in the well of a qanat was dissipated along the channel.

Farmitan, Vakilabad and Farizan were all different from Gauhariz and far less amenable to investigation: I drove back with Azraq to ponder over them. Philip had spent the day seeing what was growing and trying to find the reason why; as every evening found us as guests of some influential person of the town, this question of his was continually pressed forward: what were the factors deciding the planting of a particular crop?

There was little agreement among those landlords and there was always apparent irrationality in their method. For instance, in the past thirteen years one field had had seven years fallow, one year of wheat, two more fallow and then three of wheat. It was not believed that land left fallow was ever improved by this treatment and only one landlord in the whole of Jupar had ever ploughed his fallow fields; others had been ploughed, but by accident. Instead, the policy was that a field was left dry (or fallow) if it could not be made moist (or productive); thus fallow did not hold quite the same meaning, for water was a factor so overbearing as to render the increase in fertility relatively negligible. The second factor concerned the labour that would be involved in cultivating the field and guarding it from birds and thieves: where much labour would be required the fields near the village were selected. When the possibility of water and the degree of accessibility had been considered, only then would the fertility be taken into account. In fields where water was always sufficient they would never be left fallow; even if the water level dropped, the smaller demands of an opium crop would enable it to be grown: at Karan Sara Sang in 1950, a dry year, nothing else was grown but opium.

They did agree that certain crops improved the soil; peas and beans were acknowledged by all to do this. But not lucerne, or only incidentally; for it is always manured beforehand, although no more improvement is said to result than after opium, or potatoes, or melons which have been given the same manuring treatment. There was discrepancy over lucerne. Sajat Pur said, for instance, that five or six years of the crop much improved a field. Another called Esau, the barrel-chested man at Japur, said that if lucerne was grown continuously on one spot then that land deteriorated considerably and more so if much water was used upon it; he grew melons to restore the fertility.

In short, they are all apathetic to the fertility question and Philip collected his soil samples to see if they had any right to be so. Their point of view was not culpable in that without water the arid fields and the sandy desert looked just the same, except that the fields usually had fewer stones and the deserts had more camel thorn. The difference between such a dry field and one which has been irrigated is so large that it is only too easy to pour scorn on the head of anyone who asks whether this dry field, which grew wheat, is any different from that dry field, which drew millet. Water was their major problem and they considered that sufficient.

At one of these suppers the landlord formed an interlude by introducing us to his brother, a retired General. This man had only recently left the Army, had seen service fighting bandits of many types and, although not the red-faced, explosive type of General, he was definitely from the Army. He never looked sure that we were not pulling his leg; which made Philip and me even less sure of whether we were in fact doing so. He would laugh at some harmless joke of ours and then stop, quite suddenly, to give us both a most terrifying stare: our remarks to him got more and more harmless and correspondingly useless. He even noticed their pointlessness and stared more fiercely. This made Philip extremely jocular and he arranged a whole lot of fruit in strategic and cryptic positions and said: 'Let's pretend these are bandits'. The General relaxed immediately, became himself again and played excitedly.

On the second day we announced to our breakfast guests that we intended to go up the valley of Sagutch, the valley down which came the stream. The Kadkhoda was insistent that he should guide us to the village of Sagutch, which was situated at the entrance to the valley. We needed no guide; for the village was only fifteen miles away and quite visible from Mahun, but he was adamant: he only admitted that it was his home after he had loaded much fruit and two friends onto the truck. He was glad of this simple carriage of the fruit and we were appeased by his offer of food when we reached his house and of lunch when we returned from the valley.

The valley proved to be one of the most charming that I have ever seen. Perpetual cascades of water over giant boulders is how the valley of a stream should be; but add that to the shapes of gaunt mountains high above, which taper down steeply to the stream in powerful angular designs, and you have the valley of Sagutch. The detail of the rock and its harsh nature were noticeable because there was no vegetation: only by the stream did green things grow. The rest was just rock, hard and beautiful.

We showered curses upon ourselves for having arranged the lunch, as we were only such a little way up the valley when it became time to return. No one was hungry, but the invitation had been given and some lunch would certainly be cooked for us. Philip's respect for the invitation and Ahmed's for his stomach influenced the voting. We returned down the stream.

A big discussion on sincerity started on the way back. It was a good argument, enlivened by our general discontent and by the sun which was then at its height. I thought over all the occasions when we had met with complete falsehoods coupled with an equally complete brazenness in the telling of them. Why should the Kadkhoda have pretended that he wanted to guide us to the valley when he really wanted to have a day at his home? There was no question of a need for a guide; all we had to do was to drive out of Mahun and then leave the road when we were opposite the village: on that side of the road there was no village, save for Sagutch, for at least twenty miles. Why should the finance man assert that we had given him the happiest evening of his life? He did not say it jokingly, but it was one of a string of complimentary phrases; what was the use of a compliment if it was so obviously out of reach? Anyone will grab at one if it is reasonable, but this one was so hopelessly untrue. The custom of great hospitality is most widespread, but it vitiates its good intentions if any deceitfulness is suspected by the guest: once he realises that his host is producing pleasant phrases according not to feeling but to custom, then that guest no longer appreciates the hospitality. 'Befarmaid,' said Hassan, 'I will be unhappy if you don't come to have some tea in my house'; but only two minutes before he had expressed his intention of going straight to bed when we reached it. Abdul Samdi once told me that he was going to set his trap for the jerboas that night. The next day he said he had forgotten. This went on for seven days and on the seventh I discovered that he had no trap. There was no crestfallen appearance on his part when he finally admitted this fact. Naturally the catching of a jerboa is not of great importance but I could not understand why false promises should be carried into the realms of deceitfulness.

I hurled these accusations around me and Ahmed defended them: he proclaimed that we should not be so sensitive whether a statement was true or false; the important thing was whether kindness was intended and if this is always to be the case then false answers will sometimes have to be given. I agreed that for seven days I had been joyful at the prospect of receiving a jerboa and admitted that my irritation of discovering that he was trapless did not last so long. Ahmed considered he had gained the point and became silent.

In England we had been told never to ask the way in Persia; for the answer would be 'straight on', irrespective of where the place happened to be. The first time it occurred, near Kirman, we laughed at it, and when we repassed the man a good while later, on our way back and to our destination, he waved airily at us. We didn't stop; for he would have won by giving us quite contrary instructions with a similarly disarming smile. Such incidents happened increasingly as our knowledge of the language and our ability to ask questions grew: we waved less and less airily at our misinformer, but still there was nothing which could be said to him. Even on foot, when we repassed him more slowly, and some remark was necessary, there was a tendency only to tell him where our destination was really situated; but then he was told in a politely informative manner, as if he had never known. He accepted the news kindly and probably felt happier that now you were not only going to the place, but going in the right direction. Ahmed was quite correct; the desire to please was uppermost, the future did not concern him and was far too long a prospect. A short-sighted man reacts only according to what he can observe; he picks out a smooth path for himself and sees only for the present: in neither him nor the man who misdirects you does the vision extend very far.

We could not accept this: it irritated us more than it ought to have done and we knew it, but some sort of complacent acceptance did not arise within us, at least, never in the day when the sun was shining. Sometimes in the evening as you lay on your back, having just eaten much too much; when the stars were really bright and the air was nicely warm; when the snakes had ceased to hiss and the buz majjeh had shut his eyes; when the moon had paused awhile and the earth had ceased to move, then it came. It came suddenly and filled you with sorrow and remorse; sorrow that the flurry of earthly things should ever seem important and remorse that you had taken part in them. It came with elation that there was yet life to live and excitement that the new life should be fuller and more aware of itself. How right they were to say what they pleased.

Like the soil which had been watered at night it cracked again in the daytime. I was reminded again of the Kadkhoda at Jupar who had boldly announced one day that he had a map of the Gauhariz qanat system; no question of mine had brought forth this remark. I was taken in and asked to see it. When the map had been reported lost he drew another for me, quite wrong and quite useless; when I began correcting it for him he exclaimed joyfully how glad he was to discover that I did not need the map, for I knew it all: but this was in the daytime. So was it when we arrived at Mahun. Sultan Ahmed built it, my ancestor Izzatullah Khan built the mosque, the landlord of Mahun built it, an ancestor of Shah Abbas's built it; and all these answers were wrong. Nevertheless, I think we improved in time; we were all most effusive in our greetings to the Kadkhoda. 'How pleasant it is to return, hungry and tired, to a house where food, such excellent food, has been prepared, and is at once set down before you'.

That afternoon Philip dug holes for soil and I caught insects. He attracted a bigger crowd than I, as he was less mobile and the interest was more continuous. Those gaping crowds were composed of those members of the village who were not working and had nothing else to do other than watch what other people did; Ahmed called them the stupidest fellows of them all: even when he repeated this denunciation in Persian, no more light shone in their eyes. Philip dug holes wide and deep, made a cloud of dust and wrote lengthy notes in his book. I wandered for miles over the desert, singing Negro spirituals into the air. I suppose that the gawking tendency of the villagers was justifiable, for extremely few foreigners must ever frequent that place: then, when two of them do come, one digs pits in the ground and fills them in again, while the other sings loud and sorrowful dirges interspersed only by large entomological leaps.

The abbreviated visit had been unsatisfying; so, on our fourth day in Mahun, Philip and I returned to the valley of Sagutch. Refusing all tea invitations in the village, reluctantly from a nice one-legged teacher called Ahmad and emphatically from a hairy, English-speaking youth who called us Americans, we walked quickly away to the valley. It was to be a day solely of recreation and there was no desire to waste any of it. By ten we had reached the stream, by twelve we were quite a way up and eating the grapes, by one we were bathing in a fine pool bounded by many smooth rocks. We flippered our way about and flapped to and fro. The mermaid at Copenhagen has similar round smooth rocks, but there the similarity ends and abruptly, except that she is content. We looked at our bodies, a thing rarely done in this well-clad world; the bright light made them all too conspicuous. There was the naked white flesh that never saw the sun, there were the deep brown chunks that saw it all too often, there were the scabs and clots of blood that are present at all times on a body which leads a physical existence, there were my feet with hardened soles and the little craters where shoe nails had penetrated the outer crust but had not yet reached any part more sensitive: this was myself, this was all there was to me. I had always believed there was more somewhere: there was not. I put on my clothes quickly.

Later on came a large insurmountable waterfall, and Philip and I took independent paths to overcome it. I found myself going up a steep bit of mountain and half willing to turn back, but although unwilling, more willing to go on. For half an hour or so I scrambled up; each time I tried to advance further along the valley a precipice, the extension of the waterfall rock, was in the way. I was tempted further up to try and get over on the other side. A little squirrel hopped into a crevice. I cut my knee on a rock. I tore the butterfly net on a crag. I scrambled on. At the top of this mountain it was obvious that I was wrong, so I sat and contemplated. Far below Philip was there, far below was the stream and the path leading away from that place; but just where I was there was no path and there seemed no way: it was a spot for contemplation and all the peaks around, for no land was visible, were stolid in their approval of that place. It was a setting that I know I shall never return to in my life; I knew that then and thought about it: already, although I still believed myself very young indeed, there was no time left to return to pleasant places; already little time remained; already a third of the sands had run away.

I hurried away down another route full of scree; much thought should not be in the mountains, but only in those places where the view is restricted and the heavens are smaller. I went to join the path along which Philip was then returning. We talked a little on the way back, but not much: there was not much to say.

Back at Mahun a genial gentleman named Nahidi introduced himself. He was plump, kindly and dignified. Previously he had been named the 'Lord of Jupar' but he was nothing of the sort, only the carpet representative in that district. Recently he had been moved to Mahun to look after the industry's affairs there.

He reiterated all that we had heard about the poor state of the trade. When the English firm, the Oriental Carpet Manufacturers, left Persia, the only remaining firm was Persian and called the Iran Carpet Company. Without this company the carpet weavers would be in a greater plight today; for, as at all times when they cannot sell them otherwise, they are selling their carpets to the

Company. Now Kirman is only one of many carpet-making centres and it is reputed to have a stock of carpets worth £200,000. This was not a stock which might be likened to that occurring in any business's centre of distribution; it was a stock of carpets which had not been sold. The number which come in are in excess of the buyer's needs. Thus the Company is acquiring a debt on behalf of the weavers which is naturally backed by the Bank and presumably by the Government. The apparent altruism of the Banks can be questioned. Those carpets will not decrease greatly in value; they represent something more tangible than paper money and are being produced at an extremely small cost. The weaver cannot sell his carpet to the bazaar and has to accept the wage the Company offers him. Whether the altruism is genuine or not the weavers take advantage of it, and rarely in a scrupulous manner. In the weaver registration book at Mahun one page was devoted to the history of each man: at the top was a photograph of him, then a list of his particulars, and, all too often, at the bottom of the page was written: 'Left with bad debt of so many rials. Transferred to bad debt account, Tehran'. The man had succeeded in benefiting from the Company with only the loss of his reputation as a weaver. Never again will he be employed by the Company but, with the carpet industry in its present state, that is not considered by him as a loss. His debt may be big or small; in either case the Company cannot extract the money from him and the debt is pushed off onto Tehran. The size of his debt only shows the extent to which he was able to defraud the Company.

This is done in various ways. A weaver who has no capital, and this covers most of them, hires what he needs to make a carpet from the company. He hires the wood for the loom and the tools which he requires. The thread and the wool are carefully weighed and then given to him. He is lent a pattern and is expected to sell his carpet to the company. When the carpet is handed in and the weight of wool is found correct, then he receives his money; this wage is low and, as the only punishment for any duplicity is expulsion, he sets about expelling himself in the most profitable manner. Nothing can be done with the looms or the tools, for they can be traced: it is the wool which enables him to make his debt and he achieves his aim by making the double knot; such a knot is made by twisting the wool round four strands instead of two before cutting it: naturally it is impossible to make a knot without employing a certain length of wool, usually about two inches, but the double knot uses very little more and the carpet is made twice as quickly; also very nearly half the wool is left over. A carpet made with this knot feels thin, lasts for less than half the time and from the back each pair of knots appears much too evenly tied; instead of a row of knots slightly unevenly hammered down there is a regularity which is abnormal. With the carpet finished in half the number of days, he has time to make another carpet with the surplus wool before the company inspector wonders if that particular weaver has finished.

This second carpet is sold to the bazaar; the first is taken to be weighed: so it is that the company, which has been presented with a carpet under the agreement, finds it cannot retrieve the money, calculates the debt and possesses another carpet which it will be hard to sell. No regular carpet buyer would be deceived by the knotting and if sold it will be at a lower price, for the large buyers know the knot when they see it and know that it may pass unnoticed by those to whom they sell. The price will then have reverted to the normal. The weaver returns his loom and tools to the company and then wonders about another job. He is quite happy for, apart from the money he got from the bazaar, he made certain the money for the other carpet was paid to him in instalments. The company knows that the contract has been fulfilled, for they have received a carpet of the right size and pattern; therefore no action can be brought against the man.

Nahidi, of course, hated this practice and found that he could do little to stop it. He took Philip and me round to some carpet houses and the very first one we went into was guilty. Nahidi leapt round the other side of the vertical threads, grabbed the knife from the man and cut at the carpet with vertical strokes which severed the weft and the work the man had done. He cut it right down to the place where the double knotting had begun. The weaver whimpered quietly to himself at seeing this destruction of days of work, but Nahidi was distraught. He shouted at the man and began picking at all the knots he could see which were paired. The weaver protested, but only feebly: partly because he was crying and partly because he knew he was in the wrong. Further along a small boy of seven was working; when Nahidi saw that his work too was just as bad, he rushed out of the room. The little boy parted the threads with his fingers and his wide eyes looked out at us; they were not sorrowful or insensitive, they were just bewildered. His father was still whimpering when we too walked out of the room. Our host was almost in tears himself and poured out his plight. 'What am I to do to stop them ruining their own work and spoiling their own chances? I do not wish to hurt them, for I am a religious man. Yet what am I to do?'

There is very little he might do. He could not inspect every carpet every day; he could only hope for times when weavers should wish to remain with the company; until then, the chances of earning the same amount of money in half the time would be far too tempting for most to resist. However, we all felt better after he had taken us to some other houses which he knew could always be relied upon to make good carpets.

I spoke later to two muqannis on this subject, for I discovered they had been carpet weavers. 'Oh yes', they said, 'we always used the double knot as much as possible and we found it was well worth it. Sometimes the inspectors would come and cut at our carpets with knives so that work would have to be done again; but they did not inspect every day and often the bad part would form part of the roll at the bottom before the inspection. Anyway they could never notice it as much as we did it.' They were impenitent and cared not for the wailing of Nahidi. I remembered a story told to me long before which said that all Moslem carpets must have at least one flaw in them, for only Allah was perfect. Later on I learnt that the story was false, but only at Mahun did I begin to realise the extent of its fallaciousness.

In Jupar Nahidi had been happier. Fewer openings were possible for the villagers and they were thankful to have a job. Mahun was very definitely a town; it was large and did not have such a convivial atmosphere. The arrogance of our high garden wall and the necessity of going everywhere by truck prevented the people from acquainting themselves with us, as had apparently been the sole occupation and interest of some at Jupar. Some animals were brought in to us after Ahmed had laughingly announced the financial benefits to be received when he was in the main street one day; a few house mice and a few lizards, but very few. Once the Bakhshdar gave me a scorpion, but unfortunately his satellites, who followed him in every other way, made an exception for scorpions. The real trouble was that we were away for most of the day; Philip in the fields and I at the qanats.

Farmitan was the qanat in which Azraq and I had made so little progress; the wells were all old and wide and, without another man holding on to a thick rope, it was impossible to climb down them. Instead I tied a piece of wood on to the bottom of each net and then lowered them down the well; the wood was supposed to ensure that the net faced the stream correctly. Nevertheless it was unsatisfactory; for the nets scooped in gravel from the sides as I pulled them up and then some of them became stuck.

Vakilabad was the new qanat near the town along which we had been able to go. I thought it would be interesting to find out if the animals living in it were any different from those living in the old qanats, but did not expect to find very much; for the medical men of Mahun recommended it as being the purest water in the district and totally devoid of worms: all Mahun drew their drinking water from it. Luckily its bottom surface was stony and I did not cause quantities of mud to flow down, as had always been the case at Gauhariz; for water thick with mud had poured out whenever I had been in it, but never once did anybody complain at this disturbance: I don't know how I could have made less mud, but I had been touched by their reluctance to interrupt me, however worthless my affairs must have appeared to all of them.

Vakilabad was very slow flowing and, in order to collect a reasonable quantity of life, I left the nets there on the first occasion for twenty-four hours. When I returned, the little jar and part of the net were full of reptile droppings and I began to doubt the purity so loudly proclaimed by the doctors. On the second occasion I left it there for only six hours, hoping to have a quarter the droppings and four times the visibility, but when I put my hand into the net to swish all that it had collected down into the bottle, I felt a large amount of vegetation. I pulled it out and, with the lamp, had a closer look at what it was. I found myself clutching a long snake and a fat lizard. My reactionary jerk brought down a tremendous shower of gravel and caused my feet to be caught up in the net. As the speed of flight backwards could never have been swift, as my feet were held by the net and as I had a considerable burden of gravel upon my back, I had not gone far before I realised, firstly, that I was still holding the snake and, secondly, that the snake was dead.

For however short a time I left the net, the droppings collected made any life invisible. I speculated on the number of reptiles, presumably all swept in during the floods, that must be living in Vakilabad and wondered how the muqannis fared when they worked in it. It was strange, though, that there were no worms; for they should have thrived in that decaying atmosphere of reptilian manure. We continued to have our water collected from there; for Azraq insisted that, as it was the newest qanat, it was the cleanest. Mirza had held the same belief about a small fast qanat in Jupar; the water had been so pure and clean that it was only too easy to see the water spiders swimming about in it. As the qanat water was probably the last place from which we would catch diseases, we did not worry unduly and gulped deeply when the spider happened to be swimming the other way.

Farizan was the big one which went for 25 miles under the central plain. As all the wells were covered, no light and no vegetation entered the qanat; and I wanted to know if anything lived at the top, 25 miles away from more normal conditions. With a well 300 feet deep it is not possible to climb down by placing your feet against one side and your back against the other: apart from the exhaustion which would result, such a length of well is likely to have slightly wider portions which cannot be overcome. The muqanni climbs down a well by turning his toes outwards and sticking them into the niches in the sides, but even he does not climb down a deep well and would be equally thwarted by the wide parts. As the question of walking up from the bottom end did not arise, it was obviously necessary to hire labour so that someone could be pulled up and down the well.

Together with Ahmed and Azraq, who knew all the muqannis, I went to meet the foreman. He was emphatic, and politely I was told that I would have to hire four men for a whole day: this was too expensive, considering that I only wanted to put the nets down one day and pull them up the next. I asked for two men, who would be paid and required for only half a day. Less politely I was told that the English customs about hiring muqannis could not be used in Persia. Before I had time to correct him, he had stated an outlandish sum for the hire of rope, reminded me that I would have to use our truck for the transport of everything and pointed out that, as the next day was Friday, the day of rest, and Saturday and Sunday were always busy for a muqanni, it would be four days before I could hire the men. Ahmed translated, Azraq walked away a little and I sat down weakly on the ground. In response to Ahmed's request I told him to thank the man and say that he was one of the most helpful people that I had met in Persia. Then I lay flat on my back, only to sit up again almost instantly on realising that this sarcasm had been ineffective; for a broad smile was there and increasing the wrinkles on his face.

Azraq then took us to Hassan Muqanni, a 'skilful man ready to earn money', but who happened at that time to be helping to build a new hospital. Again there was the discussion of half a day's wage for half a day's work. This time it took much longer; for the crackling of wood under the brick kiln made hearing difficult. Certainly an hour passed before Hassan let it out that his contract with the hospital did not allow him to leave his work.

The third man we visited was reputed to be overseer of all the muqannis in Mahun. From the beginning he did not look promising. We had found him on the Kirman road just past the hitch-hiker. This last was a man who got up from the side of the road and thumbed us whenever we went past; but as we were never going to Kirman we never picked him up. He was there for six days before someone took him away. He had sat down again and gone to sleep long before we had finished our third conversation. As it was a drawn-out repetition of the first, I too sat down, gazed at the hitch-hiker and listened sleepily to Ahmed arguing with the man: poor Ahmed, I sympathised with him; for the overseer was being difficult. Half to myself I said: 'For a qanat expert you have changed your mind too frequently this evening. As an expert I consider you valueless; as for being helpful, I do not consider you at all.' It was only when Azraq sniggered that I realised that it had been interpreted; one minute later we were all on our feet; for he was promising two men for half a day to be paid for half a day.

This had taken five hours and I drove the truck cruelly back to Mahun, nearly running over a leg which belonged to the sleeping hitch-hiker. These three men had proved to me that I was no longer such a patient being; both this realisation and their method of enlightenment caused me to refuse food and go straight to bed. The deep rumblings of my stomach sounded rather pleasant and I went to sleep thinking less harshly of the three; after all they had only taken a very long time and they had used their own just as much as mine.

We were to meet the muqannis one hour after sunrise, but unfortunately we started late. As a cat had eaten the stuffed dormouse, a method had to be found of shutting the door. Some things of little value had been stolen from the truck and, as it was placed just by the door of the Gendarmerie, an act recommended by the Gendarme Officer himself, for there was an all night guard, the Gendarmes had to be informed. Also, time was spent looking for a net which had been left in a qanat and subsequently stolen. They were all small affairs but made us late.

On the way Ahmed reprimanded me for inflicting my customs of honesty onto Persia, whose custom was dishonesty. He told a story of a Swiss who had left his suitcase outside the bazaar, as was the custom on entering the Bon Marché of his own town; of course it disappeared. The police had reprimanded him for encouraging the criminals of Persia. Ahmed said it was equally wrong of me to leave the nets in the qanats and the empty petrol cans with the truck. Then he tried to smooth everything over by saying how nice it was to see the coolheadedness of the English; for if he had spent six hours stuffing an animal and then found it had been eaten, he would have been mad, as mad as a lion. The picture he drew of his own anger was, I considered, full recompense for the loss of the dormouse.

The muqannis were not there. For three hours we looked for them by driving over the land to any house or tree which we believed might possibly be sheltering them. Then, by the side of a wall near the town they were found; both of them admitted that they thought the grey truck had belonged to the Englishmen for whom they were to work but, as they were not sure, they stayed beside the wall. They climbed into the back of the truck and were driven rapidly to the qanat well which I had selected, namely, the fourth from the Madar chah (the mother well); for the top two wells are liable to have little water beneath them. As I had tripped over certain laws referring to the lowering of persons other than muqannis into the wells, the descent had to be made by one of the two.

Down he went with my net and my instructions; down he went uttering fierce prayers to all the prophets to protect him from suffocation and death; up came these prayers while the rope slithered round the stick placed over the hole. The rope cut into that stick, making the air feel hotter with the smell of burnt wood: only when the cut became deep was the rope jerked along to a thicker and stronger portion. We at the top slowly lowered the rope down the well and the cries from the man grew fainter; then suddenly, when he was only 200 feet down, the length of rope finished: these men had brought 200 feet of it for a 300 foot well. Both expressed curiosity that this should have happened and the bottom man was the more curious of the two. I lent them my thin Nylon rope, reputedly strong, and tried not to think of the consequences should it break.

He continued downwards again, but the prayers gave way to enquiries about the rope; a much thinner groove was burnt in the stick, and the enquiries grew less and less clear: the rope slackened in our hands when the man reached the bottom. We then began to talk to him. As 300 feet of well shaft distorts the normal shouts of a man into a homogeneous rumble, a special language of abbreviations is used. Thus the sounds which floated up conveyed nothing even if understood, except to one who knew the code. 'How deep are you?' was just 'approximately'; in Persian it was 'Nigar kun', a union of vowel sounds and recognizable because of them. No prayers other than the single name Ali were shouted by the top man for the succour of the man below: confusion must not be caused at any price. With these single word sentences we were informed that there was a lot of mud, sufficient water and that the net had been affixed above the mud level.

Then he came up. He climbed up for a lot of the way, with us pulling in the slack; until a jerk came which meant that he had fallen off. Then the weight decreased and he climbed once more. There was no occasion for praying save a short one by me when all the nylon rope had appeared. When he reached the top, his clothes were wet with sweat; nothing was said and he rushed for his coat; more, I felt, with an inexpressible relief at having come out of the well than with any desire for warmth. The sun dried his clothes and he became himself once more.

Then we drove out to Farmitan to collect the nets which had become stuck in its wells; this was easier and, after knotting the ropes, we all climbed up and down to fetch them. We gave the muqannis their money and arranged to meet again at one hour after sunrise on the following day. Then they went, together with a handkerchief of mine which had disappeared during the drive.

My affairs with the qanats brought strange people before me, the blind one at Jupar, the foreman at Mahun. Each qanat study brought forward some completely different individual and never was there the uniformity of those who sat behind the carpets. The muqannis were all distinct and that most definitely. This one might remove a handkerchief and another might walk three miles to return a knife you had dropped: they might both have the same opinions on life, but their habits were different. That these habits were freely expressed made those that had them more appealing. When their friend said, 'Oh yes, this one takes things', or 'That one returns them', there was no condemnation there, no question of right or wrong; they just happened to do things differently, like a man who cleans his ears with his middle finger. The qanat people always spoke more freely and there was no hesitation while they formed their sentences. The foreman was ruder to me than any other man I met, Azraq was more kind, the overseer more irritating and no one had been more attentive than my original guide at Gauhariz. While many qanat workers became known to me, they did not form the majority of my acquaintances; for the animal catchers were more numerous and formed a fair cross section of the community. Yet they were, in general, more hesitant in their manner, less forthright and nearer the norm. The muqannis formed the extremities of the population; the rest formed the trunk, the stem from which the outlying parts arose.

The doubts and fears which had passed through the man hanging on the rope had been aptly expressed when he grabbed his coat and ran around in a way a Persian never does; for he had arrived at the top and all danger and horror had been left in the well: all land affairs and surface fears are trivial in comparison. By surviving the greater dangers the man from the qanat has acquired self respect; with this acquisition comes the fulfilment of all that exists within him, the rudeness and the kindness, the callousness and the thoughtfulness. When a man is subjected regularly to danger, it is likely that some change should occur within him; usually he is made more aware of himself and of the fabric of which he is made: this awareness and the self respect make for the uniformity of the muqannis and for their variations.

On the next day we were not late but our two muqannis were not there. They were not at the qanat or at their wall. The hitch-hiker hadn't seen them and the trees were not shading them. We searched then for their houses. At the first his wife said that her man had gone to work for an Englishman. At the second we were informed that, as his daughter had sneezed when he was leaving the house, he might be anywhere and certainly with no intention of going down a qanat. I presumed that this man had discouraged the other and both were keeping away from the place.

Ahmed and I succeeded in finding one substitute and Azraq found another. Hassan Muqanni suddenly appeared with the full intention of helping us; he went to borrow rope and returned with the owner of the rope, who also wished to help. Then the two muqannis arrived and, as the same one was prepared to go down, I was saved the trouble of explaining the business of the nets to another: neither of them made any apologies and I let the matter slide. With so many men holding onto the rope the descent of the muqanni was most rapid; usually this is not the practice with deep wells, as the genuine possibility of areas with insufficient oxygen make them lower the man more cautiously. With that well, not only had he not been asphyxiated on the day before, but the well had been open all night: thus he went down as fast as we could pass the rope through our hands. There was little sympathy up above for the man who was going down, as I discovered when we came to a knot in the rope. It was not possible to tie small knots with those stiff, thick ropes of hemp and much length was entwined within each of them. Naturally this growth did not slide easily over the bar. Then it was that the man in the well felt himself stop, wondered why and, before he had time to wonder very much, dropped many feet into the darkness below him before the original rapid pace was resumed.

He arrived at the bottom without having said a single prayer. His sudden precipitation in the channel had totally immersed him in the water and he shouted very little up to us except that he was cold. Possibly he was shivering as a result of his speedy journey; but they were chilly places, with a temperature around 65° Fahrenheit. This is not a low temperature in itself; but when your clothes are wet and the air, the walls and the water are all at that temperature, it seems much colder. At Gauhariz there were two neighbouring channels of which one was warm and the other cold. I even named them accordingly and always returned at intervals to the warm one after becoming too cold in the other: at the junction of these two the change was most marked. I wondered why this should be and took down a thermometer, only to find that the difference was slightly less than 1° Fahrenheit. With the temperature of the whole environment so uniform, the human body is not insensitive to very small changes. Certain fish have been credited with an ability to detect changes of one tenth of a degree Fahrenheit: this is remarkable, but then so was the difference between the two channels.

The man announced that he had emptied the contents of the net into the jar and he was hauled up. With five men at the other end of the rope he had no time to climb up; instead, he swung helplessly from side to side and scraped himself against the walls as we all heaved jerkily on the rope: this time he appeared shivering with cold and sat down limply on the ground. I wrapped the jar in a wet towel, distributed money according to worth and received a polite promise that my handkerchief would be returned.

I spent the rest of the day examining the contents of the jar, but the tranquillity of our garden was disrupted that afternoon, for it teemed with people. In the mosque there lay the body of a rich young landlord who had died the previous night. The relatives wanted him buried in that place and the Mullas agreed on condition that 1,000 tomans were paid; the relatives were only offering 500. This argument took place around the body and those who became temporarily uninterested overflowed into the grounds of the school.

Also, the election of the Mayor was taking place in the room next to ours. Everybody knew that the Kadkhoda would be elected, but nobody was sure what time the election was due to start; for the authorities had only decided upon a day. Some of the electorate had been there since early morning and no important official was seen to arrive until the afternoon. The voters were all either prominent men of the professions or prominent men who had no profession; whoever they were they walked around in the garden and occasionally lay down to go to sleep.

Later, great cheers announced that the Mullas had capitulated: arguments about burial are inevitably curtailed in a hot climate. Further cheers punctuated the voting until the final reckoning, which stated that the Kadkhoda had been elected. The people all left and I opened the windows and doors of our workroom. When I returned from the qanats I had done this and unintentionally admitted about fifty people; they only left after, by a lucky chance, someone knocked over the bottle containing my largest scorpion.

Two hours before sunset Mahdevi came: he invited me to see the work of repair on the mosque. Together we climbed onto the roof and examined all that was being done under his instructions; for he had been elected to an office, the duties of which were to ensure that the mosque did not fall into disrepair. Mahdevi had only held the post a short time and it was obvious that many of his predecessors had neglected their obligations. As much land had been given in former years to the mosque, so that there should be sufficient income for its upkeep, Mahdevi had justification for his vehemence in decrying those who had absconded with the money rented from that land. For the first time in a good many years the mosque's money would be spent only on the mosque.

We climbed up the minarets by the winding staircases within them until we could see the view from the top. The bulbous shaped roofs, the many trees, the interesting sounds and the people in the street all joined to form a harmonious picture of the town. The two thin lines of green that flanked the streams which came in from the east tapered away into the distance. So too did the road, on the one side to Kirman and on the other to Bam. The lines of qanat wells were all quite clear. Everything was orderly and neatly displayed. A group of winnowers, a man washing carpets in a stream, some donkeys coming in from the desert, a woman with a load on her back, a car being driven along the road: everything could be seen. It did not have the momentary quality of an English view; that car could be followed on its journey from the time when it was a speck of dust 30 miles away on one side until it disappeared as a similar speck on the other. The winnowers could be followed back to their houses and the old woman to the place where she deposited her load. She was out in the desert again fetching another when we left the minaret, for we waited until the camels had arrived. They had lumbered their way from a village near the hills right down to the town, at first appearing only as a slender line, then as a series of distinct shapes until finally, with much jangling of their bells, they had been persuaded to sit down in the shade of the trees which were beneath us.

The roof of the mosque was a pleasant place on which to spend the evenings. The round curves of the smaller domes were comfortable to lean against and the heat which they had absorbed in the day was given up at night. When Ahmed sat up there he was always most eloquent and full of praises for the English. He considered them hard-working, sincere, kind and cool-headed: these four qualities he enumerated singly and with much deliberation. Upon my proffering thanks on behalf of myself and the others he rapidly denied that he had acquired this information recently; always he had been aware of it, for it was a well known fact. To him we naturally fitted into the pattern he already knew, we were all casts from the same mould, we were Englishmen. He would continue on this theme until he left the roof; he was never forthright on the topic except up there and always, in spite of the vicissitudes of the day, our qualities remained unaltered. There was never any reference to our discreditable faculties, for, he said, being sincere, we knew them. This last remark of his was particularly inconclusive and meaningless, but then so are most things before one goes to bed.

As Philip didn't have far to go to work, I used the truck and he a horse. Although they had been promised by the Governor General, there were no horses in Mahun for the first four days and arrived only after Philip had requested that two of the Jupar horses came over with their attendant soldiers. Every horse in the Gendarmerie is owned by a soldier who receives, as reward, a little more money for the fodder. One day Philip wished to make a trip by horse back to Jupar and the soldiers decided that he should have a guard: Philip declined this but they insisted. Now the journey there and back would take two days and the horse would have to be fed at night; but neither soldier could trust the other to feed his horse for him: both believed that all the fodder would go to one horse. Philip offered to witness the feeding, but they rated very highly the guile which might be employed by the one who had gone with him. It was a stupid situation and only the restlessness of Philip's horse, which started off for Jupar, put an end to the problem for which there was no other solution. The soldier who happened, at that moment, to be on the other horse went after him and then compromised the affair by continuing as escort. When Philip returned, he brought with him an impressive document written in two languages and with many signatures, all certifying the witnessing of the fact of the horse being fed. I wondered what would have happened if the horse had not bolted and for how long two soldiers could have pursued a topic of such a shallow nature. These men did not earn greatly of our respect.

Eric had had similar difficulty, namely the inability to see round problems so contorted that solutions were not easily found. For five days he and a soldier had used a horse to carry the surveying equipment up into the hills which he was then mapping. It was on the fifth and at midday when the soldier declared that the horse needed water; on none of the previous days had it done so, but the soldier was adamant. Eric agreed wonderingly and asked him to come back before dark: he refused to do this and Eric, who could not have carried all the equipment by himself, asked him to remain. The soldier was furious and began whipping the horse until Eric managed to intervene; but not before blood had appeared where the whip had fallen: this incident stopped any idea of work and they both returned to Jupar long before the day was over. The Gendarme officer, however, was informed that Eric had whipped the animal and he, without an interpreter, was not convincing in his protestations of innocence. When he applied on the next day for a horse his request was refused. Ahmed eventually put the matter right and received our praises; for it is only the most material of problems that have easy solutions: a problem which is founded on the mistaken belief that a horse needs water is not. Admittedly that served only as an excuse for the soldier, but the difficulty centred around that point, and there is no evasion of such problems when the thing really at issue is never discussed. Naturally he would deny that a personal distaste for the heat at midday had any bearing at all on the matter; he would stick to his story about the horse and make evasion impossible. With such problems we could only evade those who had created them.

I had little to do with the Military. As the Governor had charged them to salute us at all times, we had to accept these salutes; but otherwise there was only rare communion with them. They caused Ahmed to make one of his grosser generalisations, briefly: 'The soldiers are the stupidest people in all Persia'. However, there was one occasion when I had to associate with them and that was over the case of Askar Sorah Gul, known to his friends and to the police as Aqbar. He was a lorry driver, his lorry was old and he drove just wherever a commission might charter him to go, though mainly he plied between Kirman and Afghanistan. But first I must describe the environment in which he lived.

One might expect the main road to India to be well used, but it was a rare sight to see a cloud of dust curling its way along it and slowly materialising into a vehicle. Occasionally cars came along and sometimes there passed through those who were making some eventful and lengthy trip: four Dutchmen travelling from Java to the Netherlands and an Englishman going from England to New Zealand came along it. In Kirman there was a jeep trailer with 'Enterprise Australia' painted on the side together with a flourish of European capitals: its owner had had to sell it. But more often there were the lorries, always old and always loaded to excess with people or with goods.

They never had punctures; the tyres were old and exploded.

They never possessed anything which might be called an accessory; those things, when they became broken, were removed; for they were observed not to be absolutely vital: the hand-brake, the self-starters and the filters were never there, only the bare necessities which enabled the engine to continue its clanking rhythm and the truck to be pulled along the road.

When the tyres become old they are sewn up with wire, and a large piece of old tyre is put inside to prevent the inner tube becoming unnecessarily conspicuous. A tyre is thrown away when there is not enough of it left to be sewn together; but just before this final abandonment there is a stage in which layers of old carpets are placed inside to give additional strength. When this tyre explodes a piece of rubber about a foot long is blown out, but I do not know why. We had first seen these pieces in the Syrian desert; for the sand was slow in covering them up. Like orange peel beside a railway, they are a reminder of those who have been that way.

One day, when I was waiting for a net to catch something in Farmitan and pursuing Damsel flies at its exit, a lorry passed. It was the familiar scene with four men in the cab, three on top of it and the back laden high with the baggage of those who were sitting on the very summit of it all. It had just passed by me when a front tyre exploded. I looked up to see the piece of rubber and carpet lying in the road and the lorry lurch to a halt. This was nothing new, and I continued to catch the Damsel flies. The passengers came down to drink from the stream, but they didn't talk: they didn't even talk to each other. Then the driver came up to speak to me. He said that he had no spare tyre, that he had to get these people to Kirman by nightfall and that he had seen that I too possessed a Bedford. I had not noticed that his vehicle was of the same make and instantly regretted that our two spare tyres were so much in evidence. All common sense, wisdom and experience denied the man the tyre, but I was soon watching him wheeling one away, to be left musing wistfully on my own incredible foolishness. He had promised to return it on the next day to the Gendarmerie, but as there was every possibility of this not occurring, I found a flat piece of stone and scratched on it his engine number, our tyre number and the number of the vehicle which had been done in chalk and on the side: the driver gave me his name as Aqbar. Together with his assistant he fitted on the tyre, blew it up, gave further assurance that it would be returned, drove away and left me alone in the dust.

Ahmed was indignant when he heard about it and more so when the Gendarmerie informed me that it had not been returned on time. Somehow Aqbar had given me the impression of being an honest man: there was nothing tangible in this belief and everything pointed to the contrary in connection with an individual whose occupation was mainly in the transport of goods, in all probability unlawfully, along the India road. But honesty is in a different category from lawfulness and, likely as it was that the latter category did not apply to Aqbar, my impression was associated with the former and so was the tyre.

The Gendarmerie received all the particulars, saluted and sent off a telegram to Kirman. Many salutes and telegrams followed as time passed by and on the fourth day after the loss a round, fat man was brought before me. He was talking very fast and telling me how he had been in Bandar Abbas four days before and could not have stolen my tyre; it was rapidly brought home to me that the number I had copied from the side of Aqbar's lorry was this man's number and he received effusive apologies from me. In spite of his arrest in Kirman and subsequent dispatch to Mahun, he was sympathetic towards me in my loss, until he was informed by another that the tyre had not been stolen but lent.

Without the number of the vehicle there was little hope of finding it; but while Philip, Ahmed and I were packing to leave Mahun, a youth came up and asked us about the tyre. It was already dark, and as we intended to reach Kirman that night I answered his questions curtly. When he had satisfied himself about the facts, he suddenly announced that he was a friend of Aqbar's, that Aqbar had been drunk enough to stab a man on the evening of the same day as I had lent him the tyre and had since gone into hiding: in short, that his reason for coming to Mahun was to tell me my tyre was still on the lorry and the lorry had been apprehended by the police. This youth then walked away and Ahmed told the crowd to go and lose themselves.

One man of the crowd stayed behind and said that Aqbar was

a great criminal and well known to all men. He had made a bank
robbery in Tehran before fleeing to Isfahan and doing the same
thing there. With that money he had moved on once more and
to Kirman: his business with the lorry had lasted for about a year.
Then this informer also walked away. Philip said Aqbar didn't
seem the sort of man who was likely to return mere tyres.

We then left Mahun. It was a windy night and the sand was
being blown into the air. Wisps of it played about in the road
in front of us while some flicked itself against the windows of the
cab. Inside we talked about Aqbar for a while and then thought
about him: with Tehran, Isfahan and Kirman as forbidden cities,
he would have to move on once more, to begin again with little
to help him. Presumably he would stay in hiding for a short time
and then make his way to another town to look for a job, with
everyone knowing that he was new to that town and rightly
suspecting why he had left the other. In a world tied down with
references, certificates and diplomas it is refreshing to think of a
man having no more than that which he is, with his only qualifi-
cations being bound up in himself and not just things of the past.
The big ditch in the road outside Kirman woke us up from these
thoughts and we drove slowly through the town to the Consulate.

In the morning I went to settle the tyre question. The
Gendarmes had not been able to find the tyre because a different
part of the police had been responsible for the apprehension of the
lorry. Everybody else in the town seemed to know about the
tyre, for a lorry which comes into Kirman with one clean new
tyre is a lorry to be remembered. With Ahmed I visited the various
Gendarmeries until we found the right one, and a soldier then
accompanied us to the garage so that I could identify the tyre in
his presence. The yard of the garage was full of apprehended
vehicles, all dissimilar and all so very much alike. The three of us
climbed over them until I pointed out Aqbar's lorry and then,
like the bright star in the east, our famous tyre. We returned to
the Gendarmerie for permission to remove it; this was given
verbally by a police officer who happened at the time to be
underneath his desk and looking, so he said, for a drawing pin.
Back at the garage the foreman contrived to prevent us removing
the tyre, he hauled me out of the cab by my trousers when I was

looking for a jack and pushed some boy away who was offering us a wheel brace. Ahmed muttered something derogatory about all mechanics and I went to fetch our own tools from the truck. The lorries had to be shunted a bit in order to get at the wheel, and as the foreman always shoved in the opposite direction to that which I was pushing, the job took longer than it should have done.

Finally Ahmed produced a relative of his; he frequently did this and the relative always beamed obligingly and assisted us. This one removed the foreman and helped me to take off the tyre. We left the lorry resting on its jack, something which would not inconvenience Aqbar, for he would never see it again. The three of us and the gendarme, who had been so impotent in warding off the foreman, returned to the Gendarmerie. The tyre had to be wheeled throughout the building, through plush carpeted offices, and past many gaily uniformed officials. It took a long time, as each official had to call in a servant to read the tyre number, and all the while we three hung about, knowing that our presence made the place untidy. Finally the whole history of the case was written down and we were allowed to leave.

That was the case of Askar Sorah Gul and the parts which had been recorded were only the necessary facts of it: the significances were omitted. Did robbery, drunkenness and violence confirm that he was a dishonest man? In spite of everything we at least had been informed of the location of the tyre. In the garage, I had asked the mechanics to convey my thanks to Aqbar for his final gesture, but their unresponsive faces made me feel that I might have saved my words, as if I had thrown a bottle with its message into the sea and then realised the futile pathos of the act. The Gendarme reprimanded me and said how glad he was to think that this criminal would be leaving the town; for the police in each district were responsible for keeping law and order only in that place; there was very little assistance afforded to other towns. Thus Aqbar, like all the evil-doers in days gone by, could flee from the town and begin again: the doubtful and only merit of such a system is that law-breakers are kept on the move.

Ahmed's brother, Photo Saam, gave us lunch that day. The walls were bedecked with tinted photos of ethereal children, but they didn't stop us from appreciating quite the best melons that had ever been set before us; dates were provided for the first time and tasted good in their fresh juiciness. After buying many tins of petrol we set off across the plain for Jupar. These tins are not only maltreated when they become empty but while they are full; for, by resoldering the caps and transferring some of the contents, five full tins can be made to stand where only four had been full before. When a defective cap is noticed and pointed out the man makes no retort, save possibly against the Oil Company, and meekly brings another. I liked this attitude, never before had I seen such guiltless guilt.

At Jupar we met Louis, who had returned a few days before. Eric and Mirza were up in the mountains and the most southerly part of his map was being completed. I greeted the animals and loaded them onto the truck; for the third part of our stay was due to begin. Louis and I were to be in Negar, 25 miles south-west of Jupar, while Philip and Eric were to be in the Kuh-i-Badimu, 22 miles west of Kirman: about fifty miles separated the two places. The distances necessitated a lot of driving in the truck. The plan was that Philip should take me to Negar before returning to Jupar, picking up Eric and Louis and proceeding to his own destination. Louis was to return to join me at Negar. This operation could not be done in one day; it was expected that Louis should arrive in Negar two days after me.

CHAPTER IX

Negar

WE loaded all of my equipment onto the truck and made room for the Kadkhoda, who insisted on coming to ensure that we experienced no difficulties on our arrival in Negar. The Kadkhoda's son, Ma'shallah, also climbed on board and wedged himself between Ahmed and his father. The animal cages had been covered with mosquito netting, but the issuing hisses caused a tenseness of expression in the round face of the Kadkhoda which lasted throughout the journey.

The first part of the drive was over the desert to the west of Jupar, then we turned south to go through a narrow valley which connected the plain of Kirman with the small plain in which Negar was situated. Through this valley there ran a road which constantly led us down into the dry bed of the stream and up the steep bank on the other side. It was important to drive fast into those beds in order to get out of them again. If you failed the returning momentum was utilised in reversing back up the original bank before you drove at it again. The lurchings of the truck brought no sound from the three in the back; they cared for nothing but the mosquito netting.

At the other end of the valley was a small Gendarmerie which had once temporarily apprehended Philip for behaving suspiciously: he had had no papers with him and was riding an Army horse. In order to prevent the occurrence of similar brief arrests the Governor gave us all official letters which were addressed 'To all Gendarmes, Police and Government Officials'. As two of that Gendarmerie had been shot in the spring the remainder were naturally more cautious. Philip waved at the one who had apprehended him and received no greetings in return: I do not know why the man let Philip go free, but he did not seem elated at discovering that he had not done wrong to do so; most likely he considered the wave to be a mocking one.

Negar is in the centre of its plain and the track to meet it led straight over the desert. We had visited it once before in the company of Peter Wild, as the landlord, Muhammad Ameri, was a friend of his and it was with him that we had noticed the relative abundance of flowers and the accessibility of the qanats. Muhammad Ameri had been most helpful and offered us his hospitality for as long as we should wish it; it was a conjunction of all these facts which made Louis and me decide to spend the final days in that village. We arrived as it was getting dark, for there had been various stops on the way; Philip collected many samples of sand which he thought revealing and I picked up a camel's skull which I believed to be decorative.

Our host at that time was away. We had known that, but we did not know that his two brothers were also absent from the house. His sister-in-law, however, was inside and informed us that these two would be returning an hour or so later and only then could we be let in. Until they came we sat sleepily beneath the trees and worked up an appetite for the food which would surely come. The necessary time passed and the brothers arrived; they did give us a meal, but they made us sit on chairs to eat it; they were hard chairs, uncomfortable and out of place; the soft warmth of a carpet was lacking. A wireless was afterwards produced by that insensitive pair and everybody listened respectfully to a speech by the Prime Minister; but it caused little comment and the knob controlling the wave-length was turned restlessly for the rest of the evening.

In the morning Philip unloaded the things from the truck and drove away with the other three. I had woken up with a great feeling of indifference, having slept next to a room where a herb with some violently pungent smell was being dried. After half the night had passed, further sleep was impossible; for the smell of that herb was quite acrid in my nose and a feeling of sickness gradually asserted itself. When the truck had left, a muqanni came to take me on a qanat tour which had been wretchedly arranged the night before. Everything we did caused me to pant: climbing up and down the smallest wells necessitated long pauses for air. Everything was difficult. No qanat was satisfactory. Everything annoyed me. My guide was stupid. His face was grinning. He laughed at me. It was only with an effort that I took longer breaths and then they sounded much louder. The guide thought the longer breathing was even funnier. His gaping face blew in and out as I looked at it. The land around wavered uncertainly.

We returned to the house and I went to sleep; it was just midday. I awoke in the evening, explained that I was tired and went to sleep at once. I dreamt vividly: the land was dotted with wells and I ran about, but always jumping over them in an effort to avoid sliding into them. There was no variety in the dream, just deep holes and wells; so it was with a great feeling of relief that I woke up just as it was reaching the middle of the following day. The fever had gone and I went to the qanats to decide where to put my nets.

On the second day the sickness reversed itself: everything went slowly. The heart was slow, with a beat that was tired; its thump was not heard and the pulse was most weak. On the day before it had raced along at a furious pace. In order to placate the Ameri household, I went out into the desert with the butterfly net and lay down beside a mound which had a little shade. As the sun moved so did I, only to flop down in some other place. That night there was no dream and I woke knowing that whatever it had been had passed.

Ever since we had been in Kirman we had all had occasions of this sort; strange fevers knocked us down and then left just as suddenly. Louis had woken one night feeling rather odd and while he was rummaging in the medicine box for an aspirin he put the thermometer in his mouth instead of on the dirty floor. He glanced at it on replacing the things and found it registered 104°F. This so horrified him that he forgot to take the pill and went straight back to bed and to sleep. The incident provided an amusing story at breakfast, but otherwise there were no after effects. Never did these fevers cause any concern; when they were present they were far too vitriolic in their actions for any rational thought to accrue; when they had gone, they had gone absolutely. Some of the fevers are well known and precautions can be taken. For instance, sand-fly fever is deterred by the use of a thin-meshed and stifling sand-fly net, but the animal is just as liable to bite you before you go to bed. We took Paludrine spasmodically, as a counter to malaria; but there was not much of it in the area. Against the others we did nothing and accepted the nonchalant attitude of Peter Wild as being the most satisfactory. He had suffered from a large number of the local fevers and then was immune to the majority of those which he had had. Such immunity as we acquired did not benefit us for, with so short a time in the country, there were quite enough new fevers to last us out; but the attitude of nonchalance appealed to us all. That is why there was a tendency to crawl out into lonely desert places until they were over; the shivering and sweating caused concern only in those of us who weren't shivering or sweating at the time.

Peter Wild had complained that his patients only came to him when the disease was very firmly established. I did not see how this indolence in the sick population could be dispelled. If you are to accept fever, headaches, vomiting, lack of appetite and dysentery as being regular and normal affairs, then there is a time before the disease in question has started symptoms of its own. Most diseases start in association with one of those five ailments; and, as the ailment is the better known, the characteristics of the disease, as they show themselves, are considered secondary. Worms are blamed for many of the major illnesses. A woman at Jupar who had been coughing up blood for six weeks blamed it upon a leech; she knew they lived in the drinking water, she knew that they sucked blood and no realisation more ominous came into her mind. Her husband had come to visit me, although we loudly proclaimed that we knew nothing of medicine; Louis' departure with dysentery helped to impress this fact upon them. As the man believed it was a leech and refused to send her to the hospital for such a trivial matter, I made him watch the effect of salt upon a leech; he went with instructions that if salt did not stop the bleeding, he must take her to the hospital. With such a facility nearby, we did not have the problem of sick people on our hands; with our subsequent welfare dependent upon the result of the treatment.

Philip occasionally visited the hospital in order to do a little blood group work. He had come with a small amount of serum and got his blood samples for testing from the out-patients; in the same way as they had given their names to the clerk, so did they allow a drop of blood to be taken, as if it was a normal and necessary part of an out-patient's examination. Once they had stepped over the threshold of the surgery, their resignation to medical affairs was complete; they resisted nothing and waited patiently for their subjection to finish.

On the evening of the passing of the illness, I collected insects. It was a blustery evening, big clouds were filling up most of the space in the sky and they rolled rapidly over the land: it was a good time for dust devils, those wild mixtures of earth and air which are such fun to watch and so unpleasant to experience. On desert strips of the journey we had found them an interesting relief in a countryside which was otherwise so static. Once we saw one of those winding columns 100 feet high twisting its way along just beside us: the thing was only a short distance from the truck and we chatted haughtily about the forces involved. A gentle breeze had been blowing through the cab when suddenly a mass of hot gravel was showered in on top of us and the dust devil wound itself away on the other side. We cleaned out our ears; everybody shook the sand out of their clothes and talked glibly about a necessary experience: a section of melon which I had been eating had fossilised upon the instant and had to be discarded.

The peasants were returning to Negar from the fields and I sat on a hill to watch. They would shriek with joy while one of their number, only a few yards away, was immersed in swirling sand. As there was an abundance of peasants the reward was worth the temporary and blinding chaos which I occasionally suffered.

I returned, but Louis had not arrived as he should have done. Now Philip had, during his unloading of the truck, omitted to unload either my nets or the books and it was important to me that Louis should arrive soon; for I could not start upon the work which I had gone to Negar to do.

On the next day I contracted an evil form of diarrhoea and worried about the nets; although cold qanats would not have been agreeable, I seethed with discontent. All petty illnesses are lessened if the mind is occupied with things other than self-pity, but I had nothing to do except wait for the truck. At the top of the village there was no sign of a vehicle and I walked back following a man whose donkey had a monkey on its back. Only the fact that children were laughing at it reminded me that a monkey was not a usual sight in Persia. The multifarious peculiarities of the land did not sharpen one's observation of those things that were abnormal there. If a man wearing only a shirt walked down the street with you it would be difficult to notice other contradictions with eyes that had been deliberately blunted for the sake of politeness. The man may be surprised, after he has made a feeble joke, to find you hopelessly doubled up with uncontrollable laughter; but he cannot be offended, for you have restrained it till a suitable time had arisen. Even then the shirt dominates your attention and things of wider significance pass by unnoticed: thus it was with the monkey.

I made enquiries about the monkey and was told that a party of Dervishes were visiting Negar. A large group of them were in Ameri's courtyard and begging from those who passed through it; but they were not diseased or crippled as are most beggars; for just because a man is a Dervish he receives food and money from the poorer people of the village. The peasants have a great respect for them on account of their strange talents. They said that the Dervish has power over animals; if I wanted to know whether an animal was poisonous or wished to find a particular snake then I should send for a Dervish. Because of the powers, which were never persuaded to assert themselves for our benefit, the people believe that he has control over the health of human beings. Therefore they are fearful of incurring his wrath and, when he knocks at their door, will give him hospitality and kindness. The guest is never asked to perform treatment; his beneficence has a protracted effect and lasts long after he has gone.

The Dervish has little money and less education; thus he is despised by those who possess these distinctions and he receives only from the others who have the least to give. Although many of their race live permanently in Persia, the ones who beg have come over the border from India and thrive upon the enforced goodwill of the peasant: without any confirmation of his powers he is asked indoors and the Dervish is content. The monkey is

carried as a symbol. That particular one looked cold and unhappy on the donkey; the large round eyes in the little face
blinked at the children; they became quiet and stopped running
behind the donkey, for he was a very pathetic, little monkey.

Back at Ameri's house I wrote a note to Jupar requesting that
whoever was still in that village should hand the nets to the bearer.
I assumed that one of the other three was still there; for I could
think of no other reason for the delay; probably Louis had not
finished his work in time. I imagined that he had taken Philip and
Eric to the Kuh-i-Badimu and was spending a day or two more in
Jupar: there was no harm in that except that I wanted the nets.
What attracted Philip and Eric into that mountain valley was
that there were coal mines there which had been talked of volubly
and proudly by the Kirmanis. Those two had visited it once
before and found it consisted of many short adits leading into the
hillside; they were about thirty yards long and the seams were not
high. The coal was not good, being powdery and soft; it could
be cut with a spade. The output in the summer was only 3 tons per
week, but this increased towards the winter; for the rich men's
houses could consume 300 tons during one cold season. The coal
was transported to them first by donkey and then by truck: it is
true that it was not a major industry, but it did provide yet another
aspect of the Persian scene.

In Negar a man named Ali had made himself known to me by
handing in a dead snake and he promised to take the note to Jupar;
as it was eight hours' walk he could not be expected back for at
least a day. Such sickness as there was still within my system did
not encourage me to go with him or in his place: he left in the
morning. Scarcely had the garden gate banged when it banged
again repeatedly as a crowd of villagers came in with the foremost
carrying a snake: it was a thin tree snake which was capable of
holding most of its body stiff and motionless. We put it in a jar
and everyone admired it. The cause of the excitement was,
however, not this small one but a far larger one which had been
seen. As the average length demonstrated was seven feet and as
every wrist was held out as a sign of its thickness, it was obviously
an animal of greater portent. They took me to the spot with much
haste, but it had gone; the party split up and inspected all the

likely places with much recklessness. Cobras do exist in southern Persia, but this one did not reappear; if it had still been in the vicinity someone would undoubtedly have trodden on it, for a thick weed covered the ground.

For the rest of that day I festered. I did a little collecting, jabbing my net at unsuspecting creatures and killing those which I caught with much enjoyment. A hairy old man met with me and amused himself by finding scorpions; I became appeased a little and remained with him even when it rained. But it became colder, my diarrhoea got worse and I returned to the reptilian whisperings of my room. Disagreeability increased, and each of the ten times I got out of bed that night, I stopped progressively shorter of the lavatory. Self-pity was rampant.

Everything was out of perspective; nothing occupied its proper position of importance. More insects saw with their last glance a distorted and demoniacal face peering in at them through the glass of the killing bottle. At midday Ali returned to say that all the Englishmen had left Jupar and gone to Kirman; he had not continued into Kirman to pick up the nets which he knew were required and, due to the inversion of things, his blistered feet, which he exhibited to all, received little sympathy from me and I decided to walk to Kirman. Everybody protested; they said it was twelve hours' walk and I must eat before I go: they flapped around like agitated vultures when the carrion begins to move. After watching two spare shoes and a water bottle being thrust hurriedly into a rucksack, the onlookers were left to themselves; but they were soon to see me return; for one of the landlords had caught me up to say there was a horse for my use in the Gendarmerie. No effort had been made to inform me of its existence; this was not wilful, it was just that no one had told me. The Gendarmes said that the horse and the one for a guard—he was inevitable—would be saddled in half an hour. I spent the time eating lunch.

As I entered the Gendarmerie, the soldier on duty said that the horses were ready, but I found them quite bare-backed and munching lucerne in their stable; again there was no question of malice. 'Ready' in Persian cannot be translated into English in one word: it means—there is nothing except time preventing the readiness. It took five soldiers two hours to saddle those horses. Neither were accustomed to harness and a saddle on the back; one was very young and the other quite old and both, with their present state of training, would have been useless in an emergency. There are no geldings amongst the Army horses; the resultant lack of vigour is said to be unsatisfactory.

We had just clattered out of the Gendarmerie, wondering how many of the fifty miles would be left in front of us after the four more hours of daylight had expired, when a peasant ran up shouting that the truck was coming. This was silly; it hadn't come for the last three days and this was the most unlikely time for it to arrive. The man insisted, and then the familiar popping, made distinctive ever since the silencer had been lost on the French roads, could be heard: the truck came into view and there was Louis being bounced about in the driver's seat. All that had been pent up immediately disappeared; the horses were led back to the stable and greatly assisted us in divesting themselves of their equipment.

Louis, after being introduced to those peasants of note who were standing nearby, explained what had happened. Philip had contracted amoebic dysentery; he had felt ill on his way back from Negar and retired to his bed with the diagnostic abdominal pain. He remained there for two days, while Louis and Eric completed not only their own work but his also: then they drove him across the plain to the hospital. On the next day Eric and Ahmed had been taken to the Kuh-i-Badimu and then Louis had driven to Negar. All quite simple and straightforward. But Philip in his illness had omitted to observe that he had taken all my nets back again to Jupar and Louis had unloaded them at Kirman, believing that all things still on the truck were not wanted by me. Therefore I drove back to Kirman, away out of Negar and over the mountain road, pausing awhile at the top of the pass to let the engine cool. In front was the Kirman plain and behind the plain of Negar. It was not a clear evening; for a wind was blowing and the two areas appeared brown and dry, dusty and devoid of life. The qanat wells were an assurance that water existed down there, but they looked like dry and empty pits, numerous and frantic excavations for moisture. The intense optimism involved and the ingenuity displayed makes the development of the qanat technique fascinating speculation.

I slept at Kirman, collected the nets, breakfasted off dates and condensed milk, and set off for Negar, along the road to the pass. It was always our custom to give lifts to all who asked for them: going into Kirman four ebullient road-menders had been taken to their village and on the way back I picked up an old man shortly before the hills. My intention had been to stop, if he should give me any intimation of wanting me to do so, and, as I passed him, he yelled at me to stop 'for the love of Husain'; but it was also for the sake of this old man that I picked him up. He thanked me and became silent. Going up the hill the lorry pulled badly until, after a mild and feeble bout of coughing, it stopped. The old man raised his hands in despair and asked if it was ill. I said I thought it was. He said that perhaps it did not like travelling in the heat of the day and he settled down to await the cool of the evening, then seven hours distant.

However, the truck was more than ill, for one of the back tyres was flat. I informed my companion and he immediately came round to inspect it. After comparing that wheel with the others, he announced that it was that tyre which was ill and had caused the general sickness. We had had two punctures before and had experienced great difficulty in loosening the wheel nuts: the garage men who tightened them during the overhauls possessed far stronger tools than the slender one which we carried. The old man could not be expected to give any physical assistance; but, after the truck had been jacked up, for he was then showing a fanatical interest in the proceedings, I told him that it was the nuts which were the problem. He watched me attempt to unloosen the first one and, at what he judged to be the critical moment, he called in a rush upon all the Imams so that they should come to my assistance. He did not shout to the heavens but leant forward and directed all his words at the nut in question. The first time he did this sudden incantation just by my ear it weakened me considerably, but afterwards we united our efforts and the wheel came off very easily. I was grateful to all of them, but especially to my earthly benefactor, the old man. We shook hands over the event and put on the spare wheel.

He looked with me into the engine, but as no part of that looked sicker to him than any other part he had nothing to say. However, no petrol was coming through even though there was plenty left; so I switched over to the other tank. This had not been observed by him and he chanted a long prayer requesting that the engine be made well again; after this he intimated that I should try and start it. He began his refrain to the Imams immediately he saw the ignition turned on and kept it up until the engine spluttered once more; only then did he relax his stare upon the air filter and we both climbed back into the cab.

When the place was reached where his road branched off from mine, he extolled his way and told me of its virtues; he offered me food and drink at his house: I wished to get back to Negar and refused. He then said that he had no food and his family were all hungry and there must be something that could be given to him. There was bread which I had brought from Negar the day before, but he said it was too hard and stepped down to the ground, only to step up again when he realised it was profitable to go along my way for a short distance before the roads really diverged.

I liked the old man. He was an individual and fell into a group all by himself and was only one of a large number of others who also had this distinction. They could all be described by a single and perfectly adequate title. It was as if only the real personalities were being paraded before us. What better man was there with whom to change a wheel? Who else should have led us to the buz majjeh but the sage with the warts on his nose? This parade had not been arranged, as our activities in the land led us along no straight line; the people were just the outcome of such a way of life. Between the solitary man eating flesh up in the mountains and the blind man picking away in the darkness of the qanat there were so very many others, each living in his own particular style. As the livelihood of the muqanni made him more definite in his behaviour, so did the bare brown earth throw into greater contrast the irregularity of those who worked upon it. Esau, Abu Ali, Mirza and the Kadkhoda were all so different; Eric's soldier, Aqbar, and the opium smuggling donkey driver, had quite independent and immutable qualities. The interest in the environment lay in the characters which it created. The old man was nowhere to be seen as I entered Negar; his part had been played and he had disappeared into the distant haze.

For the rest of that day the nets were put down into the qanats, either by myself in the wells which were not difficult to descend or, in the deeper ones, by Ali. Luckily some of the qanats were being repaired and it was necessary only to tie the rope round his waist and let him slowly down by restraining the wooden wheel over which the rope was wound. Pulling him up took longer, but the wheel obviated the need for many men.

There were seven qanats at Negar. They were all slow, nearly the same length and flowed parallel to one another towards Negar: the village was long and narrow in consequence. There was little difference between them except in the output; but Tabakulabad and Negarjelali were chosen as they each had wheels erected over one of their highest wells. The nets were placed beneath these wheels and also fairly near the exits, in order to discover if fewer animals existed at the head of the qanat; the pairs of nets were ten miles apart.

Although Jupar was only 25 miles away from Negar, the qanat technical terms they used were peculiarly useless at Negar: Ali and those working by the wheel had been associated with qanats all their lives, but did not understand many of the words in common usage 25 miles away. That this specialisation of language has grown up in each qanat area emphasises the isolated nature of the villages and of that barrenness which lies in between. In Jupar the jarib was the cubic measure for water and a term used by all: in Negar this was unknown and qassat was the word. However, in both cases it was an indefinable quantity; for it referred to the number of square metres which can be irrigated in twenty-four hours. As the water required for irrigation varies according to the time of the year and to the crop, it surprised us that there should have been such uniformity of opinion that Gauhariz produced 3,000 daily. Only later did we learn that this assessing is done by yet another type of qanat expert; he does nothing except assess outputs and upon his word does the distribution of water depend.

Muhammad Ameri had arrived on the same day as Louis; he was one of the few men who took more than a financial interest in their estates; the peasants liked him and talked about him respectfully. In appearance he was quite different to all other landlords we had met; he did not have a fleshy face and a flabby appearance; he did not have a loud laugh, but spoke quietly; his servants were not ordered about with an air akin to petty officialdom; he never twiddled with the wireless or spent the evenings playing poker; no arak was produced for him at meals and he did not make a point of overeating himself: in fact there was a vast difference between him and the majority of Persian landlords. This was made most noticeable when the bailiff and his brother sat with us three at supper time; these two knew no French and spent the meal eating competitively and throwing the arak down their throats avidly before resorting to the evening's poker. At least they realised the worthier position held by Ameri for, when he was with them, they became considerably more authoritative to the servants than when he was not. The servants, with Ameri there, did not disobey.

The new houses at Negar, the well-being of the estate, the readiness with which the peasants talked about their landlord and the building of a new qanat, all showed that he was a man who put his money back into the land. Such rare treatment was appreciated by the peasants, as we noticed by their deference to him whenever we walked about together. One day he drove up to Louis and me, who were fatiguing lizards in the desert, and invited us to see his pistaccio village. For the benefit of his inquisitive chauffeur we explained that our previous meanderings were the result of following the fast sand lizards until they became too fatigued to run any more and could be caught: Ameri's bailiff, who was with him, said that we should have employed servants for so menial a task.

At the village of the pistachios, as Ameri had recently been informed, the whole nut crop had failed. Each one had not developed because a small insect was living at the end of the stem; with the leader of the peasants, we looked in at all the orchards and the sight was exactly the same. Ameri told us that the insect was slowly making its way throughout the country; many areas were as yet quite unaffected, but in others the practice of growing pistachios had ceased; no attempt was being made by the authorities to check its devastation. It is true that the pistachio nut does not provide an important part of the country's food; but it does provide a part and apparently nothing is being done to stop the ravages of the insect: thus Ameri has to be content to observe the fruitless years, for he is incapable of preventing them.

On the way back the chauffeur saw a wolf and Ameri, who was driving, immediately set off after it. The bailiff had brought a gun, as everybody knew, for it had been flaunted proudly on all occasions. That weapon thrashed about in the car while he attempted to load and then to point it out of the window: the wolf bounded along with a pleasantly easy stride. The various dried up flood valleys and the patches of soft sand were to its advantage; although its speed was only about 25 miles per hour, the speed of the car, due to these detours, had to be very much faster. Our sudden swervings in flurries of sand, the rapid descent down steep unsuspected inclines and Ameri's continual efforts to avoid the hard hummocks of sand at the bases of the camel thorn clumps, were all invigorating, but did not shorten the distance between us and the wolf, which was then aiming for a hilly piece of ground.

A smooth patch enabled us to catch it up and, to our surprise, when the gun went off the wolf was reduced to a whining heap. The wretched animal examined its shattered front leg and great howls filled the air. We all leaped out and the brother fired another shot; this caused sand to fly up into its eye and encouraged it to lollop off towards the hills. We followed, brandishing knives and feeling very primitive; but the wolf had lost little of its former speed and we were left gesticulating fiercely with our weapons; but impotently, like the central element of a tribal dance. Back in the car, we bore down on it again, but the third shot went very wide; the wolf looked round at us before disappearing into the hills. The chauffeur exclaimed how bad he thought the shooting had been and thus let off a little of his suppressed rage, which had been increasing noticeably with each fresh order he received from the bailiff. The maiming of the wolf and the subsequent outburst from the chauffeur had, however, stunned him into silence and he spoke no word for the remainder of the journey.

Ali had promised to come at seven in the morning in order to help me pick up the nets. Not only had he not arrived by eight, but the self-starter of the truck did not work; I asked a man to take me to Ali's house and Louis offered to look at the truck. It was three miles and the peasant with me showed increasing reluctance to continue; his speed was governed by my attitude towards him, for if I smiled, he stopped immediately. Even on Ameri's land this respect for brutality existed; no amount of kindness and gentleness would have goaded that man into action, especially for the part of the walk which was through the village, for there his inversions increased. Only with the appearance of a hardhearted and callous expression on my face did the disagreeable one leave his; and when I addressed him in the same words as the garage foreman had used to me he walked quite amicably by my side. He respected me in inverse proportion to the respect that was due; but on that day it did not matter; for he was treated with little consideration and, however sweet his temperament had been, he would not have received much more Certainly, absolute tyranny and despotism have had plenty of followers in the past.

At Ali's house his wife told us that he had gone to work for me; this tale was becoming familiar and was brushed aside firmly. She then said that he had gone to work in the fields and finally said that he was ill, but had left the house. She was a fat woman with bare muddy feet, a spotty face and hair which hung down in clotted ringlets. My guide informed me proudly that his wife was more beautiful.

For quite a time he and I stood on the top of Ali's house and shouted. This was the customary procedure for finding somebody, as most men worked within sight or hearing distance of their home; but Ali did not come. We returned to the rooms to discover that he had not arrived there either. Ameri's bailiff offered to find him before the next day; I thanked him for his offer and said that half an hour would be better. Louis had meanwhile removed the sand from the starter and Ali appeared after an hour.

He was full of apologies; he said that he had seen me at his house and was too ill to come and speak; in short, he had been sleeping off some opium, as was shown by his sudden recovery and by the effusiveness of his apologies. No man is ever so apologetic about some attack of genuine sickness; he admitted the fact and then implored me not to tell Ameri. As his bailiff undoubtedly knew the cause for his lateness, the story would reach Ameri's ears whether I told him or not, but Ali seemed relieved that he would not hear it from me. Together we drove along the qanats; his face leered over the top of the shafts that I descended and mine when he went down. In the short wells we used a primitive rope ladder made from nylon rope; if such a ladder 300 feet long had been brought from England, then all difficulties of descent into the qanat would have been negligible; also, it would have saved considerable time which was otherwise expended in walking up and down the channels. In the deeper wells Ali went down on the end of a normal rope for, unfortunately, the muqannis were not there and it was impossible for one man to manipulate the wheel: thus he had to climb up and down with the rope supporting him whenever he fell. He twisted it around my waist before lowering himself into the shaft, after he had made certain that my feet were suitably entrenched to prevent me being dragged helplessly towards the hole when the pull came.

He went down in the customary manner, lodging his bare feet in the recesses on the side; I let the rope out slowly as he pulled on it. He did fall off once or twice in the wider parts of the wells, but as he was never allowed excess of rope, he did not fall far. The wells were only ninety feet deep and ordinary conversation was possible. He collected the nets and their contents and told me to get into position. Save for the vigorous tug he always gave to test whether I was in my place and reliably secure, he never caused the rope to tighten on the way up: it was easier to see the suitable niches as you climbed past them. All Ameri's wells had three nars, the oval-shaped bricks used normally for support in the channels, at the top; this procedure lengthened the life of the well and gave them a neat, instead of a yawning appearance. Wells which were untended in any way reached a stage by which the ant-lion might have devised its conical trap; for both were as fatal once the sliding descent into them had begun. Ameri's wells, being walled in this way, removed the fear of a descent in which the only hope lay in being able to straddle the mouth until somebody pulled you away. The ant which slips into the trap is less fortunate, for the ant-lion offers no way out. Dropping ants into these holes is one of the main diversions of the boys looking after the sheep; with a strong ant the fight lasts for just as long as that between two evenly matched scorpions.

We drove back slowly along the fifteen miles to Negar, for it was a beautiful evening. It moved Ali into eloquence; he recounted the virtues of opium, for he had discovered that I didn't smoke it; and then, when he learnt that I was not married, he entered upon a lengthy appraisal of that way of life; the clotted hair of his wife leapt into my thoughts and then was hurriedly dismissed. Ali continued his eulogy, repeating the phrases over to himself with much shaking of his head. He put his feet out of the window, settled back in the seat and I heard for the first time a Persian say how good it was to live. He became thoroughly absorbed in himself and then broke into song. This was a pity, for their idea of singing is not sweet to our ears; but it was a song and, settling back in my seat, I joined in with a collection of sea shanties: somehow they seemed appropriate to the occasion and in that unmelodious manner we drove once more into Negar. Ali climbed out, put on his shirt without tucking it into his trousers and stuck each foot into its heel-trodden shoe: clothes are rarely worn otherwise. We had quickly adapted ourselves to this practice, as well as to that of wearing pyjama trousers below the shirt: for all those whose work does not require strong garments this was the daily wear and it formed a cool combination. If an occasion had arisen which required smarter clothes, then better clothes were put on as well; the coolness had been retained and the smartness had been added: even the Mahun Bakhshdar's immaculate suit had pyjama trousers protruding at the bottom. The shoes which are worn must have the backs trodden down, so that you can step out of them immediately you step onto the carpet, whether it be yours or someone elses. Naturally, there are variations in this theme according to the trades; those who dig always have their right trouser leg rolled up to the thigh. It is with this foot that they tread the spade into the ground and then step back, perfectly in time with all the others in the row, to lift the earth from its position: the unison of these digging teams is very exact; for the soil is lifted more easily if their efforts are united. Ali had put on the shirt of a muqanni, which had no sleeves to be torn, and after removing both shoes to shake out the stones, he shook hands with me and disappeared up the street.

The next day was our last in Negar. Louis sat transferring his dried plants from thick drying paper to the thinner sheets in which they would travel back to England. I sat staring into dishes of mud and withdrawing whatever moved to put it into a tube of formalin: our stay in the villages was quietly coming to an end, for in two days we had to leave Kirman. It was in the evening of the day when I pressed a cork into a full tube of formalin to make it squirt up into my eyes. I straightway went out towards the stream, but my eyes refused to open: Louis came and took me to it. Below the water a head appeared; its eyes blinked as the formalin was washed from them, the fishes pulled at the strands of hair and bumped into the face. After two months of working with those fish, I found myself prostrate before the water in which they lived. It was very fitting that that last association with a qanat stream should be, not with its small impurities, but with an appreciation of the qualities of clear running water. How apt is the name of the flowing jewels; how very right that a stream of water should be religiously believed to be the essence of purity and the acme of cleanliness; how natural that the purification of the spirit should be by water and that the first baptisms were in the stream which flowed through the wilderness of Judaea, with the waters of Jordan. I removed my head and the fish swam away; but the flow of the stream continued, swiftly and relentlessly: as long as it does so it will be revered by men.

In the morning Ameri was not in the house when the time came for us to leave; I wrote him a long note of thanks in indifferent French and gave it to his bailiff. Just before the final departure from Jupar the other three had been beset by various people for letters of appreciation; individuals like the Kadkhoda wished to have some tangible proof of the indebtedness towards him for his kindness. Ahmed translated the flowery phrases into Persian, and underneath Philip wrote his own version of their behaviour in English; the notes will be treasured as valuable references and the English part will be prized just as highly by those it condemns as by those it does not. The peasants who would have received the warmest notes did not turn up to the ceremony.

We had not been so long in Negar and were not asked for any letters. But as the loading of the truck had taken some time a lot of people wandered up to watch us go; these groups gathered always when anything was happening or when anything was about to happen. Unfortunately, the petrol was only checked at the last minute and there was not enough: Ameri had told me before that petrol could be bought in Negar, but his bailiff began saying that there was none for thirty miles. A small boy of about seven was standing next to him and I then asked this boy; he said that there was and immediately went off to get a can. It wasn't that the bailiff had any particular malevolence towards Louis or me; he just never stirred himself into thinking of anyone else. That he was not in the habit of doing so was exemplified by his behaviour when I was ill; he was my acting host and became disturbed when his servants told him that I had refused food all day. So in the evening, when I was asleep, he thrust a hurricane lamp near my face to wake me up; he told me that it was necessary to eat and in spite of my protestations, he bellowed out for some food to be brought: it came and was placed by my side. He stayed there and waited for it to be eaten, reminding me every now and then that that was what I should do: there are times in everyone's life when food cannot be eaten but this did not strike him. After my stubbornness had been sufficiently displayed, he shouted again, for the food to be taken away, before leaving me to myself. Not that night but later on I realised that the act had been prompted by kindness.

A man bought the petrol and we said our goodbyes. From the crowd we selected those who had been kind to us or who had helped us in any way and thanked them; perhaps they had just nodded to us when we passed them in the mornings or had had a chat about the buz majjeh. Whatever it was, we shook their hands, with those more especial acquaintances being greeted effusively. In this way we felt we were showing our honest opinion of those we had met in the village. The formal hand-shake is of little worth but when your hand is not shaken it increases in value. Our judgement was effected upon the crowd: 'Two men were working in a field, the one was taken and the other left'.

We drove round the courtyard amongst the peasants and out of the gate; the dust rose up and hid them from us. But after the corner we saw them again, just a line of Persian peasants, some tall and some short, some with hats and some without, and all looking very much the same. They had blended together so quickly that the ones we had liked were no different from the others; the young were the same as the toothless and only the grey suit of the bailiff marked him out. They were rendered obscure and too similar: we waved before reaching the turning but not all of them waved back.

CHAPTER X

Kirman to the Persian Frontier

WHEN we reached Kirman Louis deposited me at the Consulate and then went to fetch Eric and Ahmed from the Kuh-i-Badimu. I went to see Philip at the hospital and discovered he had every intention of coming back with us in spite of the emetine injections. I also arranged with Shaikh-al-Islami for two camels to be ready at sunrise, as we wished to make a final bid with those animals; for in England we had been asked to investigate the effectiveness of Kwells pills against the motion sickness occasionally experienced when riding camels. This request was the result of an enquiring letter sent to the makers of the pills when we heard of the camel sickness. Our offer of research had been immediately accepted: £25 and 164 pills had come by return of post. We had used camels before at Kirman in connection with the pills and, with and without the pills inside us, we had ridden on them, but none of us had ever felt any inclination to be sick. This was annoying and due to three reasons: firstly, the Kirman camels never ran; it was only with difficulty that they could be goaded into that swaying motion, the most potent as regards motion sickness. Secondly, the truck had rendered us quite immune to any internal queasiness. Thirdly, the type of saddle and the peculiarities of the camels never let us consider other possible discomforts; they formed a sufficiency. The inconsequential results obtained were to be supplemented by a film on the subject: for that reason the two were chartered for sunrise.

Louis, Eric and Ahmed returned in the evening. The stay in the area had been fruitful and the map had been made. Due to a casual remark by Eric that England had not enough coal for her needs, it was assumed by all up there to be an explanation of his visit to

that place; not only the oil, but the coal of Persia was to be removed. This belief did not hinder Eric at all, in fact it helped; for
the miners regarded their industry more boastfully; they watched
the short line of donkeys taking down the day's excavations in a
happier mood, for the Englishmen had come to look at their mine.
Thus he was shown over any part of it whenever he so desired.
His only complaint was the cold; the recent windy weather which
had caused cool breezes 2,000 feet lower down in Negar had
been extremely cold in the hills. Those in Tehran who had
assured us of the torpid and soul-destroying heat of Kirman could
never have been there; never was the heat unpleasant, as it had
been, for instance, in Mesopotamia. With such a dry atmosphere,
a temperature of 90°F. does not constitute a menace to the body
or to the soul. Nevertheless, it was strange that Eric should have
longed for gloves at midday near the end of August in southern
Persia.

The Governor General had, during the time Louis and I were
in Negar, sent a message to the Consulate inviting us all to dinner.
Eric happened to return to Kirman on that day and found the
invitation: Philip was in hospital, we were too far away and it was
up to him to go. Finding some presentable clothes out of those
we had all left in the rooms, he went to the Governor's residence.
There, in the great luxury which might be expected to exist in
such a place on such an occasion, did Eric fill himself with food;
he is not one whose appetite would be diminished by nothing
more than a change in surroundings. Before the meal began, he
remembered to extend his sympathies towards the Governor
concerning the murder of his brother by tribesmen. This brought
much laughter from the Governor and then, as the example had
been given, from everyone else. It was in this vein that the meal
was eaten by the Governor, by Eric and by the other guests of
the evening.

The same jocular air was in us all on the morning of the camel
film. The two animals had, after their arrival, been dispatched to a
suitably barren piece of desert on the Baghin road. Shaikh-al-
Islami gave us breakfast and then we all drove out together to meet
the camels. That they were not there did not disturb us greatly,
for we had been in Persia long enough and the drive continued

into the desert until we spotted a herd. Their sleeping attendant was woken up and informed that his herd was to be used for a couple of hours. He consented and we worked out the general plan of the film; fashioned on the advertisement style there should be initial gaiety transformed quickly into deep gloom and then, miraculously, in this case by the pills, into lasting happiness.

The first shot was to be of the expedition leaving camp. But scarce had Louis got his legs astride a camel before it reared up and trotted him 400 yards away, grazed a little and then sat down: obviously my job with the camera was going to require boundless agility and exceptional foresight. Shots were taken of Eric getting on a camel merely by starting the film long before he was within reach of it; as the animal's distaste for a rider was exactly similar, the lengthy shot of the camel doing nothing ended shortly after Eric's arrival into the viewfinder; for he and the camel rapidly left the area. Louis returned wearily and was put on another camel; and while he and Eric were paced restlessly around, I was able to take them at long intervals as they passed by me. At first Louis and Eric had gleeful faces, but this happy phase soon changed into one of distress; with gesticulations of despair and clutchings at their heaving stomachs the fact was forcibly expressed that they were becoming ill; in this woebegone state they fell off their camels and groped their way along the ground in a very dilapidated manner. Their plight was horrible to see, as was well reflected in the stricken expression on the face of the camels' attendant: one fumbled in the air with a butterfly net before total exasperation overcame him; the other, weighed down by a geological hammer, was more speedily subdued.

The attendant was then made to produce a packet of pills from the middle of his garments and to offer it to the recumbent scientists. Because of his complete incomprehension of all that was occurring he did it with a supreme look of bewonderment on his face; this alone would have revived the two, but they accepted the pills, rose up with excessive agility and got onto their camels. With the net swishing in the air and the hammer being waved expectantly, they trotted away into the middle distance. The film was over and Shaikh-al-Islami drove us back into Kirman.

After lunch we visited the bazaar; for Louis and I had long

intended to buy a cheap tribal carpet. I also wanted a pair of shoes; the present pair had no soles and the pedals in the truck became overwarm for comfort. The poverty of the Kirman bazaar meant that no carpet sellers had large stocks; few of them had as many as five carpets, although carpet selling was their trade. With memories hampered by the continual shouting, the copper beating, the twisting crowds and the sudden observations of dung piles as yet untrampled, we found it hard to compare the carpet being exhibited at our feet with those we had already seen. If we expressed an interest in any which pleased us, the seller was content to put it on his shoulder and pit it against the best which another could produce; once interest had been expressed the vendors doggedly pursued us, although later comparisons might have discounted the possibility of any sale of their carpets. However, they continued and the colours of the carpets mingled with the colours carried by others, the skeins of dyed wool, the bright clothes and the blood-red sides of beef. There was no difficulty in finding further carpet shops; for not only were the carpets laid out, but their owners had been tugging at your sleeve for quite some time before you reached the shops.

Finally, all the chosen carpets were laid out in a quiet back-water of the bazaar and there the decision was made. We paid, the other carpets were carried away and Louis took our bundle out to the truck. I told him I would walk back and went off to buy a pair of shoes. Although the normal Persian shoes were made of rubber soles with pliable canvas tops and their makers were most enthusiastic to sell, there was not a single pair in the whole bazaar which could be wedged onto my feet with any pretence at comfort. Some small boys had speeded up the discovery of this fact by being so elated at the first man's attempts to crush my foot into a shoe that they sped around the whole bazaar to inform all makers to bring their largest pair to the Englishman. But the arrival of each one with a retinue of small boys only brought the same frustration and the same hoots of childish delight. It was all to no avail and my sandals flapped uselessly as I walked out from the bazaar and into the sunlight.

It was on the way back to the Consulate that the soldier shouted at me. He was particularly vindictive in his manner, far more so than those who said we were Russian spies invading their land, and yet he was using none of the catch-phrases which are used to describe the western way of life by those who disagree with it. This time it was different and some other name which he was calling me, something independent of the political war associated with communism and connected not even with the Oil Company, for none of those words were there. It must, therefore, be a name which we had brought upon ourselves, some judgement of our existence, for it had not been used during the first week when we had been living in Kirman: that we never heard it initially and it was being used at the end of our stay made the opinion which it expressed more valuable. Opinions of individuals occurring through prejudice, either first hand or not, towards all the people of a country are not justifiable; any individual criticized for what he has done should not suffer through preformed convictions of his guilt. We had not received instantaneous criticisms; instead they had branded us as spies in order to give us a nationality and a reason; there was no condemnation of ourselves in that action of theirs: it was just clarification. The judgement inflicted by the soldier and by all the others who so rapidly agreed and took up the refrain occurred after observations of our behaviour: it was therefore worthy of attention.

That it was a condemnation was obvious. That the name was coined by the soldier and agreed upon by the others was equally so; but then so was the fact that only a very few of those people, for I never saw any faces which I recognized, could have had dealings with us personally. Some of the villagers might have come into the town and a few of the soldiers may have been with us; but apart from them and some scattered shop-keepers the rest relied for their opinions upon what they had seen and what they had heard.

The seeing probably came first; a strange light-grey lorry would inevitably be observed by every man in the street. A typical onlooker may have seen it on the day that it had entered Kirman; the four fair-skinned people sitting in and on it would certainly be noticed by him. On future occasions he may have seen them buying food and petrol or going into the bazaar or visiting Photo Saam; but for the most part, when he saw them they were driving through and in their truck; they occasionally went by foot and once in an army vehicle, although usually they sat in the Bedford. There was nothing more he could have seen and little cause for guilt existed in what he had observed; yet as his condemnation was so emphatic it must have been based on something which he had heard.

What story he had been told must have come from the villages; for it was in them that we had lived for all but a week, and even in that first week it had been the villages which had occupied our attention. That tales of our activities should have emanated from the villages was most natural and very reasonable; it is those occurrences which are not regular which provide conversation and we never for a moment doubted that our activities did not conform to the general plan. But which of our affairs, which of those occupations had been detrimental to our good names?

The villagers had not given us any hint as to our misdeeds or to our differences which were disliked by them. While we never laughed at their religion we were not Moslems, and the jokes they made at its expense convinced us that they had few cares about our possible beliefs. They did not worry that we were English; occasionally they would criticize the Oil Company but this did not impinge upon us; it had merely provided conversation and then, as we put forward the Company's viewpoint, discussion. That foreigners had come to live in their village was not begrudged by those of the village. These factors didn't give the soldier reason to shout, but that did not mean that he had none; of course he had reason, he had plenty of it; he could pick upon hundreds of incidents in our lives in the country and disagree with them. That was his land and not ours; he had a perfect right to criticize those who came to stay in it. Why should we inspect the district? Why should we be allowed to examine everything, ask questions and take stock of all which was theirs? With the authorities backing us the peasant could be punished because he did not conform to our wishes; why should this be so? We were not helping the country in any way; we had just decided to go to a part of it irrespective of whether we were wanted or not. Why were the feelings of the people not considered? On such accounts the soldier had reason.

Events in the villages could have given cause. Our refusal to tend the sick. The deference shown to us by the officials. The good treatment we received from the Governor. Our habit of giving money for animals; thereby, as with snakes, encouraging dangerous foolhardiness in the children which resulted, for instance, in a nasty scorpion sting; the giving of money to children could in itself be criticized. Our disregard for their day of rest. The indifference with which we passed by the open hands of beggars when, if we gave it away for insects, we had money and to spare. The casual way in which we wandered over the land with Louis hacking up plants and Philip digging holes. Still greater cause could arise from those occasions when our patience had been whittled away and resulted in a caustic attitude towards the people who were nearby. Some form of jealousy could result when the landlords gave us food which had been grown by the peasant and was only being given to us so that we would speak well of that landlord. Our blunt manners towards those we disliked could provide resentment: in fact any or all of these things; but the warm handshakes of the villagers and their huge wide smiles made us believe that they had waived over such deficiences. However, even the hairy fist of Esau could not squeeze out from us our contentions that very many errors had been committed that gave the soldier reason, should he choose to look for it.

There was yet another possibility. In a village as poor as Jupar which had experienced starvation due to the war and was very likely to suffer it again quite soon, were we not a cause for discontent? The Russian and English armies that occupied Persia after the dethronement of the Reza Shah are blamed for the shortage of corn which caused the starvation; without that corn they had died. The embitterment, and it exists, could be enhanced on the discovery that money had been spent, not on repairing the damaged economy of Persia, but on sending four people to look at the plants and animals which lived there, an expedition to them of fleeting value, although the geographical report will be useful to their developmental planners. There are various subsidiary points associated with this main one: our truck, cheap and second hand, looked most royal beside any others which entered the village; our equipment, to a man who had nothing of his own, looked valuable and important; obviously it had come from a place more opulent than that in which they lived. When one of them looked wistfully at our things, like the old man with the ice-axe, we, and then he, realised the extent of his poverty. Such enlightenment does not increase the happiness of the one who is poor: any possibility that sorrow was being increased gave the soldier the greatest reason of all.

When I turned down the side street to the Consulate and left the crowd behind, I tried to think of ways in which it could have been avoided. Had we been simple tourists they would have accepted us as such; inhabitants may consider a tourist an odd and laughable creature, but they do not have any deep hatred for him. But we had not and only by our persistence in studying what had been planned in Oxford did we come to know anything about the people and the lives they lived; we had disturbed them more than does a tourist, but he learns little about a land. This secondary occupation had the effect of increasing our persistence with the first, for the more we pursued it the more we discovered about them: the greater our persistence the more the soldier could shout, but the greater was our knowledge of the intricate ways of their lives: for that, and I turned into the Consulate, he could hurl whatsoever epithets he chose.

Considering that everything had to be packed up in readiness for our departure on the following morning, our inactivity on the evening of that day was astounding. Eric idly touched up his Kuh-i-Badimu map; Louis amused himself with lengthy calculations about our expenditure and I tried to make one pair of shoes out of the two defective pairs: no one mentioned the packing, for no one wished to declare the expedition over. When darkness came, we stirred ourselves to cook a meal, and then drove round to fetch Philip from the hospital. He was ready and, as Peter Wild was away, we did not linger there; for the last time we drove, slowly and thunderously along the narrow high-walled streets which led us from the hospital out into the broad street, and from there to the roundabout and the Consulate. Driving from one side to the other to avoid the ditches and piles of dung we observed once more the harsh night scene. The dazzling brightness of the lamps, the loud tinny wirelesses, the cracked warning cries of those with heavy loads, the eternal hammering of metal and the screechings of the children all combined to give that harshness. The enveloping softness of a Persian night did not exist in such a street; the shadows cast were jagged and the stars were sharp points of light. It was a strident scene, grating and shrill, with an edge to it like that of bitterness. It had changed, as do the eyes of a cat, when the day passed into the night.

After Shaikh-al-Islami had told us that the soldier in the street had been ridiculing those habits of ours of which we were not ashamed, the wearing of beards and shorts and our pursuit of biology, I was relieved that our defaults were apparently undiscovered. He had jibed, not at the mistakes we had committed in Jupar or in Mahun, but at the greater mistake of going to those places. The sole error in coming to Kirman was that we had exhibited our folly in not staying in Tehran, in the greatest city of their land; instead, we had come to a hotter and less modern town and then, to crown it with the most laughable factor of all, we had gone to work in the villages. Eric on his hills, Philip in his holes, Louis by the plants, and I in the qanats, all living with the villagers, working with them and laughing with them. To the soldier and those who accompanied him it was right that our laughter should be thrown back at us and that we should be told of our gross stupidity.

When we learnt of his reasons the business of packing began and at once. There was no longer the procrastination, the reluctance to put an end to our stay, the refusal to be interested in the journey home, as the expedition had already ended: for Louis and me the line of men at Negar, and for Eric the small group in the Kuh-i-Badimu had been the witnesses of its finish. It was in the villages that we had lived and when they were left behind the journey had already begun: Kirman had been the first stopping place and was then treated, as are all such places at the beginning of a trip, with much impatience.

Presented by the Northcrofts in Tehran as a remedy for all ills, a bottle of whisky had remained untouched; for there never came a time when all four of us were simultaneously smitten and the healthy ones could not bear the thought of it being poured down a throat rendered less sensitive by the sickness: envy had weighed heavily upon the cork. With a sudden and mutual agreement all envious thoughts were banished, the cork popped out and any problem concerning the contents was rapidly dismissed.

For many hours of that night, while Philip slept, we three joyously packed the boxes; his sleep was deep but it needed to be as the occasion was surprisingly light-hearted. For the sake of the Customs officials lists of the boxes' contents had to be made; so while two of us packed the other one wrote: there was luckily not to be the same trouble on the outward journey, for most of the boxes were to be sent home by Oil Company tanker, a lessening in our difficulties for which we were most grateful. Little sympathy was extended to the men of the Customs; for we cared not how things were packed, save that nothing should be left behind or should break: how would he know that 'Clothes and geological specimens' should lead him to a shirt full of coal? On that night we were not greatly concerned; for none of us would be there to argue about any points which might arise due to some other man's more finicky attention to detail. Why should not Miner's helmets, Dettol and braces go under the heading of Safety equipment? It was good, however, that the job was finished fairly quickly; for already the box labelled 'Fossils' had been misused by the addition of a Persian stone cooking pot, two stuffed jerboas and a pair of Eric's socks: we were surprised that our apparently varied equipment could be so shortly and easily classified. The lids were screwed on, the bottle was finished and, after a half-hearted search for another, which at that time was believed to exist, we went to sleep.

It took a long time to load the truck. The boxes had to be placed so that the two back springs received equal weight; this had not been done at Oxford and the subsequent unevenness was believed to have weakened the spring which had later broken. The quantity to be taken back was far greater than that with which we had arrived and nothing had been left behind except the wire netting. We would not be needing it again and, in spite of the fact that the loose sand gave each member of the Jupar bus-load a pleasant interlude to every journey, the Kadkhoda, who owned the bus, considered it a waste of the chauffeur's time and bought the netting from us. He was terribly proud of it and tied the two rolls on to the headlamps; they gave the bus a quaint, quixotic appearance.

Philip's weakness prevented him from performing any task; a place was made for him in the back of the truck where the side bars would prevent him from falling off it and he was wedged in there. Ahmed arrived with every pocket full of nuts; they had been presented by his relatives, as is the custom for anyone going on a journey; a bag of nuts thrust with a handshake makes a far more lasting and sensible farewell. The departure from the Consulate was unceremonious, for the truck was missing badly, stalled several times and finally pulled us out through the gate: the spluttering engine gave us little faith in the reality of our departure and Shaikh-al-Islami, who had always been most kind to us, received but the briefest of farewells.

Up in the town we bought petrol and oil and got a man to clean all the plugs. Then at noon on that day, with greater confidence, with Ahmed spitting nut shells over the side and with five out of the six cylinders firing, we drove out of the town of Kirman.

We passed the night forty miles short of Yezd. The day had not been eventful; after watching all the familiar Kirman landscape go by, we had given our attention to Ahmed's nuts. At Rafsinjan this supply had been replenished by pistachio nuts and pomegranates; both require much spitting and in this fashion the journey had continued. In the evening the sun set straight ahead and was to set in front of us very many more times before the trip had ended, always as a dancing, dazzling ball and blinding to the eyes until it courteously dropped behind the land. It was a reminder that the east was being left behind us and the road led away to the west.

Due to the misfiring of the cylinders, the petrol consumption of the engine increased excessively and the two tanks became dry exactly ten miles from Yezd. The town lay spread out before us, perfectly visible and enticingly near, but it would have taken someone a depressingly long time to fetch a can from it. Instead, we all sat disconsolately beside the truck and waited for something to happen; luckily only an hour had passed when a car came along. Tubes were placed in his tank and the necessary mugfuls extracted;

much bonhomie exuded from all of us and more than made up for any deficiency of his own; but our gratefulness was naturally bountiful and he received twice as much money as the precious liquid had cost him; for when you have none and are ten miles from a town, the value of it increases with the hours. Of course the stoppage should not have happened, but the two tanks had taken us seventy miles less than the usual distance and we excused ourselves on that account.

But that was not the only reason for the shortage. We were doing something which, contrary to the activities of the previous weeks, we had done already. The drive from Tehran to Kirman had not presented any difficulties and there seemed no reason why there should be any on the return journey. The thing had been achieved once and could be done again; but, as a pilot's second solo trip is always more dangerous than the first, we did not concern ourselves greatly and succeeded in doing what only stupidity will allow, namely running out of petrol. Even after the Yezd incident, when we were filling up again at Nain later on the same day, we omitted to look at the oil level: immediately after leaving the town the pressure gauge was noticed to be low, but we continued; for it was only eighty miles to Isfahan and the distance we considered to be paltry. Now there was a hill about thirty miles long just past Nain and the continual upward slope, combined with the lack of oil, made the engine boil and long before the top was in sight. Only the fear of losing all the water made us turn back for the necessary gallon of oil. Such arrogant contempt for the lengthy distances between filling stations was proving itself fatuous, even in our indifferent selves: only an overwhelming abundance of similar errors began to deflate the swollen confidence.

The pass was then ascended without difficulty and the engine never boiled. Although many warnings on the subject had been issued, we had not, on all the occasions when there was enough oil, been troubled by a boiling engine. They had advised us that a tin of water carried near the radiator would, by the connection of a suitable pipe, condense and collect all the water which had exuded as steam; in this way less water would be lost. We didn't fix such an arrangement on the front of the engine; for we wished first to have proof of its necessity, but the steam only spurted out when there was a following wind. The water, however, invariably boiled when the engine was switched off; this could be prevented by letting it idle for a few minutes before stopping it. But the business of boiling did not constitute a problem and was yet another peril which existed only in the minds of those who build bridges before they, or the people they are influencing, know whether the river has ever existed.

Many weeks previously, it had been decided that at least one day should be spent in Isfahan, but the length of this day had been imperilled by our folly with the oil. There was little of the day-time left when we reached the top of the pass and, as our intention had been to spend the night in the garden of the Oil company's representative, it would not do to descend on him at too late an hour. Philip was agitating that we ate a meal and prepared for the night while there was still day-light; the rest of us were for proceeding to Isfahan and fast, over the down-hill stretch of 45 miles which still lay before us. I happened to be driving and, suddenly becoming possessed, drove the truck along at a pace which she had never experienced before. Previously, caution had existed concerning harsh wear on the tyres and on the engine, but on that evening it was left behind to mix with the flailing mass of sand in our wake. Sheep scattered off the road, donkeys were hastily pulled to the side; the mounting enjoyment only increased the speed. Down through the villages, down into the plain and the final stretch of straight road which led to the town. Just once did we meet anything; on hurtling blindly into a village, we were suddenly confronted by a large crowd of Persians, donkeys and goats all mingling round a bus. There was only one side of it to which we could go and both Persians and animals realised it in the same moment: a space cleared miraculously and through it we flashed before careering on to Isfahan.

It was just dark when we reached the town. The lights were on, the people were all in the streets and Ahmed stood up to receive the continual directions to the Oil Company house. Our faces were warm from the wind which had so recently been rushing past us and made us feel happily aloof from all those who had so obviously not been doing the same thing.

The A.I.O.C. man offered us a piece of his garden and arranged for the truck to be overhauled at the Company's garage; we unloaded the bedding and it was taken round there. He then suggested a drink, adding that most English of all provisos: 'Perhaps you would like to wash your hands first'. The five of us disappeared into the bathroom and, as this was the first wash basin with hot water (not that we had seen any with cold water) that we had been privileged to see for more than two months, it was used diligently. All other hot water had either been made into tea or used to cook the rice: there had never been any question of using the stuff for washing. Unfortunately, just as much time had to be spent cleaning the basin with its surrounds afterwards and it was over an hour before we five finally rejoined the solitary imbiber who was our host.

For all the next day Louis, Eric and I inspected Isfahan. Philip started with us, but had retired after a short while. From the roof of Shah Abbas's palace, an uninspiring building in itself, can be seen the whole roof-top pattern of the town. Interspersed, and mainly congregated near to the palace, are the mosques; these buildings vary not so much in their style as in their size and in the money which has been spent on them. Closer examination reveals that the stones or marble slabs which form the base, and the blue and white tiles above them, are not neatly put in place; but the utmost ingenuity and skill is displayed in the squinches, the corner angles, where all the various curves resultant upon the dome and its attendant shapes are brought down to form the single right-angle of the two walls which are the base of that corner.

Inside the palace there is little of note. The remains of the paintings that once covered the walls can still be seen, but the descendants of Shah Abbas have done their best to remove them. They are said to have been made by a group of Italians brought over for the purpose, but they are not inspiring. The rooms themselves were unusually vague in their shape: they could either be considered as small and surrounded by many inter-connecting passages, or as being large, with many thick pillars about the centre; it depends whether you prefer the thought of a room surrounded by pillars or passages. In one room the walls were lined with small, almost complete, plywood boxes; their function had been the retention of the harsh discords of eastern music so that its wavering character should be greatly increased. In this manner such tempo as there had been was lost and music of a dying nature was produced long after the musicians had relaxed.

It was after eating a doubtful piece of meat in a presentable café that we went into the bazaar. Now the Kirman bazaar, although long and rambling, was a squalid affair. Very little of any value was being produced; car tyres were made into shoes, petrol cans into water jugs, and sugar into sugar lumps: things had not been made so much as changed into something else. Isfahan was different. In the first place, the covered streets were wider and higher; there were large well-lit courtyards at the junctions of the streets and the shops were more spacious. The copper and silver sections were producing some excellent work, graceful jugs with long slender spouts and large trays with intricate design. The sale of Kirman carpets had not merited a definite section, but in Isfahan there were many displays of them and all along one street. Kirman muddled everything up too much. There is no enjoyment in examining a carpet if a man is making camel bells in the next shop; there is even less in eating sweet cakes if the neighbour deals in charcoal. Numerous coffee houses existed at Isfahan which was, as we remarked each time on entering, a great improvement.

For six hours we were in that place. Louis bought a hat, I found a pair of shoes and Eric spent an insane half-hour testing the tone of every camel bell the largest dealer possessed. Otherwise we just watched, except for the time spent eating a meal of dates and coffee and then another of macaroons and coffee. It was after the macaroons that we felt like a bit of fresh air; so choosing the weakest looking droshky horse in sight we had a pleasant and unhurried drive back to our home.

As Philip had taken a lot of film of various incidents on our outward journey, we decided to finish the film off for him. Most earlier shootings had been of the truck hurrying by on its way to Kirman; such carefree success could not be allowed to exist throughout its sequence. Therefore, somewhere near Yezd, shots had been taken of breakdowns, while the poor truck was made to jerk to a halt. With Eric and Louis being principal actors and unenlightened mechanics, the truck was cruelly inspected and finally abandoned. The droshky, of course, provided the last shot of all.

On the next evening we arrived in Tehran. Because of an abundance of guests, the Northcrofts were not able to provide accommodation, and we descended instead upon David Bivar, the third secretary of the Embassy, whose house was in its grounds, and who had kindly invited us to stay. There existed a certain amount of exuberance within us upon arriving in Tehran, but in none of us had any survived by the end of the first day. The factors concerned were numerous.

Firstly, our Yugoslavian visas had not come through. Cheaper and quicker, the way back through Turkey, Greece and Yugoslavia had attracted us. During our previous time in Tehran, I had visited their Embassy dressed in a white cotton suit of David's and accompanied by him; in spite of the impression we felt we must have made, the visas had not arrived. This time, without any resplendent clothing, we had another interview with them: it resulted in their sending a telegram and admitting that two to three months was not an unreasonable length of time for a visa. Secondly, the truck had to undergo a major repair and have all the valves reground; this was going to take five days. Then cash calculations were upset, for neither David nor his friend, having previously arranged to travel back to England with us for a small fee, were coming, for they had been surprised by a free travel permit from the Foreign Office. Then, in the middle of the day, I became ill and felt that the sickness was not a temporary one; at the same time, the normal user of the rooms we were inhabiting wished to return there from his more wayward summer residence, as he had acquired amoebic dysentery. Also, Eric heard that his mother was seriously ill. And finally, just before it became dark, the buz majjeh escaped into the thick shrubbery of the Embassy gardens.

Naturally our stay in Tehran could not be a long one and this moulded these events into shapes more difficult to handle. If the Yugoslavian visa was going to arrive, then we would wait for it; if not, then we would have to catch the *Esperia*, the only convenient boat. It left Beirut twelve days later and it was unfortunate that places for the deck class could not be booked in Tehran. Additional uncertainty was on account of sickness: Philip was improving, I was becoming worse; Louis for the time being was stable and fit; this situation was extremely liable to alter. Only Eric simplified matters by deciding to fly home.

One way of encouraging a sickness to mature is to pretend that it does not exist. While the others visited the Banks, Agencies and Government departments in the town, I procured from the Embassy workshop, one cage to hold three snakes and another, rather optimistically, to hold a buz majjeh. After spending some time there and then an hour filling up visa forms, I weakened, found myself being sick, and went back to bed. The yellow colour of jaundice was beginning to appear.

Days passed. Eric left by air with the three snakes: apparently they were treated with hostile suspicion by the Customs and amiable kindness by the hostess before their safe arrival in England. Philip and Louis continued with the formalities and, for this was Tehran, went to the parties in the evening. The *pièce* was a gigantic wedding reception given by the Northcrofts. We were invited; for the blind fish expedition which couldn't get away was by then well known and a part of the life of that town. Their large floodlit garden provided space for the guests, who were confronted with kabobs frying on the lawn, with carpets on all paths and all the other adornments that would be produced for a Tehran wedding feast. One of the tortoises from Jupar was given as our present: on its back had been painted the Oil Company crest, for the bridegroom was one of its employees. This animal achieved distinction by being photographed with Mr. Northcroft and the other dignitaries of the Company; the negative of the photo was somehow obtained and then printed by the Nationalist press, but the tortoise had been obliterated. It showed, therefore, the Company's officials being inexplicably hearty and grouped around the expostulating hands of Mr. Northcroft. However, on the evening it was a success.

I did not attend but remained in bed. The others had moved out of the house and I alone remained; the man with the dysentery returned and occupied the next room. Most of my hours were spent sitting in the lavatory; for the journey there was always a dizzy affair and I saw little point in going back and forth so frequently to my room; so I stayed and looked out of the window to watch the Tehran traffic. While we had been in Kirman, a law was passed stating that no horns should be used in the capital; this resulted in so many crashes that even the Tehranis felt concern. Pedestrians, accustomed to crossing streets when no horn was blowing, suffered greatly. Car drivers, who had always used their klaxon to clear traffic out of the way, were thwarted and crashed. All offenders were mercilessly pounced upon by the police and fined £1. The energy of the police was encouraged by the stipulation that no receipt had to be given to the one who had made the noise and paid the money. After the initial galaxy of crashes, the stream of traffic was frightened to a slower pace: all except the klaxon sellers approved, for the town had become a quieter and a safer place.

There was another lavatory and from there I looked out onto the Embassy grounds. They were large and pleasant, with high trees, thick shrubs and a sleepy atmosphere; there were houses and a swimming pool hidden behind the trees, but for the most part it was a leafy place and full of shade. As with all the other Embassies, the grounds are a spot where, by diplomatic privilege, the police cannot pursue you. This concession had once been grossly utilized by eighty Persians who, wanted by the police for some petty infringement, walked into the gardens and encamped themselves upon the lawn. Naturally the quiet somnolence of the place was disturbed and furious negotiations ensued in order that they might be made to leave; the police, however, could do nothing and the Embassy staff were few and equally powerless. Only when a month had passed did the police concede to the request from the Ambassador suggesting that their crimes be forgotten. Then the eighty walked out and the garden resumed its former, but more desolate, peace. From the window it looked peaceful enough, but somewhere down there the buz majjeh was exploring his new environment; he was later to be joined by a family of white hedgehogs, which were not worth a special air trip and unlikely to survive a land journey. They were next heard of when, long after our departure, a frantic gardener cried that he would not work in a garden full of spiny chickens; the word chicken is often used as the word for animal and perplexed David Bivar until the creature had been pointed out to him: its inoffensiveness and friendliness had to be demonstrated before the gardener would resume his work. Long may the time be before he discovers a hissing chicken, $3\frac{1}{2}$ feet long, amongst the plants he has to tend.

After a week in Tehran, and six days before the boat was due to sail, the visas had still not come through and we decided to go via Beirut. It had taken us seven days to travel the 1,500 miles on the outward journey, but there had been an enforced stay of two days in Baghdad. It would probably not take so long to return but, as nobody could tell us how early we must arrive in Beirut in order to assure a passage for ourselves and the truck, our intention was to get there as early as possible and trust that that was early enough. The boxes had all been left at the Company's garage for eventual carriage and shipment by them to England and, although there were many things which were not in the boxes, there was space enough in the back for a camp bed. It was flanked by the jerricans, the carpets, the four spare wheels, the other beds and bedding and the rucksacks; it looked secure and extremely comfortable. I climbed into it, the other two got in the front and the engine was started to make a loud and strong noise, an infinitely better sound than that which had been the case on our outset from Kirman. Then Ahmed came, faithful as ever, and armed with a boxful of cakes. We thanked him heartily, shouted our farewells and drove out through the arched gate of the Embassy. The day was pleasantly warm, I lay back upon the bed, the tyres hummed over the tarmac road and Tehran receded into the distance.

Any thoughts which had arisen concerning the blatancy of that town and its disproportionate value of things were dispelled when the pot-holes began. On the way out they had certainly been noticed by us, but on the return such sickness as we had, like all other introvertive complaints, made us more aware of ourselves and of those holes. Moreover, the gaps had all been enlarged by the roadman; he who was in charge of that road had ordered many hundreds of labourers to make the holes into neat rectangular shapes in preparation for those who would fill them up with tar. But, and my swollen liver impressed the fact upon me for many miles of road, he had not arranged for any tar men: mile upon mile of square and tidy holes and no one to fill them in. The truck plunged about; I hung onto the roof bars and rearranged the tyres. This gibbonish attitude had been hampered by the spare wheels; for they had become dislodged by the jolting, and once a lorry tyre begins to lean it does so with all the weighty affection of a bloodhound.

When the Persian roads had been left behind the camp bed made a position to be envied; but while in Persia, and especially near Qazvin, it was not: therefore a rotation began, with no man having more than two hours in the back and that was long enough. When it was dusk and Hamadan was still forty miles further on, the road had been blocked by a line of Diesel lorries. We took our place at the end of them and a little policeman came running along shouting that a roadman had been run over. He chartered us, as we were at the end of the line, to take him back to the previous village in order that he might inform the authorities. On our return to the lorries he clattered off up the road to collect the information from all witnesses: until that happened everyone would have to wait.

The roadmen have the task of shovelling the gravel which is at the side of the road back into the middle. It was not a wonder that a man familiar with traffic should let himself be killed, but that the other three of his party were not killed too, for in spite of the loud blowing of the horn and the high column of dust which accompanied every approaching vehicle, they always oozed back to the side of the road at the very last minute. This immunity of theirs often caused braking on the part of the driver in an effort to avoid those who had been perfectly visible for some miles. The unwillingness to relinquish their task could be called diligence or stubbornness or indifference, but the consequence is the same; for the vehicle had had to slow down and they had made it do so. The one who died had, even by his death, succeeded in holding up very many lorries for three hours. Perhaps the noise of the two long lines of diesel engines starting and warming up provided a fitting requiem for his departing soul.

We stopped for a drink at the next tea-house along the road and spent the night in its yard. Mosquitoes and sniffing dogs made it an unpleasant one, and as soon as dawn began we packed up the beds and left. Up a pass and down into Hamadan, up again and down to a broad valley; so the day continued, climbing and descending, over the passes and down the other sides, until the gates were opened for us once more at the Customs house at Khosrovi. By then it was dark and we were ready for sleep; Louis and I got down the beds and Philip went in with the passports, more by way of introduction than to have them stamped. Unfortunately they dealt with them at once; neither did Louis nor I realise that the man who watched us putting the beds together and preparing the food was inspecting our kit. I had climbed into mine when somebody opened the gate and declared us free to enter Iraq. Louis couldn't think of anything to say to him and climbed into bed. Three men came; we shut our eyes. I think it was Philip who pushed the gate to again, but by then Louis and I were asleep.

It was Louis, however, who opened it in the morning and let us out. Two officials came running out of the house when they heard an engine start and stopped at the top of the stairs on seeing it was only our truck. Both yawned a bit and rubbed the sleep from their eyes; one kicked at a chicken and sat down where it had been in order to scratch his calves with long satisfying strokes; the other crouched upon the steps to put on his boots. A voice came from within that tea was ready and the two of them got up to go back through the doorway. There was nothing then to be seen except the chicken slowly hopping back to its original position at the top of the stairs. The end had come and the stage, but for the chicken, had been emptied. We gave a brief glance at the wonderful mountainous backcloth before shutting the gate on it all.

CHAPTER XI

Persian Frontier to Oxford

WITH those who leave a theatre, the few brief and cryptic remarks about the play are immediately followed by more prosaic statements concerning the journey home. Only the critics have to decide upon their opinions at once; perhaps phrases would come to their minds. Splendid scenery. Variety of personalities and activities. Variety of beliefs and way of life. In fact the word variety might stick, to be used as a theme for the piece he would write. Then of course hospitality, kindness, insincerity of behaviour, much pathos, perhaps too much. Maybe certain scenes would be remembered and then utilized in an inadequate and hopeless attempt to describe the whole. The boy with the scorpion, the girl of five being taught to make a carpet, or the view from the minaret. Yet even he is liable to be interrupted in his thoughts as he travels to his home.

With us, we made one or two pert comments about the affairs at Khosrovi and then discussed what things had to be done in Baghdad: then, as you can't talk for eighteen hours a day over the noise from a loud engine, we relapsed into silence. For the whole of the rest of the journey, whether the engine was making a noise or not, each one of us had the habit of producing a remark about that country we had visited. Beginning usually with the introductory phrase 'funny thing that . . . ', the point would be uttered, provide conversation for a few minutes and then die. They weren't descriptions of incidents, for each of us was aware of what had happened, but were rather more from occurrences which had never received any attention before and later, to the one who had remembered them, seemed full of poignancy and interest. After 'it was odd that Mirza never thought of any way of cooking an egg other than by leaning it against a piece of red hot charcoal' there was a short discussion on the monotony of Persian cooking, until the silence returned once more to leave us with remembrances of our own. These pronouncements were of little depth, but were at the end of a long train of thought which had been initiated by something that had passed by and occasionally gave the other person entertaining speculation as to what had caused them. But they had to occur; for the picture of Mirza cooking his eggs was so strong that, once it had materialised, the only way to replace it by another was to mention it: these arresting images formed conversation, but could hardly be said to be our reasoned opinions; only verbal exhaust ever came out of our lorry.

'The Persians are an ignorant and suspicious lot' had been said to us just before we left England; that was a criticism and, to its maker, a fair one. Nevertheless, it told us nothing about them; naturally they would be ignorant, for how can a country which is mainly illiterate be otherwise. That they are suspicious is equally likely, for their oil, their proximity to Russia and the ease with which foreign armies have encamped themselves on their soil during the past two wars, will have made them so: he who had told us this was not surprising anybody with facts about the land.

Perhaps the distinguishing features of a country are its surprises, but they would be dependent upon the home country of the one who is surprised. Another way might be to remove one of its inhabitants, place him in that other country and observe which things surprised him. There had been a little Persian at Oxford who had gone there to learn more about diesel engines. He explained to us, while we were trying to acquire certain facts from him, that England was as he had imagined, save that the diesel engines were not of the quality he expected them to be. Later, we took him with us to be given tea by a friend of ours who is one of those people that expects some help from his guests in the garden before they are rewarded with tea. Levelling land for a tennis court was the task of that day. Many others had arrived before we joined them and all, except our Persian, carried some earth and levelled something before the time came for tea: not much maybe, but industrious appearances were exhibited. On the way back the Persian said he had been surprised; for not only did we work, but we had made ourselves look like workers. If more attention had been paid to his remark then, it would have come as less of a jolt to hear Ameri's bailiff informing us that servants should be employed for so menial a task as the fatiguing of lizards.

It is necessary to be surprised by the whole country; for the few outside it are dismissed as eccentrics, certainly the diesel expert was indicted in this way. The Persian Ambassador at Baghdad was similarly labelled and the habit continued for a while, even after we had driven through the Customs post at the border of their country and were definitely ensconced within Persia. Only repetition of so called eccentricity will transfer that label to the land in which they live and then be called a national characteristic.

The disease had surprised us. Infantile mortality and lack of longevity provide startling figures, but they do not make the same impression as the constant witnessing of people with disease. The swollen red eyes thick with flies, the quivering bodies, the twisted spines; they occur with a horrible frequency amongst the people that you pass: others take little notice of the maimed ones and so confirm that it is a sight seen all too often. The Persian is not averse to staring at whatever interests him and it is not for sympathy or kindness that his eyes look elsewhere. When a man staggers down a street on his hands as well as his feet and nobody looks at him, then familiarity with disease is most forcibly expressed.

Wealth is another feature. The difference between the rich and the poor is obvious and made so by the rich man; for 'what is money', they appear to say, 'if it cannot be flaunted'. Similarly the ones who are poor cannot conceal the fact, and those in the extremes of poverty seem to flaunt their state as loudly as do the rich; their shoes and hats are pitiful and have long since failed to protect the soles of their feet and the tops of their heads. Neither of the groups would say that a small landowner was a person with a medium income: he is either able to present himself as a rich man or he is not.

The books had said that Persia was the size of Germany, Italy, France and the British Isles; we had measured the mileage between their towns and there had been talk about Land's End and John o' Groats, but we had not learnt the real meaning of distance. When there is nothing between two towns but desert and the road which connects them, then its conception becomes clearer and is almost understood. It was this absence of anything except ground to be walked over that gave us some idea of its meaning: if you went north from the village of Jupar you would come across its town, Kirman; but there was 25 miles of sand between them. All distances there are measured in farsakhs, in the hours they take to walk for only then do they become comprehensible, as the space separating them means nothing. We found ourselves saying that the petrol debacle occurred just outside Yezd, yet it would have taken one of us five hours to fetch another can. No one ever considered calling Negar an oasis, although the nearest village, the nearest water, was fifteen miles away. These figures weakly demonstrate our inability to understand the long empty distances, but only in such bewilderment can the reality of distance arise.

The greatest underestimation concerned the omnipotence of water. It is true that this is always so, but its brutal authority and autocracy were made manifest. The type of life follows directly from its laws; the isolation, the poverty and the disease with which it is afflicted.

It took four hours to arrive at Baghdad. The road, in general, was straight and had a good surface; the truck went along at a constant speed and our few remarks were made long before its outskirts had been reached. Certainly, little enough was said in the town itself, as the traffic dominated all our thoughts, particularly in the one long main street which forms the centre of Baghdad. There we stopped and the hooting, swirling stream swept past us. Food was bought, vain enquiries were made about the *Esperia*, and after the petrol and water cans had been filled and the exit visas obtained, we drove out of the town and over the Tigris into Mesopotamia. Past Habbaniya, over the Euphrates, into the Iraqi Customs at Ramadi and along the road to Rutba Wells. But this time, when we reached that solitary spot, it was night and very different to our midday remembrance of it; the wirelesses blared out into the vast expanse of surrounding desert and the streets were crowded with people. Louis, who carried our

money, spent time with a sinister money-changer, for although
Rutba accepted any sort of money, there was no point in carrying
Persian and Iraqi currency into Transjordan, Syria and the
Lebanon. The Nairn bus came in from Damascus and the café
which had provided us with tea became filled with many others
who believed that there are times when one shilling for a cup of
tea is not a sufficient deterrent. We left them there and continued
along the way they had come. Another hundred miles further on
and twenty hours after leaving Khosrovi, we stopped once more,
drove over the ditch by the side of the road and spread out the
bedding upon the ground. It was our custom to drive some way
into the desert to escape the glare from the head-lights flashing
along the road, but I do not think they would have disturbed us
greatly during those four hours of sleep.

Due to the necessity to get to Beirut as quickly as possible, we
went by the pipe-line road and not over the desert, for on the road
we could travel in the dark. This route led through places with the
hyperfunctional names of H.3, H.4 and H.5 and to Mafraq, a
town of petrol tanks and shining tin huts. From there we turned
north up to Deraa and the Transjordan-Syrian border. The
country then became less flat and undulated smoothly round the
little railway which ran to Damascus. The trains puffed ener-
getically up and down it and all looked old enough to have been
the survivors of the numerous explosions which occurred along
the line in 1917. But at Deraa there were more Customs and plenty
of time to watch those trains.

It was the task of the man who was neither driving nor sleeping
on the bed to attend to the Customs-house formalities. He would
collect all the documents he thought relevant and wander into the
building. Tin or concrete, wood or canvas, the scene inside would
be approximately the same; two or three desks, a lot of paper
and a few officials: with one of these he would come out to inspect
the truck. The man in the back was always deep in rucksacks and
tins and well embedded into the chaos; sometimes the Customs
man would discover him, gasp and say 'But here is a man' with
all the hoarse vigour of a matron inspecting a faulty girls'
dormitory. The other would have to acknowledge him calmly
and point out his likeness on page three of the passport. The

officer would then search, but carelessly, and forever glancing at the sleeping figure as if he were an unclean thing.

Whatever language was hazarded between us and the Customs men, our names always had to be transcribed into Arabic script. The wealth of consonants in Armstrong perplexed them and a horrible distortion of sounds was written down. This did not worry us until, as in the applications for visas, our names were reversed into Roman script. That Armstrong became Sam, and Gordon Goddam caused confusion on certain occasions. Many weeks before, when we had been waiting for our frontier passes for the Caspian, a man came in carrying our documents and a few belonging to some Persians who were also cluttering up the room: no one answered the first four names which he read out. It was suspicious that four people applying to visit the frontier should not attend to collect their passes. He read the nationality on the cards and said 'Où sont les Anglais'; we made a strong show of hands. He then read them again. At the third name, Eric guessed and said 'Peut-être c'est moi'. The man looked at Eric's face and saw that the passport photo, even allowing for the characteristic distortion, could never have been a representation of it; he said 'Non' rather unkindly. A fourth name was read out and Eric, feeling slightly hurt, but who then stood a better chance than the rest of us, guessed again. This time the official just looked at Eric and went out of the room. We had a short and hurried conversation which convinced those around us that we were indeed villains who, posing as Englishmen, had omitted to remember their English names. A rapid decision that I should say 'C'est moi' emphatically to the only monosyllabic pronouncement and that Eric should claim one of the names he had not ventured upon succeeded without a hitch when the man returned. Louis and I, given each other's passports, signed accordingly. Our obvious relief that the situation had been clarified must have, to the cluttering Persians, convinced them of our guilt.

Customs men and passport officials are rarely treated with any sympathy by those whom they are delaying and we fell in with the general practice. Our passports, written in French and English, were meaningless documents to the men familiar only with the Arabic script; therefore they had to rely upon our help and that was their undoing. When a question came in Persian, French or German we occasionally understood, but not when it came in Arabic; this ignorance, coupled with our customary inability to understand their idea of how Germans, French or Persians speak, forced us to rely upon the bluntness of our fingers in pointing out an appropriate column. They always and unquestioningly accepted whichever column it appeared to be, and we found our names being written down as our birth places and the dates of birth as our passport numbers. At first there was a tendency to protest when your name went down as Buckinghamshire, but after a spasm of explanations and your father had received the name, it was realised that silence was more profitable. The person whose turn it was to go to the Customs would come back, smiling slightly, and tell us that Louis' mother went, according to Syria, under the alluring name of Calcutta, or that someone's occupation was described as Blue-grey. I think it was Philip's father who acquired the quite impersonal name of 'student'. Of course, once this game had been started, the blunt finger became blunter; for those we played against were, after all, only passport officials.

On from Deraa and to Damascus. At that time, I was on the bed and watched the tall white houses go floating by. Pleasant trees passed overhead and then, as we approached the centre, the houses came closer together and the smell of a town began. Louis and Philip in the front were looking for a bank and, in their efforts to find one, turned up a side street: loud shouts came from the vendors as their fruit was disinfected by our exhaust, louder cries came from those who were trying to sell us some of it and the donkeys brayed at being pulled to the side of the road. Some people looked in at the back, but the one who was there made an uninteresting sight; for he saw only those things which chanced to be above him and he lay completely relaxed. Instead of the road ahead, thick with people, there were the high walls of the houses for him to see, the drunken sign-boards nailed to them, the broken window frames and the fascinating darkness that lay within. The truck stopped just opposite a shop whose sign said, in most ill-spelt French, that bread and charcoal could be bought there, but the stoppage caused a most hysterical approach from the red-cloaked man whose loaves were receiving our undivided attention: his feet flapped around to the front and the truck jerked on again. The streets widened, the boards disappeared and the buildings announced their business in thick black letters fixed to the window panes. We stopped again outside one of them where the activities of a bank were advertised in many languages. Then on again and down a street where the boards were neatly painted and the walls were clean. We were going slowly and, as we travelled, bags of bread and fruit were dropped into the back: the business of shopping was being completed. Another stop, and the smell of petrol dominated all others. The different measures by which oil and petrol were sold, their varying prices and the several currencies which we had been forced to use, always caused great calculations by those in the front; their distant murmurings permeated through to the back. Another jerk, and the roof of the garage disappeared from view. The houses thinned out, the avenues of trees became less regular and then they too were left behind. We had passed through the town of Damascus.

On past the place where our first night in Asia had been finished, past the place where it had begun and then up the valley to the frontier with the Lebanon. It chanced to be my turn to deal with the Customs. It was the President's birthday and there was much gaiety within the hut; our particulars were written down whimsically, but when it came to putting the big entry stamp in my passport, the man could find no space; although others had stamped on top of stamps, he insisted that space should be found. Then, with an expression of relief, he banged it down on the place reserved for the photo of the accompanying wife. 'Elle est très, très belle', he said, and took it to show the others. 'Ah oui, elle est ravissante, magnifique.' 'Monsieur, vous avez la bonne fortune.' 'La plus belle du monde,' and they gazed at it lovingly. I left to go back to the truck and my underpants, suddenly becoming buttonless, slipped down from their normal position and forced me to walk in very short paces. All the time 'Ravissante', 'Charmante' issued from the hut, until I regained my seat and we drove away. Louis driving, and amazed at the turn of events, was curious, but the backfiring of the exhaust, caused by our coasting down into the valley, obviated any explanation.

Beirut was in a lively mood. Fireworks were thrown about,

rockets shot in all directions and the town was brilliant with light. The winding road which led up from the sea flickered with the headlamps of the many cars driving up to the cooler air above the town. No one was going down, when the evening had just begun, except for us and we didn't go far. A road led into a wood and a short distance along it we stopped. Although the various sounds of the fireworks and the motor horns were muffled by the trees, they could not have concerned us; for just as soon as the food was finished, just as soon as there was no further reason for staying awake, the three of us were asleep.

When breakfast was over we drove down to the town and, after discovering that it was not too late, booked our passages for the *Esperia*. The truck had brought us more than 1,500 miles in a little over three days and was congratulated. 'Mosheen' is the Persian for vehicle, and with this name, firstly by the Persians and then by us, it became known. Our complete dependence upon the Mosheen and her reliability had formed a sentimental attachment. Every time another 1,000 miles was registered by the milometer, those in front would cheer a little and clap their hands; a ritual which, when uttered, sounded ridiculous but always took place. Since leaving Tehran the engine had developed the fault of continuing to fire even when the ignition had been switched off: when we stopped the carbon in the faulty cylinder would be hot enough to keep the whole engine turning over very silently. The petrol from the cylinders would be pushed along the exhaust pipe and, about ten seconds after the engine had been silenced, there came a great explosion. Just before it happened a surly group of onlookers would be certain to be peering into the cab, while we waited feverishly for the bang which never failed us. The crowd would leap back, falling over each other in their efforts to remove themselves from the area: whether we laughed or paid no attention, the crowd was always much smaller when it peered in again.

An unnecessarily large amount of spare parts had been taken; but advisers are very quick to think up yet another part of an internal combustion engine which has, in their experience, required replacement. The tyres behaved normally; they did not wear down rapidly and then explode as had been the warning:

the hot sun had little effect on the pressure and, although care was taken in noting their pressures on the first two days, we omitted this precaution for the rest of the time. We had some old smooth tyres with us and these proved much more satisfactory on soft sand; those with deep castellated surfaces, called track grip, cut deeply into the sand and couldn't cut themselves out again; nevertheless they were better for the loose gravelly roads which were steep.

Practically all of the trouble came from the valves. Most of them burnt out to a greater or lesser degree and, until they were ground down or replaced on our return through Tehran, oil seeped into the cylinders; the sparking plugs, therefore, had to be constantly changed and cleaned. This did not happen so frequently on the longer journeys, but mainly on the short trips, where the soft sand and bad roads made the speed of the engine very irregular. Apart from this difficulty the spares were untouched save for a small valve part and the large back spring of the chassis. The two major overhauls given by the A.I.O.C. garage in Tehran very greatly helped in preventing further trouble. It was their help which made our large number of spare parts superfluous.

The drive from Persia acted beneficially upon our healths. Philip and Louis had forgotten about their dysentery and I began eating again as soon as we arrived in Beirut. We had two days there before the boat sailed and, living in a boarding house just by the sea, spent the days simply. The long coast line, the port and the hills behind it, make Beirut a pleasant place in which to pass the time.

Although the town provides many places for the man who wishes to lead a leisured life, there are also certain universities there. It was vacation time and we were unable to compare the activities of the students with the stories of Mahmud concerning himself and his fellow students at the University of Tehran. Mahmud had accompanied me on my initiation into Gauhariz qanat at Jupar and had afterwards given me and Louis lunch at his home. There he had told us about the parades, the marchings of the students and the method of acquiring their demands. It seems that if a particular department has a grudge, whether they are short of books or that their prices are too high, then the whole of that faculty makes a parade about it. With banners stating their case they march through the streets of Tehran so that all may read of their distress. The displays are kept up until the point in question has been amended to meet their desires. Mahmud said he approved of the system in general, but there had been so very many marchings during the previous term that he had failed the exam at the end of it. The large number had been initiated by some trivial affair, but the University authorities, after adjusting that particular law, had expelled the ringleader of the protesting students. Promptly the marchings began again; for a few weeks the authorities were stubborn, while all the students had a regular routine of breakfast, first parade, work, lunch, work and another parade before the evening meal. Most of them became so tired from the long walks that they could do no work in the allotted periods. Eventually, one week before the exams began, the authorities relented, returned the leader and were relieved by the cessation of parades. However, as a point of punitive policy, they failed everybody who took the exam and the parades began again: this second point had not been settled when the students dispersed for the summer vacation.

The tendency of all eastern students to demonstrate their dislikes publicly is utilized, to become a very potent factor, by politicians. The student population of a town is sufficiently large to make quite presentable parades for the most trivial of matters; but when the question is one which affects them all, some national outburst, then they are all in the street and present themselves as a formidable array. But on the previous day they may have been doing the same thing for microscopes or blackboards or slide rules; exactly the same performance, but at the second time the words and banners have been changed. Mahmud said that everybody turned up to the parades so long as they might be affected by the result; even if they had nothing to gain, if they possessed a slide rule already, their interest in the case would persuade them to attend: for that reason everyone in his faculty, the Medical school, had failed the exam. Such altruistic self-discipline could be called thoughtless obedience to the majority; but it does explain why quite so many students suddenly become intrigued in a problem of their country, put a stop to the traffic in the centre of a large town and infect its people with their own enthusiasm.

Mahmud returned from Jupar to the University before the term started in order to have caught up with his work when the parades began again. A revealing point would be if the University authorities waived over the far greater time spent on the oil parades and passed all those whom they had failed during the previous summer for displays which, though the chantings were less nationalistic, had been precisely similar in their nature.

It was while we were at Beirut that I decided to have my beard removed. In its earlier days, it had taken an interest in itself and had grown vigorously, but in the previous month it had lost that interest and growth had practically ceased: it was time that it came off. I wandered into the poorer part of the town to find a barber who would do this cheaply. Shortly afterwards, a shop which looked sufficiently decrepit presented itself before me. The man in the next chair wore no shoes and only a rolled up pair of dungarees, but he spoke a type of French; through him I demanded that 'toute la barbe' should be removed. The barber, who possessed a massive hairy chest, agreed to remove the beard for forty piastres and the whole lot, that is including the moustache, for fifty piastres: I demanded that my ten piastre moustache should go as well. The interpreter relaxed and munched an apple while his hair was cut. I produced a banana from the bag that I had bought on the way to the shop and the barber paused good-naturedly every time another piece of it was bitten off. After offering bananas all round, my furtive generosity was well rewarded, for in every mirror were visions of banana eaters. Bananas and dungarees, bananas and fuzzy ginger beards; dozens of hairy hands were holding half-peeled bananas. The view in the mirrors was most pleasing and was occasionally enlivened by a sight of the barber trying to manipulate the razor, the shaving brush, and a cigar as well as his banana while he removed the hair from my face.

When the beard lay on the floor with all the banana skins, he started, purely by habit, to run a comb through my hair. Little did he know that no comb had been through that hair for three months, that a tarpaulin just by banging up and down on it can cause a bewilderment of knots; he knew nothing of the effect of the damp, sandy roof of a qanat upon such an entanglement; nor did he know that Louis spent two hours in Tehran cutting out the knots with dissecting scissors and had then failed with a large-mesh dog comb. He should have been warned by its pitted and twisted appearance, but he started and out of habit: it was out of pride that he determined to finish it. Oil was poured on to trickle down my face and neck. Knotted tufts clogged up the comb. More oil was applied and it reached the small of my back just as the remaining strands of hair were made smooth again. Louis said he needn't have bothered; for the knots would have grown out with time, but even if the problem was only temporary, he had solved it and deserved the five other piastres he had omitted to give with the change.

The *Esperia* arrived late, so the chaos at the dock was greater than had been anticipated. Thirty policemen composed the only inactive group and were waiting for some important personage. They lounged about with their white gloves on for three hours before the man arrived; he walked hurriedly past the line which they had equally hurriedly formed and disappeared up the gang-way into the ship. I don't know who he was and never came nearer to him than the first class bathroom, out of which a steward expelled me and into which I had repaired to remove the oil from my hair.

We had seen quite a lot of this colourful pomp in the Lebanon. While cruising down the road into Beirut after our sleep on its outskirts, a band of motor cyclists came up the hill blowing sirens and whistles and motioning us to the side of the road. We did; so did the rest of the traffic. Many more lines of motor cyclists came roaring past, then their noisy blur changed into a blur of motor cycles plus side-cars and finally a longer and smoother blur of American cars. These all shot by two or three abreast and we drove off once more into the beautiful silence which they left in their wake. That was the nearest we ever came to the President of the Lebanon.

It was dark when the *Esperia* left the dock. Many people stood on the shore; many people were lined on the boat. The lights of Beirut were all twinkling at the ship and the lights of the ship were all twinkling at Beirut. There should have been three more people leaning over the rails, pondering about Asia and the time they had had there, but instead, these three were downstairs and arguing with the Cook. We called him 'Il fattore—the steward' and not just the Cook. He was given a packet of cigarettes and asked to feed us well; he was given friendly pats on the back and very nearly agreed.

When morning came Asia had disappeared. There wasn't even a glimpse of mountain on the horizon, as had been our first sight of the continent just three months before. Then we had made ready to land upon it, to find our way down to Kirman and to try and work in that place. As a blind man will, by direct reason of his shortcomings, stumble over everything that is before him so had we, through our ignorance, been tripped up to observe the things that were near. The blind man misses every obstacle in a house which is known to him, but it takes him a long time to learn the way. With us the time had been far too short for the surroundings to become familiar and the stumblings never stopped.

For the first stage of this learning, the one who does not know considers that he is in the wrong; the obstacles and difficulties are presumed always to have been like that. The second stage comes when the impatience of the learner makes him believe that the difficulties have been deliberately put in his way. Only when the patience returns can he tell himself that he has been in the wrong once more.

During the times when we felt that way everything was blamed upon Persian default. Yet our patience would have expired on occasion equally well had we been visiting an uninhabited isle; the only difference was that, as people were around us, it was they who received the reproaches. Then generalisations followed the rebukes, until all the problems of the country were attributed to certain of their characteristics, such as the practice of bribery and the smoking of opium: oblivious of our own defects, we believed that we had discovered all theirs. The same is true in reverse, as the Persian diesel expert at Oxford blamed all Britain's ills upon the lack of disrespect shown by the wealthy for the common working man. The West and the East, confused by the differences that exist, should regard each other's problems in the light of the prevalent customs and not as direct products of them: by either side solutions are readily proffered for the opposing difficulties. Since the war Persia has been discussing the operation of a seven-year plan, a scheme for economic advancement; so far there has only been discussion and the seven years have not begun. This delay could be due to the immensity of the tasks involved, but during our stay in the country we heard every other possible factor given as a reason for its prolongation.

By pursuing our various programmes of work we came to know a little of the people at the bottom of the country, those who knew nothing of the affairs beyond the hills and weren't even sure that the world was round. They spoke naturally. If the one to whom they were speaking was a foreigner, it mattered only that the language made the conversation proceed more slowly; quite where the other man's country was did not concern them terribly and they were satisfied on having learnt that he came from the direction of the sunset. The peculiarities in the customs of the two countries were something to be laughed at or even, if they were sufficiently different, ridiculed; but amicably, and with no suggestion that one set of customs, mere habits, was better than any other. There was no hint of rivalry or patriotism. 'It was likely', they appeared to say, 'that those who were born 1,000 farsakhs away should have fair hair, pale skin and eat their food differently.' When you meet a man who is also crawling along a qanat, as sometimes happened at Jupar, you both give salaams and then squat and talk. Probably he asks you about the women in your country. You reply suitably. The conversation will then proceed along this vein until one makes a disparaging remark about the past activities of the other, then much water will be splashed about before both crawl away along the channel. Meet a man as you walk along a lonely town street and you will receive a contemptuous glance: he knows that you are from the west and shows his opinion of that world. No conversation ensues and you both walk straight on. The man in the town has made his point.

However, to go and live in the villages is to become familiar, not only with the more amiable part of the community, but with some of its diseases. Hygiene can be attempted, although the flies will defeat your efforts. If plans are adopted for boiling all water and cooking all food that does not come out of a tin, then all hospitality has to be refused. Even so, every scheme is defeated when one mistake has been made, when one glass of water was not boiled, and such mistakes you are certain to make. The European readiness to catch Asiatic diseases if he lives within their community does provide a strong deterrent for him to do so. If he has confidence in a large medicine kit or in his many injections, then he will go more readily, but he is always liable to be afflicted in one way or another. We did not neglect the problem of disease, but it was regarded by all as insoluble; that Philip, Louis and Eric got amoebic dysentery, all except Philip got jaundice and each one of us brought back a host of non-pathogenic parasites within him, was afterwards said by the Medicals to have been most likely whatever precautions had been taken. At least their opinions comforted us that we had only received our share of the diseases, and that unnecessary time had not been lost by our neglect and by their occurrence.

Our plans of work were ambitious and necessitated that all possible attention should be paid to them: around them did we model the pattern of our existence. These programmes were full but, as we didn't know Persia, the manner of their fulfilment could not be stipulated or even guessed at beforehand. Therefore the events which occurred after we had stated our wishes and started our work were quite unplanned and resulted from the environment in which the wishes had been made. In the villages these were more natural; for no special behaviour, no political attitudes, no nationalistic demonstrations were being produced for our benefit. To the observer the one who plays the part most easily receives all his sympathy; it is never the one who is so obviously trying to elevate himself from his former quieter standpoint. The townsman declaims his lines with greater power and can more clearly be heard; but it is the villager, just as much as he, who provides the Persian story.

The disappearance of Asia, however, was only a stage in our journey and it led to the reappearance of Africa. For a day and a half the ship stayed in Alexandria, the derricks swung noisily

and from everywhere came the sharp, halting sound of Arabic:
the air was thick and we did nothing. It was good when the ship
moved off once more and the dolphins began to play again round
her bows. There were many more passengers than on the outward
journey, resulting in considerably less bonhomie and deck space
between them. Most of these people sat in the same spot throughout the day and slept there at night; they looked dour and stared
dreamily at whatsoever was in front of them. Others stood
strongly and valiantly as they leant against the wind until, with
their clothes flapping round them, they retired to a sheltered spot,
having had sufficient invigoration from the sea for the time being.
There were those who ate continuously, those who read fluttering
books and those who always slept; but all such people are to be
found on every boat. It just happened that there were more of
them on our return.

The second port was Syracuse. The large wide bay with its
narrow inlet was a perfect harbour when the vessels were smaller,
but now there is only a small channel through which big ships
can go. Knowing only that the Syracusans had beaten the
Athenians in a sea battle not long after the place had been col-
onized, I asked a strange Egyptian classical scholar for information;
this man had made himself known to me and professed that
Cambridge had educated him at the beginning of the century.
He had no teeth, but a wonderful sense of the dramatic. I have
never seen a man who looked less like an Athenian sea captain, yet
he recounted the fight with all the brutal love of battle which
must have been in those men. His bony fingers traced the line of
the retreating Syracusan vessels, while the other hand denoted the
pursuing course of the Athenian ships. The fingers then returned
to point out the Syracusans filling up the harbour mouth by self
destruction. His bony hand continued and then lingered; the
Athenians were waiting and guarding their land forces on the
opposite shore. So, while one hand gripped firmly onto the ship's
rail and blocked the exit of the harbour, his other arm indicated
the missiles that were being flung at the intruders from the region
of the town. At first this arm and its fingers jabbed excitedly at
the Athenian ships, but soon the wretchedness of their plight told
upon him and his tale became slower and slower. He stopped

when all of them had been sunk, shook his head gravely and was silent for a moment. Then, after discovering that I had not got a cigarette, he left me to find one of his own.

We went ashore at Syracuse and ate a large meal in a dirty little café called the 'Triumphal Arch' before hurrying back to the ship. Then along the Sicilian coast as darkness came, past Mount Etna and through the Straits of Messina. The lights from the towns on either side, the brilliantly lit ferry boats and the flashing lighthouses gave the place an atmosphere of gaiety. So different to the days when the sailing boats preferred to go round Sicily rather than entrust themselves to its currents.

Deep down below them is the home of Morgain, the wife of Sir Lancelot. There she lives and from that place she ventures to make the visions of the air, the mirages of the desert, the polar lights and those other spectacles which can make the sky so wondrous. She plays with her talents to confound the thirsty in the desert and the imaginative everywhere; the oasis looms up before them and the Aurora Borealis flickers disturbingly from the north. The revenge of mankind has been to transform the Straits of Messina; its deep and sullen waters are now swept by the beams of lighthouses and danced over with reflections from the lights on the shore. The well-lit ships make criss-cross tracks and move between the regular flashing of the buoys. For she who controls the Northern lights and has made travellers fall down on their knees in despair, the Straits of Messina are sadly different from the place it used to be when she made those depths her home.

We spent more time at Naples and ate more food. When it rained our soft Persian shoes began to disintegrate and we sheltered in an ironmonger's. Two dripping youths who had come in before us were making the place wet and were asked to leave; thus it was that each of us had bought several cheap coffee machines and two mouse traps before the weather was fine again. On the final part of the trip up to Genoa the wind became stronger. Most passengers had left at Naples and amongst the remainder, with a suitable mixture of generosity and caution, we distributed our surplus camel pills.

There had been too much confidence when we left Kirman, but it was nothing like as bad as the self-assurance which smote us at

Genoa. For there were Customs men with whom we could argue and they used a language which could be read: how could travel in Italy possibly present any difficulties? This confidence lasted with us for many miles and caused hopeless mistakes which should have shattered it to pieces. Without even bothering to ask the way, we drove out of Genoa on quite the wrong road. Fifteen gallons of petrol were put in the tanks before discovering that there was only sufficient money for thirteen. Some fruit was bought over-casually in a market and proved to be hard and inedible. Gradually this complete trust in ourselves was toned down as the stupidities accumulated, but it still accompanied us; for in England we became more lost than had been the case in any other country, far more so than in the sands of Syria or the back streets of Baghdad.

Nevertheless, it was pleasant to be on long stretches of smooth tarmac, to hear the satisfying humming of the broad tyres and to see Italy again. But nothing was in its right perspective, all was wrong somehow and gave us the feeling of a convalescent on his first day up from bed, someone to whom all commonplace things appear strange. Much too suddenly we had been forced to put on warm clothes. Rain had come and everything felt damp. We wondered where our socks had been lost and when the windscreen wipers had become defunct. Slowly the sand was washed away from the Mosheen, the locusts and hornets were sluiced from their lodgings in the radiator, our number plate became legible and our feet became cold. The old fragments of flat Asiatic bread looked, for the first time, out of place on the floor of the cab. The mouse was no longer living amongst the spares. The four spare tyres, the pick and the shovel seemed pointless and, for the rain poured in through the canvas, no less so than the water bottles.

The man on the bed no longer gazed up at a blue sky, but out of the open flap at the rear of the truck. As there was only the wet road to be seen, or the misty faces in the car behind, he wrapped himself in the carpets and the two mackintoshes before trying to go to sleep. Those two ragged garments had been left in the front cab, but no one knew when; for each of us had assumed they belonged to another. So many people had sat in that front seat: the Bedouin, the Italian escort, Tehran officials, policemen, veiled women with their babies, the Ali who sang and the old man of the puncture. To none of them could be attributed the ownership of the two mackintoshes; but that did not disturb the recumbent man in the back.

It was still raining at the top of the Mont Cenis pass; the Italians, previously so annoying, remained in their hut and inspected our kit from there. The rain had not stopped when it was time to sleep and we drove up to a hotel in Termignon. The two men fighting on the floor in the doorway made it hard to get in but, once in, it was not long before we slept.

Then on through Chambéry and Chalon, along the Côte d'Or and to stop for sleep once more; this time, for it was fine, in a field and near Seaulieu. On again to Paris for information about the channel boats. The swirling traffic of that city carried us rapidly to an agency and swiftly out again: any hesitation was noisily resented by those behind. Out and on to Pèronne, where the night was spent in the Bar des Collèges. Finally to Dunkirk. Having driven on to the boat and parked between a Rolls and a Hudson we went down to the lounge. There a reckoning was made for, throughout the trip, personal expenditure had been with expedition money and had not been recorded: therefore a list was necessary. To us these items, as we remembered them, were conventional and of no startling interest. To our neighbour they were 'just a trifle illogical'. We tried to recall everything: 2 camel bells from Isfahan, shoes from Baghdad, 2 carpets from Koshan, 1 woollen hat at Yezd, 2 tickets for the Iraq museum, dates at Alexandria, 3 toothbrushes (I was always losing them) at Kirman, an extra cup of tea at Rutba Wells, more dates; and so the list continued.

We declared most of the relevant part of this at Dover. The seeming frivolity with which the official was treated caused him to burrow deeply in the back. The forgotten coffee machines and mouse traps were pounced upon and he was burrowing to find more when I, being the theoretical owner of the Mosheen, had to show the documents. Naturally by this time the routine was well known. But 'Where is your C.D.3 covering this 29B?' I hadn't any idea. One or two people looked up. Here was a man without a C.D.3. I went back to the truck and fished out the buz majjeh cage: when that creature had not been found in the Embassy grounds its tin had been appropriated for the wealth of documents. The Customs man promised to recognise the form if I would turn the papers over. 'Receipts for damage to taxi in Beirut.' 'Contents of our rucksacks in Arabic.' 'Circular letter to all Gendarmerie in the Jupar area.' 'Addresses written in uncouth hands.' 'Sketch maps of towns with an X in one corner.' 'List of prices paid for animals.'

The Customs man was talking. 'You know, if you can't find it you will have to pay the cost of the lorry in Persian currency. That'll be difficult, won't it?'

'Frontier permits for the Caspian.' 'Permit to export snakes from Asia.' 'Statement about Lire brought into Italy.' 'List of spare parts in Persian.'

'Where would you begin to find 150 quids worth of Persian money?'

'An envelope full of visa photographs.' 'Invitations to Tehran cocktail parties.' 'Calculated mileage from Tehran to Belgrade.' 'Illegible Persian telegrams in English.'

'Dunno where I'd begin.'

'A letter from the Persian Ambassador to Iraq.'

'Glad I haven't got to.'

'Receipt from Mirza: 142 eggs, 17 melons.'

'Wonder where it went?'

'A letter from a man who thought he could supply us with bears.' And then, for no reason at all, it appeared.

'So it was in all that bumf after all.' I put everything back in the cage and drove off on the left hand side into England.

The trip was nearly over. Whether we had changed or benefited as a result of it was a different matter and I was musing on it in Guildford when Philip and Louis had gone off to get some money. A policeman wanted to know why the licence was not on the windscreen. I said it wouldn't stick. 'Can't help that. Must be visible.'

It was while I was tying it on with some string that a man came up to me from the Antique Furniture dealer's shop opposite which we had parked.

'Got anything for us today, Jack?'

'No, not much. Just a couple of carpets, but straight from Persia.'

'Oh, go and chase yourself.'

Over Magdalen bridge, up the High, around to Balliol and the trip was ended. Our Mosheen exploded with more than her customary vigour. However, no hairy Asiatic faces were peering in, no donkeys were licking the paint off the woodwork; nothing at all was happening. The sound dissipated itself into the October air.

Postscript

The sound may have dissipated, but memories of Persia did nothing of the sort. I should have been wholeheartedly aware of impending exams, but the major piece of me was still in Jupar, striding between its high mud walls, wading within qanats. I would sniff my notebooks, savouring the dusty fragrance of that other world. We all visited the Radcliffe, with awful contributions that it welcomed enthusiastically, so replete were they with novel bacteria telling of our three-month tussle with dysentery. On occasion I lit my muqanni's lamp, switched off all lights, admired its smoky flame and then reluctantly returned to that week's essay. Other students of my year had spent the long vacation in earnest preparation for the finals that lay ahead, but I had learned a thousand different things, of desert and thorn, nomad and villager, poverty and excess, fear and relief from fear, lives so very different from those around the Woodstock Road. I had profited – I was quite sure of that – but at the expense of the lists and facts that examiners require.

As happy distraction we were invited by the Anglo-Iranian Society to lecture at its premises in Belgrave Square. Louis and I accepted, drove there in our beloved Bedford and spoke flippantly of mother wells and Mirza, of kakhoda and landlord, of mosques, minarets, mountains and other kinds of men. Two poignant questions surfaced from the audience. Might there be a book about our exploits? And what about the blind white fish: were they never to be found?

As for the book, an offer came from George Allen and Unwin to publish an account of those Persian days. More amazingly, it was accompanied by a £25 cheque, an 'advance on royalties to be earned'. (What joy partnered all those words!) Not only was the letter straightforwardly flattering, but it also helped to postpone all thoughts of career. After

Oxford I would write a book about our search for the blind white fish. And that is what I did. Having acquired a second (while many of the earnest preparers were rewarded with a first), I departed for Germany. I knew that friends there would provide a room where I could write, and eke out such savings as I possessed, until the book was done. Unfortunately I fell ill almost at once, and the local doctor muttered about diphtheria. It need not have been – a lengthy session with a terrifying medical volume told me that – but I was no longer so welcome. A recently bereaved aunt of theirs, they decided, would solve the issue. I therefore travelled to find the enchanting Zillerthalbahn, to Zell am Ziller and Felicitas von Kraus, who had been informed, by crackling phone, she would be my hostess for an uncertain length of time.

The arrangement proved to be ideal – from my viewpoint. She taught at the local school. We met, for *Dampf Knödeln*, *Blutwurst* and the like at midday. I wrote mainly in the afternoons and evenings, with occasional breaks for chat or, better still, singing. With Felicitas at the piano and Schubert (usually) as our choice, we would belt out his *Lieder* before I returned to my desk, to qanats, Mahun, irrigation ditches and valleys like Sagutch. Eventually, as Christmas loomed, the book was finished, and I set out to hitch back home.

'Herewith "The Blind White Fish",' I wrote to Allen and Unwin. In my mind that had always been its title. I was therefore taken aback when they requested a more informative title. The compromise was *Blind White Fish in Persia* – but where, a reader might ask (and readers did), were the pages about these creatures? The reason, unexplained within the text, lay in our many forms of failure. Our expedition, for all the buoyancy embedded in the book, had not succeeded in its aims. Louis's plants, gathered and processed into hay, were never described. My collected animals were eaten by ants, liberated in Tehran or became desiccated remnants of their former selves. Eric had made his maps, and Philip had amassed a great deal of information, but all of us had been devastated by disease. The business of getting to and from our chosen destination had also been demanding of our time, energy and resources. Our mistakes had indeed been numerous but were the strength of such youthful endeavour. Learn about faults, of every kind, and be less inclined to make them – or so it is hoped – in future forays of any kind.

The blind fish were in a more disastrous category of error. We, and particularly I, had pinned so many hopes on finding them. In Tehran, more at the start than at the end, the British community had called *us* the blind white fish, partly for our quarry but also for our pale faces and general naivety, as we blundered in and out of the land they knew so well. Our failure to find our namesakes was compounded after our return to Oxford. There we learned, from a scientific paper published late that year, of two Danes who had discovered a species of cave fish in the country we had visited. They had been laggardly about rushing into print, having found the fish in 1937, and had been in the Zagros mountains rather than Kirman, but they firmly described *Iranocypris typhlops*, a blind Iranian carp. It was the first true cave fish to be encountered on the Eurasian landmass. Not only had we not found such a fish; we had not even known such a prize had been found thirteen years earlier. Our failure was absolute.

I made no mention of this dismal fact when, in between Schubert and blood-sausage, I was writing *Blind White Fish*. Why publicise such unsuccess? As punishment for untruthfulness, worse was to come. After the book's publication, and when I was working in Africa, a letter reached me from Iraq. Its author, with words only an Englishman could use, explained that he 'happened to be down a pot-hole 300 feet deep the other day' when he found some blind white fish. He had read my book, had realised they might be of interest and had 'kept them alive on one corn flake each every other day, but they are now dead'. I looked up from the palm trees, my Star beer and the God-be-Willing Bar, to think again of that distant student expedition; then I wrote to the Natural History Museum. Its Fish Department contacted Mr A. G. Widdowson, suggesting that 'if he happened to be down that same pot-hole again' he should refrain from pisciculture in general and corn flakes in particular, but should 'place his catch forth-

with inside the tubes of alcohol enclosed for that purpose'.
The refrigeration engineer by trade, and pot-holer by recreation, performed perfectly. Several specimens arrived at the
Cromwell Road and were adjudged a new species. *Typhlogarra widdowsoni* was therefore added to the scientific list.
Down in Africa I received this news with some gratification
and a further sense of loss. We had not found the first fish;
now we had not even found the second. That honour belonged to a man who was even less of an icthyologist than I
had been, but had merely read the book.

Many more years passed. I travelled to lots of other countries and, after a time, seemed to be evading Persia (or Iran, as
it preferred to call itself). Perhaps I had no wish to be dis-
illusioned, as second bites at a cherry can be disappointing.
The original experience had been so astonishing that nothing
could equal that first rapture. (Today's young, frequently well-
travelled before dispensing with nappies, cannot begin to
comprehend the delight and euphoria on travelling abroad
after being confined by non-travelling parents, by war and
then by post-war restriction before the gates were finally
opened.)

A quarter of a century after the student expedition I suggested to some television friends that a film on qanats might
intrigue its audience. They wrote to Tehran, inquiring if such
underground channels were still in existence, and were informed by return that Iran was now a modern country, that
diesel engines pumped water to the surface and that qanats
were a matter for history alone. My inhibitions about returning vanished instantly. The Iranians were undeniably wealth-
ier in 1976 than in 1950, but I could not believe their several-
thousand-year-old tradition of subterranean adits had vanished
overnight.

'They are talking nonsense,' I protested firmly.

'Well, you had better go and see,' said the television men.

So I did go and see. I hurried down to Kirman, to Jupar,
and met Gauhariz again, the qanat of the flowing jewels.
Once more I waded in its waters, savoured paraffin smoke,
learned things again I had not even known I knew, and won-

dered where the twenty-six years had gone, so vivid were the memories. 'Qanats Alive and Well,' I cabled home.

On returning to Tehran (which also receives a large portion of its water via qanats) I realised that a few days loomed before I could travel home. Why not journey to the site where the two Danes had made their find? Admittedly, thirty-nine years had passed since they had captured Eurasia's first cave fish, but I was curious to see where they had succeeded. I had their scientific paper with me and was enchanted with its casual tone. 'At 382 kms from Bendar Shapur . . . the small rivulet Ab-i-Serum runs into Ab-i-Zezar . . . To reach the place where the water pours out from the rocks, and where the cave-fishes were caught, one first has to pass a waterfall of 10–15 m's height . . . At the base of the wall is seen a basin, which is supplied with subterranean water . . . in it the blind pink cave-fishes were found swimming apathetically around.' It all seemed so easy – far, far easier than splashing around in qanats, collecting disease and experiencing Mirza's cooking. The Danish paper concluded with a fuzzy photograph of the valley of Ab-i-Serum, home of the famous fish.

'We do not know the location of km 382,' said the railway authorities. 'The line has been greatly changed since those far-off days.' I then showed the fuzzy photograph to a most helpful geographer who enthused, 'All geography is unique.' Equipped with a detailed map of the Zagros mountains, knowledge of the railway's current route between Tehran and Bendar Shapur and the photograph's (few detectable) physical features, such as a couple of sharp peaks in the distance, he pronounced that Tang-e-Haft was the nearest railway halt.

Somewhere called Seventh Gorge sounded unimposing, and indeed a train did not stop there every day. The place was accessible, however, and within a few days I had arrived, together with a Farsi-speaking friend. After descending on to a modest platform and seeing that Tang-e-Haft was not much bigger, we set off by the west bank of the Ab-i-Zezar towards the rivulet of the Ab-i-Serum. The air was pleasant, the warmth perfect, the view supreme, and I missed only my companions from the earlier foray. How delighted they too would have been to be on the track of genuine cave fish.

Every passer-by, or rather stopper and talker, enquired about our mission. For some the quest was too exciting to be disregarded, and our party swelled in numbers. The more it grew, the greater the excitement and the greater the encouragement for others to join the throng. One old man was particularly inquisitive before being equally dismissive. 'Not another group to see the cave fish?' was the gist of his remarks, but he too joined us. After all, thirty-nine years had elapsed since the earlier inspection. Most of the multitude were children, as they are always readiest to take part in any adventure, and I and the old man strode ahead like Pied Pipers taking them far from home.

We passed the '500 metres of myrtle' mentioned by the Danes. We saw their waterfall, and then headed upstream towards a solid wall of mountain, feeling more Pied Piperish than ever. At its foot was a basin, entirely as described. I looked into its water – we all looked into its water – and there, amazingly, were half a dozen 'blind pink cave fishes . . . swimming apathetically around'. It was incredible. Here were some Iranocypris, exactly as the Danes had seen them, and there was I, looking at a quarry that had been so elusive when four of us had driven from England to experience almost everything except such a sight.

Unfortunately the sight was brief. Every single one of my companions leaped into that pool. Not one had a net, but all had hands and bits of rag that had been handkerchiefs. Somebody produced a plastic pot with a mauve screw-on lid. My extreme joy was now misery, as capture seemed impossible. Then I saw one fish being carefully coerced from handkerchief to pot, then another and finally a third, but that was it. The pot was passed from muddy hand to muddy hand so that all could see the catch. I feared for the fishes' wellbeing. The original glimpse had been short, but the captured lives might last only a little longer.

Over glasses of tea, hot, sugary and entirely welcome, at the old man's house I realised the fish were hardier than the average minnow in the average childhood jar. Perhaps apathy had something to do with it because they continued to cruise as casually within their plastic pot as in the well-like outlet that emerged from their subterranean home. As we walked downhill to the station, and others wished to see our catch, the water must have warmed with every group we passed, but still the trio of fish did not die.

On the following morning, after a night in the waiting room, we looked poorly but the fish were quite unchanged. (There were two of them by now: the third had been donated to a helpful but insistent government employee, part of the posse that had set forth from Tang-e-Haft; but the two in my possession were more than sufficiently intriguing.) On the lengthy journey to Tehran I kept their pot within a sodden shirt. At every station I would leap out, gather more water from the inevitable tap, pour it liberally over my charges and be continually amazed by their tenacity. The ticket collector skidded nastily on the tide swirling from my compartment and gave me an evil look. His expression changed to beaming happiness when he discovered that my water had doused a little fire on the next compartment's floor. A group of Luri tribesmen, migrating to higher pastures by train, had decided to brew tea in the standard fashion. Eventually, a dozen hours after they had departed to make another fire somewhere on the hard, dry earth, we reached Tehran. The poor fish then had their first taxi ride (never to be taken casually in that city), their first sojourn in a hotel wardrobe, and then, when my plane was due, their second taxi ride.

Emigration was no problem, but Security wished to inspect the pot with the mauve screw-lid. The men looked and then shook the little occupants, subjecting them to a force 30 gale. Next came the relatively minor hazard of modest decompression as we headed west for Europe. Of course, I inspected my catch frequently and noticed that one favoured climbing out of the water, if the slope permitted, and reclining like some indolent swimmer. The other would cruise upside-down, grazing the surface in a most un-fish-like fashion.

Neither was white, as suggested by the title of my book,

but pink, as the Danes had reported. Lack of pigment permitted the colour of their blood to be visible. Their size was
modest, the upside-downer being an inch in length and the
indolent recliner about half as much again, but I could see
their hearts clearly, double blobs of red. The gills were also
steeped in blood, and the visible guts showed that both had
eaten recently. Humans who savour fishes somewhat larger
than my minute pair should remember – before mocking my
exuberance – that time span of 1950 to 1976. There had been
the expedition. We had been dubbed the 'blind white fish'. I
had named the book accordingly and yet had encountered
nothing of the sort for all that span of years. Suddenly, and in
a little pot, I was holding a pair, and I knew tremendous joy.

I and my cargo arrived in London on a Friday. No point in
confusing Customs, I muttered to myself on passing through
the green exit. Then I realised the Natural History Museum
would be closing for the weekend. Both fish, still jauntily
alive, still casual about gravity and the normal rules of fish
procedure, would have to spend another sixty-six or so hours
in my company before being handed over to Science. Surely,
now that they had lived this long and through such trials, a
mere weekend in a London home would present no
problems?

Friends came to see the catch, now transferred from plastic
pot to handsome bowl. The grazer continued to crop the
surface from underneath, and the more energetic, larger fish
wriggled constantly, so that some two-thirds of its length
rested above the water-line. As for their eyes, there was a cup-
shaped opaqueness the same size as the original sockets, but
nothing else remained of the original organs. The fish were
therefore totally blind. Because of their lack of pigment it was
possible to see even the brain's outline, as well as the viscera
and where capillaries were at their densest. The larger and
more gymnastic of the two had three pairs of barbels protruding from the region of the mouth, but in almost all other
respects the two fish were similar. Their pinkness was striking,
as were their blindness and lack of fear of any sudden movements we might make and their overall dissimilarity from

other kinds of fish. They were different from each other, but so are cousins or even brothers, and those of us who peered into their bowl considered that the discrepancy in size might explain the other variations.

On Monday morning, with the fish re-potted, I caught the bus for Cromwell Road. 'Please contact the Fish Section,' I demanded, holding up my pot while bits and pieces of dead natural history stared down at me. Humphry Greenwood came to Reception and then, proudly, I padded along behind him on the final, labyrinthine stretch of the long journey from Zagros pool to Icthyology. It is not every day that cave fishes, let alone cave fishes collected only once before (and then by Danes), arrive in the formalin-scented bowels of the Natural History Museum. So coffee cups and forceps were put down, and a small crowd gathered round the pot.

Alas for total recall, but I cannot remember precisely what happened next, mainly because of the hubbub. 'That's a cyprinid, certainly,' said someone. 'But the other? It can't be. Yet it has to be. It must be. It's a cobitid.' I asked for an explanation and received it jerkily. 'One's the Danish fish, *Iranocypris*. But the other's quite different. It's a loach, no two ways about that. And it's a cave loach. But there aren't any cave loaches. Or rather there weren't. But here is one. So it's the first. It's the world's first cave loach. What a find. Congratulations! It's a brand-new blind white fish.'

Coffee had never tasted quite so good. I had not suspected my Persian contingent had scooped up two species, the Danish carp being the contrary grazer and the loach, the new loach, being the acrobat so disdainful of water. A further curiosity was the cohabitation of two cave fishes in the same locality, a partnership found in only one other cave system (Mammoth Cave, Kentucky). As I savoured the coffee, relished the praise and listened to the technical pronouncements on all five centimetres of the brand-new fish, I could not imagine such contentment being so speedily dashed. 'Of course they must be killed at once,' said Dr Greenwood, department chief.

My coffee turned to ash. I protested instantly. Was all that effort, involving ticket-collectors, thirsty Luris and considerable time, to be pushed aside so swiftly? A compromise was therefore reached. They would present me with a tube of alcohol in which I should immerse each fish the moment its life ended. They said that decay was swift and could render certain features valueless even within hours. Death at midnight, they insisted, would be the worst, as some eight hours would then elapse before its discovery. 'Better to kill them now,' they urged.

'Nothing of the sort,' I retorted, before leaving with the two fish and one tube. It was like transporting a coffin in case someone should drop down dead.

Three unnerving weeks after my return, when the new loach was being closely filmed (its fame demanding such attention), it floated to the surface. Within a minute at most the poor little form was embalmed in alcohol. I delivered the corpse, plus its still living but already documented companion, to Humphry Greenwood. His glee at the death was considerable, and his pleasure, on learning that preserving immersion had been almost immediate, was also wholehearted. I searched his face for any signs of grief, but he then played an ace with disarming dexterity. 'I shall call the new fish after you. *Noemacheilus smithi* is its name.'

Later that year, in the *Journal of Zoology*, appeared 'A new and eyeless cobitid fish (Pisces, Cypriniformes) from the Zagros Mountains, Iran'. The paper described *N. smithi* in considerable and necessary detail, thus forming the conclusion of the Oxford University Expedition to Persia 1950. Louis happened to be over from Pittsburgh that same year, and Eric, Philip and I, who all live in England, met him for a most agreeable reunion. Longer in the tooth and shorter in the hair, we cared not a fig for the years that had passed and relished each other's company.

Perhaps no stories ever truly end. We filmed the qanats the following year and then revisited the Zagros site with two divers. They discovered no entranceway into the cave system from which my catch had temporarily emerged, and there is possibly no such entrance large enough for humans. We discovered no more normacheilines; only half a dozen *Iranocypris* were there to greet us on our return. However, the film, when transmitted by the BBC, was seen by an Iraqi student at an English university. A mixture of national pride and academic rivalry prompted him, after returning home, to seek out the location of the pot-holer's find, *Typhlogarra widdowsoni*, whose relatives had lived – and died – on corn flakes. Amazingly, he discovered that they shared the habitat with yet another species of blind carp, now named for the student. Yet another was then located in Oman, a fair distance from either Tang-e-Haft or Iraq's pot-holes near Haditha, but the subterranean water system may be linked more closely than the surface mileage suggests. Finally, the Chinese have reported the finding of a cave loach, the world's second and a partner of a kind for *smithi*, despite the fact that most of a continent lies in between.

It had been late in 1949 when we at Oxford read in a travel book: 'Blind white fish live in the qanats and make for excellent eating.' The qanats were never their home, but they are surfacing in the Eurasian landmass in an exciting manner – six species so far, with surely more to come. The blind white fish do exist and are more alive and well than we would have thought possible when we stopped our mosheen outside Balliol and 'the sound dissipated into the October air'.

FOR THE BEST IN PAPERBACKS, LOOK FOR THE 🐧

In every corner of the world, on every subject under the sun, Penguin represents quality and variety – the very best in publishing today.

For complete information about books available from Penguin – including Puffins, Penguin Classics and Arkana – and how to order them, write to us at the appropriate address below. Please note that for copyright reasons the selection of books varies from country to country.

In the United Kingdom: Please write to *Dept E.P., Penguin Books Ltd, Harmondsworth, Middlesex, UB7 0DA.*

If you have any difficulty in obtaining a title, please send your order with the correct money, plus ten per cent for postage and packaging, to *PO Box No 11, West Drayton, Middlesex*

In the United States: Please write to *Dept BA, Penguin, 299 Murray Hill Parkway, East Rutherford, New Jersey 07073*

In Canada: Please write to *Penguin Books Canada Ltd, 2801 John Street, Markham, Ontario L3R 1B4*

In Australia: Please write to the *Marketing Department, Penguin Books Australia Ltd, P.O. Box 257, Ringwood, Victoria 3134*

In New Zealand: Please write to the *Marketing Department, Penguin Books (NZ) Ltd, Private Bag, Takapuna, Auckland 9*

In India: Please write to *Penguin Overseas Ltd, 706 Eros Apartments, 56 Nehru Place, New Delhi, 110019*

In the Netherlands: Please write to *Penguin Books Netherlands B.V., Postbus 195, NL–1380AD Weesp*

In West Germany: Please write to *Penguin Books Ltd, Friedrichstrasse 10–12, D–6000 Frankfurt/Main 1*

In Spain: Please write to *Longman Penguin España, Calle San Nicolas 15, E–28013 Madrid*

In Italy: Please write to *Penguin Italia s.r.l., Via Como 4, I-20096 Pioltello (Milano)*

In France: Please write to *Penguin Books Ltd, 39 Rue de Montmorency, F-75003 Paris*

In Japan: Please write to *Longman Penguin Japan Co Ltd, Yamaguchi Building, 2–12–9 Kanda Jimbocho, Chiyoda-Ku, Tokyo 101*

A CHOICE OF PENGUINS

The Secret Lives of Trebitsch Lincoln   Bernard Wasserstein

Trebitsch Lincoln was Member of Parliament, international spy, right-wing revolutionary, Buddhist monk – and this century's most extraordinary conman. 'Surely the final work on a truly extraordinary career' – Hugh Trevor-Roper. 'An utterly improbable story ... a biographical coup' – *Guardian*

Out of Africa   Karen Blixen (Isak Dinesen)

After the failure of her coffee-farm in Kenya, where she lived from 1913 to 1931, Karen Blixen went home to Denmark and wrote this unforgettable account of her experiences. 'No reader can put the book down without some share in the author's poignant farewell to her farm' – *Observer*

In My Wildest Dreams   Leslie Thomas

The autobiography of Leslie Thomas, author of *The Magic Army* and *The Dearest and the Best*. From Barnardo boy to original virgin soldier, from apprentice journalist to famous novelist, it is an amazing story. 'Hugely enjoyable' – *Daily Express*

The Winning Streak   Walter Goldsmith and David Clutterbuck

Marks and Spencer, Saatchi and Saatchi, United Biscuits, GEC ... The UK's top companies reveal their formulas for success, in an important and stimulating book that no British manager can afford to ignore.

Bird of Life, Bird of Death   Jonathan Evan Maslow

In the summer of 1983 Jonathan Maslow set out to find the quetzal. In doing so, he placed himself between the natural and unnatural histories of Central America, between the vulnerable magnificence of nature and the terrible destructiveness of man. 'A wonderful book' – *The New York Times Book Review*

Mob Star   Gene Mustain and Jerry Capeci

Handsome, charming, deadly, John Gotti is the real-life Mafia boss at the head of New York's most feared criminal family. *Mob Star* tells the chilling and compelling story of the rise to power of the most powerful criminal in America.

The Assassination of Federico García Lorca   Ian Gibson

Lorca's 'crime' was his antipathy to pomposity, conformity and intolerance. His punishment was murder. Ian Gibson – author of the acclaimed new biography of Lorca – reveals the truth about his death and the atmosphere in Spain that allowed it to happen.

Between the Woods and the Water   Patrick Leigh Fermor

Patrick Leigh Fermor continues his celebrated account – begun in *A Time of Gifts* – of his journey on foot from the Hook of Holland to Constantinople. 'Even better than everyone says it is' – Peter Levi. 'Indescribably rich and beautiful' – *Guardian*

The Hunting of the Whale   Jeremy Cherfas

'*The Hunting of the Whale* is a story of declining profits and mounting pigheadedness ... it involves a catalogue of crass carelessness ... Jeremy Cherfas brings a fresh eye to [his] material ... for anyone wanting a whale in a nutshell this must be the book to choose' – *The Times Literary Supplement*

Metamagical Themas   Douglas R. Hofstadter

This astonishing sequel to the bestselling, Pulitzer Prize-winning *Gödel, Escher, Bach* swarms with 'extraordinary ideas, brilliant fables, deep philosophical questions and Carrollian word play' – Martin Gardner

Into the Heart of Borneo   Redmond O'Hanlon

'Perceptive, hilarious and at the same time a serious natural-history journey into one of the last remaining unspoilt paradises' – *New Statesman*. 'Consistently exciting, often funny and erudite without ever being overwhelming' – *Punch*

When the Wind Blows   Raymond Briggs

'A visual parable against nuclear war: all the more chilling for being in the form of a strip cartoon' – *Sunday Times*. 'The most eloquent anti-Bomb statement you are likely to read' – *Daily Mail*

A CHOICE OF PENGUINS

Better Together   Christian Partnership in a Hurt City
David Sheppard and Derek Warlock

The Anglican and Roman Catholic Bishops of Liverpool tell the uplifting and heartening story of their alliance in the fight for their city – an alliance that has again and again reached out to heal a community torn by sectarian loyalties and bitter deprivation.

Fantastic Invasion   Patrick Marnham

Explored and exploited, Africa has carried a different meaning for each wave of foreign invaders – from ivory traders to aid workers. Now, in the crisis that has followed Independence, which way should Africa turn? 'A courageous and brilliant effort' – Paul Theroux

Jean Rhys: Letters 1931–66
Edited by Francis Wyndham and Diana Melly

'Eloquent and invaluable … her life emerges, and with it a portrait of an unexpectedly indomitable figure' – Marina Warner in the *Sunday Times*

Among the Russians   Colin Thubron

One man's solitary journey by car across Russia provides an enthralling and revealing account of the habits and idiosyncrasies of a fascinating people. 'He sees things with the freshness of an innocent and the erudition of a scholar' – *Daily Telegraph*

They Went to Portugal   Rose Macaulay

An exotic and entertaining account of travellers to Portugal from the pirate-crusaders, through poets, aesthetes and ambassadors, to the new wave of romantic travellers. A wonderful mixture of literature, history and adventure, by one of our most stylish and seductive writers.

The Separation Survival Handbook   Helen Garlick

Separation and divorce almost inevitably entail a long journey through a morass of legal, financial, custodial and emotional problems. Stripping the experience of both jargon and guilt, marital lawyer Helen Garlick maps clearly the various routes that can be taken.

A CHOICE OF PENGUINS

The Russian Album Michael Ignatieff

Michael Ignatieff movingly comes to terms with the meaning of his own family's memories and histories, in a book that is both an extraordinary account of the search for roots and a dramatic and poignant chronicle of four generations of a Russian family.

Beyond the Blue Horizon Alexander Frater

The romance and excitement of the legendary Imperial Airways East-bound Empire service – the world's longest and most adventurous scheduled air route – relived fifty years later in one of the most original travel books of the decade. 'The find of the year' – *Today*

Getting to Know the General Graham Greene

'In August 1981 my bag was packed for my fifth visit to Panama when the news came to me over the telephone of the death of General Omar Torrijos Herrera, my friend and host...' 'Vigorous, deeply felt, at times funny, and for Greene surprisingly frank' – *Sunday Times*

The Search for the Virus Steve Connor and Sharon Kingman

In this gripping book, two leading *New Scientist* journalists tell the remarkable story of how researchers discovered the AIDS virus and examine the links between AIDS and lifestyles. They also look at the progress being made in isolating the virus and finding a cure.

Arabian Sands Wilfred Thesiger

'In the tradition of Burton, Doughty, Lawrence, Philby and Thomas, it is, very likely, the book about Arabia to end all books about Arabia' – *Daily Telegraph*

Adieux: A Farewell to Sartre Simone de Beauvoir

A devastatingly frank account of the last years of Sartre's life, and his death, by the woman who for more than half a century shared that life. 'A true labour of love, there is about it a touching sadness, a mingling of the personal with the impersonal and timeless which Sartre himself would surely have liked and understood' – *Listener*

A CHOICE OF PENGUINS

Riding the Iron Rooster Paul Theroux

An eye-opening and entertaining account of travels in old and new China, from the author of *The Great Railway Bazaar*. 'Mr Theroux cannot write badly ... in the course of a year there was almost no train in the vast Chinese rail network on which he did not travel' – Ludovic Kennedy

The Markets of London Alex Forshaw and Theo Bergstrom

From Camden Lock and Columbia Road to Petticoat Lane and Portobello Road, from the world-famous to the well-kept secrets, here is the ultimate guide to London's markets: as old, as entertaining and as diverse as the capital itself.

The Chinese David Bonavia

'I can think of no other work which so urbanely and entertainingly succeeds in introducing the general Western reader to China' – *Sunday Telegraph*. 'Strongly recommended' – *The Times Literary Supplement*

The Diary of Virginia Woolf
Five volumes edited by Quentin Bell and Anne Olivier Bell

'As an account of intellectual and cultural life of our century, Virginia Woolf's diaries are invaluable; as the record of one bruised and unquiet mind, they are unique' – Peter Ackroyd in the *Sunday Times*

Voices of the Old Sea Norman Lewis

'I will wager that *Voices of the Old Sea* will be a classic in the literature about Spain' – *Mail on Sunday*. 'Limpidly and lovingly, Norman Lewis has caught the helpless, unwitting, often foolish, but always hopeful village in its dying summers, and saved the tragedy with sublime comedy' – *Observer*

Ninety-Two Days Evelyn Waugh

With characteristic honesty, Evelyn Waugh here debunks the romantic notions attached to rough travelling. His journey in Guiana and Brazil is difficult, dangerous and extremely uncomfortable, and his account of it is witty and unquestionably compelling.

FOR THE BEST IN PAPERBACKS, LOOK FOR THE 🐧

A CHOICE OF PENGUINS

Return to the Marshes Gavin Young

His remarkable portrait of the remote and beautiful world of the Marsh Arabs, whose centuries-old existence is now threatened with extinction by twentieth-century warfare. 'A talent for vivid description rarely found outside good fiction' – Jonathan Raban in the *Sunday Times*

Manhattan '45 Jan Morris

Disembarking with the victorious GIs returning after the war, Jan Morris takes us on a wonderfully nostalgic exploration of Manhattan in 1945; an affectionate portrait of an unrepeatable moment in history.

Britain's Poisoned Water Frances and Phil Craig

Every day millions of British families drink water containing toxic chemicals. But what are we doing about it? This startling investigation is essential and shocking reading for anyone concerned about our environment, our health, and the health of our children.

How I Grew Mary McCarthy

Mary McCarthy's account of her formative years possesses all the insight, wit and intelligence of her classic *Memories of a Catholic Girlhood* and her international bestseller *The Group*. 'Rich, generous stuff ... it leaves one licking one's lips for what is yet to come' – Penelope Lively

Who Should be Sleeping in Your Bed – and Why James Oliver

Should a Little Princess be faithful to a Wimp? This series of simple quizzes and personality profiles devised by clinical psychologist James Oliver will show you why infidelity happens – and how to make sure it doesn't happen to you.

The Big Red Train Ride Eric Newby

From Moscow to the Pacific on the Trans-Siberian Railway is an eight-day journey of nearly six thousand miles through seven time zones. In 1977 Eric Newby set out with his wife, an official guide and a photographer on this journey. 'The best kind of travel book' – Paul Theroux

FOR THE BEST IN PAPERBACKS, LOOK FOR THE 🐧

A CHOICE OF PENGUINS

Trail of Havoc Patrick Marnham

In this brilliant piece of detective work, Patrick Marnham has traced the steps of Lord Lucan from the fateful night of 7 November 1974 when he murdered his children's nanny and attempted to kill his ex-wife. As well as being a fascinating investigation, the book is also a brilliant portrayal of a privileged section of society living under great stress.

Light Years Gary Kinder

Eduard Meier, an uneducated Swiss farmer, claims since 1975 to have had over 100 UFO sightings and encounters with 'beamships' from the Pleiades. His evidence is such that even the most die-hard sceptics have been unable to explain away the phenomenon.

And the Band Played On Politics, People and the AIDS Epidemic
Randy Shilts

Written after years of extensive research by the only American journalist to cover the epidemic full-time, *And the Band Played On* is a masterpiece of reportage and a tragic record of mismanaged institutions and scientific vendettas, of sexual politics and personal suffering.

The Return of a Native Reporter Robert Chesshyre

Robert Chesshyre returned to Britain in 1985 from the United States, where he had spent four years as the *Observer*'s correspondent. This is his devastating account of the country he came home to: intolerant, brutal, grasping and politically and economically divided. It is a nation, he asserts, struggling to find a role.

Women and Love Shere Hite

In this culmination of *The Hite Report* trilogy, 4,500 women provide an eloquent testimony to the disturbingly unsatisfying nature of their emotional relationships and point to what they see as the causes. *Women and Love* reveals a new cultural perspective in formation: as women change the emotional structure of their lives, they are defining a fundamental debate over the future of our society.

THE PENGUIN TRAVEL LIBRARY – A SELECTION

Hindoo Holiday J. R. Ackerley

The Flight of Ikaros Kevin Andrews

A Desert Dies Michael Asher

The Innocent Anthropologist Nigel Barley

The Deer Cry Pavilion Pat Barr

The Path to Rome Hilaire Belloc

Looking for Dilmun Geoffrey Bibby

First Russia, Then Tibet Robert Byron

Granite Island Dorothy Carrington

An Indian Summer James Cameron

Siren Land Norman Douglas

Brazilian Adventure Peter Fleming

Caucasian Journey Negley Farson

The Hill of Devi E. M. Forster

Journey to Kars Philip Glazebrook

Pattern of Islands Arthur Grimble

Writings from Japan Lafcadio Hearn

A Little Tour in France Henry James

Mornings in Mexico D. H. Lawrence

The Stones of Florence and **Venice Observed** Mary McCarthy

They Went to Portugal Rose Macaulay

The Colossus of Maroussi Henry Miller

Calcutta Geoffrey Moorhouse

Spain Jan Morris

The Big Red Train Ride Eric Newby

The Other Nile Charlie Pye-Smith

The Marsh Arabs Wilfred Thesiger

Journey into Cyprus Colin Thubron

Ninety-Two Days Evelyn Waugh

Maiden Voyage Denton Welch